Table

Contents

Table of Contents

Introduction
Welcome to the World of Website Building

About This Book
How to Use This Guide
Module 1: Introduction to Website Development

Lesson 1: Understanding the Basics of Website Development
Lesson 2: Introduction to Wix and Its Features
Lesson 3: Signing Up for a Wix Account
Lesson 4: Getting Started with the Wix Editor

Module 2: Getting Started with Wix

Lesson 1: Signing Up and Logging In
Lesson 2: Choosing a Template
Lesson 3: Customizing Your Website
Lesson 4: Adding Pages
Lesson 5: Creating a Navigation Menu
Lesson 6: Mobile Optimization
Lesson 7: Previewing and Publishing Your Website
Lesson 8: Choosing a Domain Name
Lesson 9: SEO Optimization
Lesson 10: Analytics

Module 3: Customizing Your Website

Lesson 1: Advanced Editing Tools
Lesson 2: Adding Custom Elements
Lesson 3: Integrating Apps and Widgets
Lesson 4: Creating Interactive Features
Lesson 5: Customizing Your Mobile Site
Lesson 6: Implementing Advanced SEO Strategies
Lesson 7: Exploring Design Trends
Lesson 8: Collaborating with Team Members
Lesson 9: A/B Testing and Optimization
Lesson 10: Monitoring Performance and Analytics

Module 4: Creating Pages and Navigation

Lesson 1: Add Pages
Lesson 2: Creating New Pages
Lesson 3: Customizing Page Layouts
Lesson 4: Adding Content to Pages
Lesson 5: Incorporating Dynamic Content
Lesson 6: Creating a Navigation Menu
Lesson 7: Designing a User-Friendly Navigation Structure

Lesson 8: Implementing Navigation Enhancements
Lesson 9: Implementing Navigation Testing and Optimization
Lesson 10: Maintaining Consistency Across Pages

Module 5: Adding Advanced Elements

Lesson 1: Exploring Advanced Elements
Lesson 2: Custom Forms
Lesson 3: Databases Integration
Lesson 4: Member Areas
Lesson 5: Bookings and Appointments
Lesson 6: Online Stores
Lesson 7: Advanced Media Elements
Lesson 8: Custom Code Integration
Lesson 9: Performance Optimization
Lesson 10: Testing and Troubleshooting

Module 6: Optimization

Lesson 1: Making Your Website Mobile-Friendly
Lesson 2: Optimizing for Search Engines (SEO)
Lesson 3: Testing and Previewing Your Website
Lesson 4: Publishing Your Website
Lesson 5: Monitoring Your Website's Performance
Lesson 6: Making Ongoing Updates and Improvements

Module 7: Publishing and Promoting Your Website

Lesson 1: Publishing Your Website
Lesson 2: Configuring Domain Settings
Lesson 3: Promoting Your Website through Social Media
Lesson 4: Email Marketing Strategies
Lesson 5: Search Engine Marketing (SEM)
Lesson 6: Analyzing and Measuring Results

Module 8: Advanced Techniques and Tips

Lesson 1: Advanced Design Techniques
Lesson 2: Customizing with Code
Lesson 3: Advanced SEO Strategies
Lesson 4: E-commerce Optimization
Lesson 5: Multilingual Websites
Lesson 6: Website Security and Maintenance

How to Build a Website using Wix
By Adarsh Gautam

Kakadeo kanpur Uttar pradesh India-208025

For any Query -akroy7342@gmail.com

Introduction

Welcome to the world of website building with Wix! In today's digital age, having a strong online presence is essential for individuals and businesses alike. Whether you're a small business owner, an entrepreneur, a freelancer, or simply someone looking to showcase your passion or portfolio, creating a professional website is key to success in the digital realm.

In this comprehensive guide, we will embark on a journey together to explore the power and versatility of Wix, one of the leading website building platforms available today. With its intuitive drag-and-drop interface, extensive customization options, and robust features, Wix empowers users of all skill levels to design stunning websites that captivate audiences and achieve their goals.

Whether you're new to website creation or looking to enhance your existing site, this book is designed to be your trusted companion every step of the way. We'll start by laying the foundation with an overview of Wix and how to get started, guiding you through setting up your account, navigating the Wix dashboard, and understanding the basics of website design.

From there, we'll dive into the exciting world of website design, exploring topics such as choosing the right template, customizing your design with fonts, colors, and media, and creating seamless navigation for your visitors. You'll learn how to incorporate advanced features, optimize your site for mobile devices, and boost your SEO performance to increase visibility and reach online.

As we progress, we'll cover essential aspects of website management, including publishing your site, updating and maintaining content, and monitoring performance with analytics. We'll also delve into advanced techniques and tips, such as setting up an online store, starting a blog, collaborating with team members, and troubleshooting common issues.

By the end of this guide, you'll not only have a fully functional and visually stunning website built with Wix but also the knowledge and confidence to continue growing and evolving your online presence. Whether you're building a personal blog, an e-commerce store, a portfolio, or a business website, the possibilities with Wix are endless, and the journey is just beginning.

So, let's embark on this exciting adventure together and unlock the potential of website building with Wix. Your digital masterpiece awaits!

Welcome to the World of Website Building

Congratulations on taking the first step into the dynamic and ever-evolving world of website building! In today's digital era, a well-designed and functional website serves as the cornerstone of your online identity, enabling you to connect with your audience, showcase your work, and achieve your goals with unprecedented reach and impact.

Whether you're a budding entrepreneur, a seasoned professional, an artist, a freelancer, or simply someone with a passion to share, the ability to create your own website opens up a world of possibilities. From launching your own business venture to establishing your personal brand, the opportunities for growth and success are limitless in the digital landscape.

With the advent of user-friendly website building platforms like Wix, the process of creating a professional and visually stunning website has never been easier or more accessible. Gone are the days of complex coding and technical expertise; now, anyone with an internet connection and a creative vision can bring their ideas to life with just a few clicks.

In this guide, we'll embark on an exciting journey together to explore the power and potential of website building with Wix. Whether you're a complete novice or have some experience with website creation, this guide is designed to equip you with the knowledge, tools, and confidence you need to design, build, and launch your own website with ease.

Throughout the pages that follow, we'll cover everything you need to know to create a stunning website that captures attention, engages visitors, and achieves your objectives. From choosing the perfect template and customizing your design to optimizing for mobile devices and enhancing your site with advanced features, we'll walk you through each step of the process, providing practical tips, expert insights, and hands-on tutorials along the way.

But more than just a technical manual, this guide is also a roadmap to realizing your digital dreams and aspirations. Whether you're looking to start a business, promote your services, showcase your portfolio, or share your passion with the world, your website is the gateway to making your mark online and leaving a lasting impression on your audience.

So, as you embark on this exciting journey of discovery and creation, remember that the possibilities are endless, and the only limit is your imagination. With Wix as your trusted partner, the world of website building is yours to explore, conquer, and transform into your own digital masterpiece.

Welcome to the world of website building with Wix. Your adventure begins now!

About This Book

Welcome to "Website Building with Wix: A Comprehensive Guide to Creating Stunning Websites". This book is your go-to resource for mastering the art of website creation using one of the most popular and versatile platforms available today – Wix.

Whether you're a small business owner, an entrepreneur, a freelancer, an artist, or simply someone looking to establish a strong online presence, this book is designed to help you unlock the full potential of Wix and build a website that stands out in the digital landscape.

What You'll Learn

In this comprehensive guide, we'll cover everything you need to know to design, build, and launch your own professional website with Wix. From the basics of getting started and navigating the Wix dashboard to advanced techniques for optimizing your site for search engines and mobile devices, we'll walk you through each step of the process with clear, step-by-step instructions and helpful tips.

Key Features

- **Comprehensive Coverage:** We cover all aspects of website creation with Wix, from choosing the right template and customizing your design to managing your site, enhancing its functionality, and optimizing its performance.
- **Practical Guidance:** Whether you're a complete beginner or have some experience with website building, our practical guidance and hands-on tutorials will help you gain the skills and confidence you need to succeed.
- **Expert Insights:** Throughout the book, you'll find expert insights, best practices, and real-world examples to inspire and inform your website-building journey.

Who This Book Is For

This book is for anyone who wants to create a professional website with Wix, regardless of their skill level or background. Whether you're a business owner, a creative professional, an aspiring blogger, or simply someone with a passion to share, this book is your ultimate guide to bringing your ideas to life online.

How to Use This Guide

You can read this book from cover to cover for a comprehensive overview of website building with Wix, or you can use it as a reference guide to find answers to specific questions or challenges as you work on your website. Each chapter is organized in a logical sequence, with clear headings and subheadings to help you navigate the content easily.

Let's Get Started

Are you ready to embark on an exciting journey into the world of website building with Wix? Then let's dive in! Turn the page and let's begin our adventure together.

Chapter 1: Introduction to Website Development

In the digital age, having an online presence is essential for businesses, organizations, and individuals alike. Websites serve as virtual storefronts, offering a platform for communication, interaction, and commerce. Understanding the basics of website development is crucial for anyone looking to create, manage, or optimize a website. This chapter provides an overview of website development, covering its importance, key components, and basic concepts.

Section 1.1: Importance of Website Development

- Discuss the significance of websites in today's interconnected world.
- Highlight how websites facilitate communication, marketing, and sales.
- Emphasize the role of websites in establishing credibility and building brand identity.
- Provide examples of successful websites and their impact on businesses and society.

Section 1.2: Key Components of Website Development

- Introduce the fundamental components of website development, including HTML, CSS, and JavaScript.
- Explain the purpose and functionality of each component.
- Discuss the role of web browsers in rendering and displaying websites.
- Outline the importance of web hosting, domain names, and server-side technologies.

Section 1.3: Basic Concepts in Website Development

- Define key terms such as frontend, backend, client-side, and server-side.
- Explain the difference between static and dynamic websites.
- Discuss responsive design and its importance in creating websites that adapt to various devices and screen sizes.
- Introduce the concept of user experience (UX) and its impact on website usability and engagement.

Chapter 2: HTML Essentials

HTML (Hypertext Markup Language) serves as the foundation of web development, providing the structure and content of web pages. This chapter delves into the essential concepts and elements of HTML, equipping learners with the knowledge to create basic web pages.

Section 2.1: Introduction to HTML

- Define HTML and its role in web development.

- Explain the structure of an HTML document, including tags, elements, and attributes.
- Provide examples of common HTML elements such as headings, paragraphs, and lists.

Section 2.2: Document Structure and Semantic HTML

- Discuss the importance of semantic HTML in enhancing accessibility and search engine optimization (SEO).
- Introduce semantic elements such as <header>, <nav>, <main>, <section>, and <footer>.
- Explain how semantic HTML improves the organization and clarity of web content.

Section 2.3: Working with Links and Images

- Explain how to create hyperlinks using the <a> element.
- Discuss the use of relative and absolute URLs in linking to web pages and resources.
- Describe the <img> element and its attributes for embedding images in HTML documents.
- Provide guidelines for optimizing images for web use, including file formats and compression techniques.

Section 2.4: HTML Forms and Input Elements

- Introduce HTML forms and their role in collecting user input.
- Explain how to create form elements such as text fields, checkboxes, radio buttons, and dropdown menus.
- Discuss form validation techniques using HTML attributes and JavaScript.

Chapter 3: CSS Fundamentals

CSS (Cascading Style Sheets) is used to control the visual presentation of HTML documents, including layout, colors, fonts, and other design aspects. This chapter explores the basics of CSS, empowering learners to style and customize web pages.

Section 3.1: Introduction to CSS

- Define CSS and its role in styling web pages.
- Explain the concept of cascading and inheritance in CSS.
- Introduce different methods of applying CSS styles, including inline, internal, and external stylesheets.

Section 3.2: Selectors and Properties

- Discuss CSS selectors and their specificity in targeting HTML elements.
- Introduce common CSS properties such as color, font-family, margin, padding, and border.

- Provide examples of using CSS shorthand properties for efficiency and readability.

Section 3.3: Layout and Box Model

- Explain the CSS box model and its components (content, padding, border, margin).
- Discuss different layout techniques, including float, flexbox, and grid.
- Provide examples of creating responsive layouts using CSS media queries.

Section 3.4: Styling Text and Images

- Describe CSS properties for styling text, including font-size, font-weight, text-align, and text-decoration.
- Discuss techniques for controlling the appearance of images using CSS, such as size, position, and alignment.

Chapter 4: Introduction to JavaScript

JavaScript is a dynamic programming language used for adding interactivity and functionality to web pages. This chapter introduces the basics of JavaScript, enabling learners to incorporate interactive elements into their websites.

Section 4.1: Introduction to JavaScript

- Define JavaScript and its role in web development.
- Discuss the characteristics of JavaScript as a scripting language.
- Introduce the concept of client-side scripting and its advantages in web development.

Section 4.2: Variables, Data Types, and Operators

- Explain how to declare variables and assign values in JavaScript.
- Introduce different data types in JavaScript, including numbers, strings, booleans, arrays, and objects.
- Discuss arithmetic, comparison, and logical operators in JavaScript.

Section 4.3: Control Structures and Functions

- Discuss control structures such as if statements, switch statements, loops (for, while), and conditional (ternary) operator.
- Introduce the concept of functions in JavaScript and how to define and call them.
- Discuss the importance of functions in organizing and reusing code.

Section 4.4: DOM Manipulation

- Explain the Document Object Model (DOM) and its representation of HTML documents as a tree structure.

- Discuss how JavaScript interacts with the DOM to manipulate HTML elements and attributes dynamically.
- Provide examples of common DOM manipulation techniques, such as selecting elements, changing content, and handling events.

Chapter 5: Putting It All Together: Building Your First Website

In this final chapter, learners apply their knowledge of HTML, CSS, and JavaScript to create a basic website from scratch. This hands-on exercise reinforces key concepts and allows learners to showcase their understanding of website development fundamentals.

Section 5.1: Planning Your Website

- Discuss the importance of planning and organization in website development.
- Outline the steps involved in planning a website, including defining objectives, identifying target audience, and creating a site map.

Section 5.2: Building the Structure with HTML

- Guide learners through the process of creating the structure and content of a website using HTML.
- Encourage the use of semantic HTML elements for improved accessibility and SEO.
- Provide tips for organizing and formatting HTML code for readability and maintainability.

Section 5.3: Styling with CSS

- Demonstrate how to apply CSS styles to HTML elements to enhance the visual presentation of the website.
- Encourage experimentation with colors, fonts, layout, and other design aspects to personalize the website's appearance.
- Emphasize the importance of responsive design principles in ensuring compatibility across different devices and screen sizes.

Section 5.4: Adding Interactivity with JavaScript

- Introduce interactive elements such as navigation menus, image sliders, and contact forms using JavaScript.
- Guide learners through the process of incorporating JavaScript code into HTML documents and linking external scripts.
- Provide examples of event handling and DOM manipulation to create dynamic and engaging user experiences.

Conclusion

Understanding the basics of website development is the first step towards mastering the art of building compelling and functional websites. By familiarizing themselves with HTML, CSS, and JavaScript, learners gain the foundation necessary to create, customize, and optimize websites to meet

Understanding Wix

Wix is a popular cloud-based website development platform that empowers users to create professional-looking websites without the need for coding knowledge. In this chapter, we'll delve into the fundamentals of Wix, its features, and how it revolutionizes the website creation process.

Section 1.1: Introduction to Wix

- Provide an overview of Wix as a website builder and content management system (CMS).
- Discuss the history and growth of Wix as a leading platform for website creation.
- Highlight the user-friendly interface and intuitive drag-and-drop editor that make Wix accessible to users of all skill levels.

Section 1.2: Key Features of Wix

- Explore the features and functionalities offered by Wix for website development, including:

- Wix ADI (Artificial Design Intelligence): An advanced AI-driven tool that creates a personalized website based on user input and preferences.
- Wix Editor: A robust drag-and-drop editor that allows users to customize every aspect of their website's design and layout.
- Wix App Market: A marketplace offering a wide range of apps and integrations to enhance website functionality, such as e-commerce, marketing, and analytics.
- Wix Templates: Professionally designed templates that serve as starting points for building various types of websites, from portfolios to online stores.
- Wix Code: A feature that enables users to add custom functionality and interactivity to their websites using JavaScript and APIs.
- Wix SEO Tools: Built-in tools and features to optimize websites for search engines and improve their visibility online.

Section 1.3: Benefits of Using Wix

- Discuss the advantages of using Wix for website development, including:

- Ease of use: Wix's user-friendly interface and intuitive editor make it easy for anyone to create a professional-looking website.
- Flexibility: Wix offers a wide range of templates, design elements, and customization options to suit different needs and preferences.
- Affordability: Wix offers a range of pricing plans, including a free plan with basic features and premium plans with additional functionalities.
- Scalability: Wix websites can easily scale as businesses grow, with options to upgrade plans and add features as needed.

- Support: Wix provides comprehensive support resources, including tutorials, forums, and customer service, to assist users at every stage of website development.

Chapter 2: Getting Started with Wix

In this chapter, we'll walk through the process of getting started with Wix, from signing up for an account to creating and customizing your first website.

Section 2.1: Signing Up for a Wix Account

- Guide users through the process of signing up for a Wix account, including choosing a username and password.
- Explain the different pricing plans offered by Wix, including the free plan and premium plans with additional features and benefits.
- Discuss the benefits of upgrading to a premium plan, such as removing ads, using a custom domain, and accessing advanced features.

Section 2.2: Choosing a Template

- Explore the various templates available on Wix and how to browse and filter them based on categories, industries, and styles.
- Provide tips for selecting a template that aligns with your website's goals, audience, and branding.

Section 2.3: Customizing Your Website

- Walk through the Wix Editor interface and its various tools and features for customizing website design and layout.
- Demonstrate how to add and edit text, images, videos, and other elements to your website using the drag-and-drop editor.
- Explore advanced customization options, such as changing fonts, colors, backgrounds, and animations.

Section 2.4: Adding Functionality with Apps

- Introduce the Wix App Market and how to browse, search, and install apps to add functionality to your website.
- Highlight popular apps and integrations for e-commerce, social media, email marketing, SEO, analytics, and more.
- Provide step-by-step instructions for installing and configuring apps to enhance your website's features and capabilities.

Chapter 3: Advanced Features and Functionality

In this chapter, we'll explore some of the more advanced features and functionalities offered by Wix, including e-commerce, blogging, SEO, and Wix Code.

Section 3.1: E-Commerce with Wix Stores

- Discuss the e-commerce capabilities of Wix, including Wix Stores, an integrated solution for building online stores.
- Walk through the process of setting up an online store, including adding products, managing inventory, and configuring payment and shipping options.
- Explore advanced e-commerce features, such as abandoned cart recovery, discount codes, and product variations.

Section 3.2: Blogging with Wix Blog

- Introduce Wix Blog, a feature that allows users to create and manage blog posts directly within their Wix websites.
- Explain how to set up a blog, create posts, add categories and tags, and customize the blog layout and design.
- Discuss the benefits of blogging for businesses, organizations, and individuals, including driving traffic, building authority, and engaging with audiences.

Section 3.3: SEO Optimization

- Explore the built-in SEO tools and features offered by Wix for optimizing websites for search engines.
- Discuss best practices for optimizing website content, including meta tags, keywords, headings, and image alt text.
- Provide tips for improving website performance, mobile responsiveness, and user experience to enhance SEO rankings.

Section 3.4: Wix Code for Custom Functionality

- Introduce Wix Code, a feature that allows users to add custom functionality and interactivity to their websites using JavaScript and APIs.
- Discuss the capabilities of Wix Code, including database collections, dynamic pages, user input forms, and third-party integrations.
- Provide examples of how Wix Code can be used to create dynamic, data-driven websites, such as directories, event calendars, and membership portals.

Chapter 4: Optimizing and Managing Your Wix Website

In this chapter, we'll cover strategies for optimizing and managing your Wix website to ensure its success and effectiveness.

Section 4.1: Website Optimization

- Discuss strategies for optimizing website performance, including speed, security, and mobile responsiveness.
- Explore tools and techniques for tracking website analytics, monitoring traffic, and measuring key performance indicators (KPIs).
- Provide tips for improving user experience, navigation, and accessibility to enhance website engagement and conversion rates.

Section 4.2: Website Maintenance

- Outline best practices for ongoing website maintenance, including updating content, monitoring security, and troubleshooting issues.
- Discuss the importance of regular backups and how to implement backup and restore procedures to protect website data.
- Provide guidance on managing domain settings, renewing subscriptions, and staying up-to-date with platform updates and developments.

Section 4.3: Promoting Your Website

- Explore strategies for promoting your Wix website and driving traffic, including search engine optimization (SEO), social media marketing, email marketing, and online advertising.
- Discuss the importance of content marketing and how to create and distribute valuable, relevant content to attract and engage your target audience.
- Provide tips for building relationships with influencers, collaborating with partners, and leveraging online communities to expand your website's reach.

Chapter 5: Conclusion and Next Steps

In conclusion, Wix offers a powerful platform for creating, customizing, and managing professional websites with ease. By understanding its features and functionalities

Introduction to Wix Account Creation

In this chapter, we'll explore the process of signing up for a Wix account, which is the first step towards creating your own website using the Wix platform. We'll cover everything from choosing a plan to setting up your account and accessing the Wix dashboard.

Section 1.1: Understanding Wix Account Creation

- Provide an overview of the importance of creating a Wix account for website development.
- Explain how a Wix account enables users to access the platform's features and tools for building and managing websites.
- Highlight the benefits of signing up for a Wix account, including access to templates, design tools, and customer support.

Section 1.2: Choosing the Right Plan

- Discuss the different pricing plans offered by Wix, including the free plan and premium plans with additional features and benefits.
- Compare the features and limitations of each plan, such as storage space, bandwidth, and e-commerce capabilities.
- Provide guidance on choosing the right plan based on your budget, needs, and goals for your website.

Section 1.3: Creating Your Wix Account

- Walk through the process of creating a Wix account step by step, including:

- Visiting the Wix website and clicking on the "Sign Up" button.
- Entering your email address and choosing a password for your account.
- Providing additional information, such as your name and location.
- Agreeing to the terms of service and privacy policy.
- Verifying your email address to activate your account.

Section 1.4: Exploring Wix's Pricing Plans

- Provide an in-depth overview of the different pricing plans offered by Wix, including:

- The Free Plan: Explore the features and limitations of the free plan, including Wix branding, limited storage, and bandwidth.
- Premium Plans: Discuss the benefits of upgrading to premium plans, such as removing ads, using a custom domain, and accessing advanced features like e-commerce and marketing tools.
- Business and E-Commerce Plans: Highlight the features and benefits of Wix's business and e-commerce plans, including online store capabilities, payment processing, and inventory management.

Chapter 2: Setting Up Your Wix Account

Now that you've created your Wix account, it's time to set it up and customize it to suit your needs. In this chapter, we'll walk through the process of setting up your Wix account, including personalizing your profile, choosing a website template, and accessing the Wix dashboard.

Section 2.1: Personalizing Your Profile

- Guide users through the process of personalizing their Wix profile, including:
  - Uploading a profile picture or logo.
  - Providing additional information, such as your business name, industry, and website goals.
  - Adding social media links to connect with your audience.
- Discuss the importance of personalizing your profile to make it more engaging and professional.

Section 2.2: Choosing a Website Template

- Explore the wide range of website templates available on Wix, categorized by industry, style, and functionality.
- Provide tips for choosing the right template for your website based on your brand identity, target audience, and website goals.
- Demonstrate how to preview and customize templates to see how they look with your content and branding.

Section 2.3: Accessing the Wix Dashboard

- Introduce users to the Wix dashboard, where they can manage their websites, settings, and account information.
- Walk through the different sections of the dashboard, including:
  - My Sites: Where users can view and manage their websites.
  - Dashboard: Where users can access tools and features for website customization, marketing, and more.
  - Upgrade: Where users can upgrade their plans and access premium features.
  - Settings: Where users can manage their account settings, billing information, and notifications.
- Provide tips for navigating the Wix dashboard efficiently and effectively.

Chapter 3: Exploring Wix Features and Tools

In this chapter, we'll explore some of the key features and tools offered by Wix that users can leverage to create and customize their websites.

Section 3.1: Wix Editor

- Introduce users to the Wix Editor, a powerful drag-and-drop editor that allows them to customize every aspect of their website's design and layout.

- Walk through the different elements of the Wix Editor, including:
  - Adding and editing text, images, videos, and other content.
  - Changing fonts, colors, backgrounds, and other design elements.
  - Arranging and resizing elements on the page.
- Provide tips and best practices for using the Wix Editor to create professional-looking websites.

Section 3.2: Wix App Market

- Explore the Wix App Market, a marketplace offering a wide range of apps and integrations to enhance website functionality.
- Highlight popular apps and integrations available on the Wix App Market, such as:
  - E-commerce: Apps for setting up online stores, managing inventory, and processing payments.
  - Marketing: Apps for email marketing, social media management, and SEO optimization.
  - Design: Apps for adding animations, galleries, and other design elements to your website.
- Provide guidance on how to browse, search, and install apps from the Wix App Market.

Section 3.3: Wix SEO Tools

- Discuss the built-in SEO tools and features offered by Wix for optimizing websites for search engines.
- Explain how to optimize website content for keywords, meta tags, headings, and image alt text.
- Provide tips and best practices for improving website visibility and rankings on search engine results pages (SERPs).

Chapter 4: Conclusion and Next Steps

In conclusion, signing up for a Wix account is the first step towards creating your own professional-looking website with ease. By understanding the process of creating a Wix account, setting it up, and exploring its features and tools, users can leverage the power of the platform to bring their website ideas to life.

Introduction to the Wix Editor

The Wix Editor is a powerful tool that allows users to create and customize their websites with ease. In this chapter, we'll explore the basics of the Wix Editor, including its interface, features, and functionality, to help users get started on building their own websites.

Section 1.1: Overview of the Wix Editor

- Provide an introduction to the Wix Editor as a web development tool.
- Explain how the Wix Editor empowers users to design and customize their websites without coding knowledge.
- Highlight the user-friendly interface and drag-and-drop functionality that make the Wix Editor accessible to users of all skill levels.

Section 1.2: Key Features of the Wix Editor

- Explore the key features and tools offered by the Wix Editor for website customization, including:
  - Drag-and-Drop Interface: Allows users to easily add, move, and resize elements on the page.
  - Design Toolbar: Provides access to design tools for editing text, images, backgrounds, and other elements.
  - Page Manager: Allows users to manage pages, navigation menus, and site structure.
  - Preview Mode: Enables users to preview their website as it will appear to visitors.
- Discuss how these features empower users to create professional-looking websites with ease.

Section 1.3: Understanding Wix Templates

- Introduce Wix templates as pre-designed layouts that serve as starting points for website creation.
- Explain how users can choose from a wide range of templates based on their industry, style, and preferences.
- Discuss the benefits of using Wix templates, including saving time and ensuring a cohesive design.

Chapter 2: Navigating the Wix Editor Interface

In this chapter, we'll explore the interface of the Wix Editor and how users can navigate its various sections and tools to customize their websites.

Section 2.1: Accessing the Wix Editor

- Guide users through the process of accessing the Wix Editor after signing in to their Wix account.

- Explain how users can access the Wix Editor from the Wix dashboard or directly from their website's dashboard.

Section 2.2: Exploring the Wix Editor Interface

- Provide an overview of the Wix Editor interface, including its main components:
  - Top Menu Bar: Contains options for saving, previewing, and publishing the website, as well as accessing help and support.
  - Sidebar: Contains tools and options for editing and customizing the website, including design, settings, and pages.
  - Canvas: The main workspace where users can drag and drop elements to design their website.
- Discuss the layout and organization of these interface components to help users navigate the Wix Editor effectively.

Section 2.3: Understanding the Canvas

- Explain the concept of the canvas in the Wix Editor as the workspace where users design their website.
- Discuss how users can interact with the canvas by adding, moving, resizing, and editing elements.
- Provide tips for organizing and structuring elements on the canvas to create visually appealing and functional layouts.

Chapter 3: Customizing Your Website with the Wix Editor

Now that we've familiarized ourselves with the Wix Editor interface, let's dive into customizing our websites using its powerful design tools and features.

Section 3.1: Editing Text and Images

- Walk users through the process of editing text and images on their website using the Wix Editor.
- Explain how users can double-click on text elements to edit them directly on the canvas, and use the text toolbar to format text.
- Discuss how users can click on image elements to replace them with their own images or edit them using the image toolbar.

Section 3.2: Adding and Editing Elements

- Explore the various elements available in the Wix Editor, including text boxes, image galleries, buttons, and more.
- Demonstrate how users can add elements to their website by dragging them from the sidebar onto the canvas.
- Discuss how users can customize elements by clicking on them to access editing options such as size, position, style, and more.

Section 3.3: Customizing Design and Style

- Introduce users to the design tools and features available in the Wix Editor for customizing the look and feel of their website.
- Explore options for customizing fonts, colors, backgrounds, and other design elements using the design toolbar.
- Provide tips and best practices for creating visually cohesive and appealing designs that align with users' branding and preferences.

Chapter 4: Previewing and Publishing Your Website

In this chapter, we'll explore how users can preview and publish their websites using the Wix Editor to share their creations with the world.

Section 4.1: Previewing Your Website

- Explain how users can preview their website as it will appear to visitors before publishing it.
- Discuss the importance of previewing the website to ensure that it looks and functions as intended across different devices and screen sizes.

Section 4.2: Publishing Your Website

- Walk users through the process of publishing their website using the Wix Editor.
- Explain how users can click on the "Publish" button in the top menu bar to make their website live on the internet.
- Discuss options for customizing the website's domain name, SEO settings, and social sharing options before publishing.

Section 4.3: Managing Your Published Website

- Provide guidance on how users can manage their published website, including:
  - Updating content and design using the Wix Editor.
  - Monitoring website traffic and analytics using the Wix dashboard.
  - Responding to visitor feedback and inquiries.
- Discuss best practices for ongoing website maintenance and optimization to ensure a positive user experience.

Chapter 5: Conclusion and Next Steps

In conclusion, the Wix Editor offers a user-friendly and powerful platform for creating and customizing professional-looking websites with ease. By understanding its interface, features, and functionality, users can leverage the Wix Editor to bring their website ideas to life and share them with the world.

Introduction to Signing Up and Logging In

In the digital world, signing up for an account and logging in are fundamental actions that allow users to access various online platforms and services. In this chapter, we'll explore the importance of signing up and logging in, the steps involved in each process, and best practices for account management and security.

Section 1.1: Importance of Signing Up and Logging In

- Discuss the significance of signing up for an account and logging in to access online platforms and services.
- Highlight the benefits of creating personalized accounts, such as personalized experiences, saved preferences, and access to exclusive features.
- Explain how logging in helps verify users' identities and protects their privacy and security online.

Section 1.2: Understanding User Accounts

- Define what constitutes a user account in the context of online platforms and services.
- Explain the purpose of user accounts, including storing personal information, preferences, and activity history.
- Discuss the types of information typically associated with user accounts, such as usernames, passwords, email addresses, and profile data.

Section 1.3: Account Security and Privacy

- Explore the importance of account security and privacy in safeguarding users' personal information and preventing unauthorized access.
- Discuss common security threats and risks associated with online accounts, such as hacking, phishing, and identity theft.
- Provide tips and best practices for enhancing account security, including creating strong passwords, enabling two-factor authentication, and avoiding sharing sensitive information.

Chapter 2: Signing Up for an Account

In this chapter, we'll delve into the process of signing up for an account on various online platforms and services, covering the steps involved and considerations for creating a new account.

Section 2.1: Choosing a Platform

- Discuss the various online platforms and services that require users to sign up for an account, such as social media networks, e-commerce websites, and productivity tools.

- Highlight factors to consider when choosing a platform, including its features, reputation, and terms of service.

Section 2.2: Steps to Sign Up

- Walk through the steps involved in signing up for an account on an online platform, including:

- Visiting the platform's website or app and locating the sign-up or registration page.
- Providing personal information, such as name, email address, and date of birth.
- Choosing a username, password, and security questions.
- Agreeing to the platform's terms of service and privacy policy.
- Verifying the account through email or SMS verification.

Section 2.3: Creating a Strong Password

- Discuss the importance of creating a strong and secure password for a new account.
- Provide guidelines for creating strong passwords, including using a combination of letters, numbers, and symbols, avoiding common words and phrases, and making passwords unique for each account.

Section 2.4: Managing Account Settings

- Explore the account settings available on the platform after signing up, including profile information, privacy settings, and notification preferences.
- Discuss the importance of reviewing and adjusting account settings to personalize the user experience and protect privacy and security.

Chapter 3: Logging In to an Account

In this chapter, we'll explore the process of logging in to an existing account on various online platforms and services, covering the steps involved and best practices for account security.

Section 3.1: Accessing the Login Page

- Explain how users can access the login page of an online platform or service, typically by visiting the platform's website or app and locating the login form.
- Discuss alternative methods for accessing the login page, such as clicking on a login link or button from the platform's homepage.

Section 3.2: Entering Credentials

- Walk through the steps involved in entering login credentials, including:

- Entering the username or email address associated with the account.
- Typing the password in the password field.

- Optionally selecting the "Remember Me" or "Stay Logged In" option for convenience.

Section 3.3: Password Recovery and Reset

- Discuss the options available for password recovery and reset in case users forget their passwords or are unable to log in to their accounts.
- Explain how users can initiate the password recovery process by clicking on the "Forgot Password" or "Reset Password" link on the login page.
- Provide guidance on verifying identity and resetting the password through email, SMS, security questions, or other verification methods.

Section 3.4: Security Measures

- Highlight the importance of practicing good security habits when logging in to online accounts.
- Discuss best practices for protecting login credentials, such as avoiding public Wi-Fi networks, using secure connections (HTTPS), and logging out of accounts after each session.
- Provide guidance on enabling additional security measures, such as two-factor authentication (2FA) or biometric authentication, where available.

Chapter 4: Conclusion and Next Steps

In conclusion, signing up for an account and logging in are essential actions that allow users to access and interact with various online platforms and services. By understanding the importance of account management and security, as well as the steps involved in signing up and logging in, users can navigate the digital landscape safely and confidently.

Introduction to Choosing a Template

Choosing the right template is a crucial step in creating a website that reflects your brand identity, engages your audience, and achieves your goals. In this chapter, we'll explore the importance of choosing a template, factors to consider when selecting a template, and tips for making the best choice for your website.

Section 1.1: Importance of Choosing a Template

- Discuss the significance of choosing a template for website development.
- Highlight how templates provide a foundation for website design, layout, and functionality.
- Explain how the right template can streamline the website creation process and help achieve a professional and cohesive look.

Section 1.2: Understanding Website Templates

- Define what website templates are and how they are used in website development.
- Explain the purpose of website templates in providing pre-designed layouts and structures for websites.
- Discuss the types of website templates available, including generic templates, industry-specific templates, and customizable templates.

Section 1.3: Benefits of Using Templates

- Explore the benefits of using templates for website creation, including:

- Time-saving: Templates reduce the need for designing layouts from scratch, saving time in the development process.
- Cost-effective: Using templates can be more cost-effective than hiring a designer to create a custom design.
- Consistency: Templates help maintain consistency in design elements, branding, and user experience across pages.
- Accessibility: Templates make website development accessible to users with varying levels of design and technical skills.

Chapter 2: Factors to Consider When Choosing a Template

In this chapter, we'll explore the key factors to consider when choosing a template for your website, including design, functionality, customization options, and compatibility.

Section 2.1: Design and Aesthetics

- Discuss the importance of design and aesthetics in choosing a template that aligns with your brand identity and target audience.

- Explore different design styles, such as minimalist, modern, classic, and bold, and how they can convey different brand personalities.
- Provide tips for evaluating design elements such as color schemes, typography, imagery, and layout options when selecting a template.

Section 2.2: Functionality and Features

- Consider the functionality and features required for your website and how they align with the template's capabilities.
- Discuss common features offered by templates, such as navigation menus, image galleries, contact forms, and e-commerce integrations.
- Evaluate whether the template provides the necessary features to support your website's goals, such as lead generation, online sales, or content publishing.

Section 2.3: Customization Options

- Explore the level of customization offered by the template and how it meets your needs for personalization and branding.
- Discuss the availability of customization options such as color palettes, fonts, layout variations, and widget integrations.
- Consider whether the template allows for easy customization without requiring advanced design or coding skills.

Section 2.4: Responsiveness and Compatibility

- Ensure that the template is responsive and compatible with a variety of devices and screen sizes, including desktops, laptops, tablets, and smartphones.
- Discuss the importance of responsive design in providing a seamless and consistent user experience across devices.
- Evaluate the template's compatibility with different web browsers, ensuring that it renders correctly and functions optimally for all users.

Chapter 3: Exploring Template Options

Now that we understand the factors to consider when choosing a template, let's explore different template options and where to find them.

Section 3.1: Wix Template Marketplace

- Introduce the Wix template marketplace as a resource for finding a wide range of professionally designed templates for various industries and purposes.
- Explore different categories and themes available in the Wix template marketplace, such as business, portfolio, e-commerce, and blog templates.
- Provide tips for browsing and filtering templates based on criteria such as industry, style, features, and popularity.

Section 3.2: Third-Party Template Providers

- Discuss the availability of templates from third-party providers outside of the Wix platform.
- Explore options for finding templates from reputable third-party providers, such as template marketplaces, design agencies, and freelance designers.
- Consider the pros and cons of using third-party templates, including customization options, support, and compatibility with the Wix platform.

Section 3.3: Customizable Templates

- Highlight the availability of customizable templates that allow for greater flexibility and personalization.
- Discuss how customizable templates provide a balance between pre-designed layouts and the ability to tailor the design to your specific needs.
- Explore options for customizing templates through the Wix Editor, including design elements, layout variations, and widget integrations.

Chapter 4: Making the Final Decision

In this chapter, we'll discuss strategies for making the final decision when choosing a template for your website, including testing, feedback, and evaluation.

Section 4.1: Testing and Previewing

- Discuss the importance of testing and previewing templates before making a final decision.
- Explore options for previewing templates in the Wix Editor, including demo sites, live previews, and interactive previews.
- Provide tips for testing template responsiveness, functionality, and customization options to ensure they meet your needs.

Section 4.2: Gathering Feedback

- Consider the value of gathering feedback from stakeholders, colleagues, or target audience members when evaluating templates.
- Discuss strategies for soliciting feedback, such as sharing prototype designs, conducting usability testing, or sending surveys.
- Explore how feedback can help identify strengths, weaknesses, and areas for improvement in potential templates.

Section 4.3: Making an Informed Decision

- Discuss how to weigh the factors discussed earlier in the chapter, such as design, functionality, customization options, and feedback, when making the final decision.
- Provide guidance on considering factors such as budget, timeline, and long-term scalability when choosing a template.
- Emphasize the importance of making an informed decision that aligns with your website's goals, audience, and branding.

Chapter 5: Conclusion and Next Steps

In conclusion, choosing the right template is a critical step in creating a successful website. By considering factors such as design, functionality, customization options, and compatibility, users can select a template that meets their needs and helps achieve their website goals.

Introduction to Website Customization

Customizing your website is a crucial step in creating a unique and engaging online presence that resonates with your audience. In this chapter, we'll explore the importance of website customization, the benefits it offers, and the various aspects of customization that you can leverage to tailor your website to your specific needs and preferences.

Section 1.1: Importance of Website Customization

- Discuss the significance of website customization in creating a memorable and impactful online presence.
- Highlight how customization allows you to differentiate your website from others, establish brand identity, and showcase your unique value proposition.
- Explain how customization enhances user experience by catering to the preferences and expectations of your target audience.

Section 1.2: Benefits of Website Customization

- Explore the benefits that website customization offers, including:

- Enhanced Branding: Customization allows you to align your website's design, content, and functionality with your brand identity, reinforcing brand recognition and credibility.
- Improved User Experience: Tailoring your website to the needs and preferences of your audience enhances usability, engagement, and satisfaction.
- Increased Conversions: Customization enables you to optimize your website for specific goals, such as lead generation, sales, or audience engagement, leading to higher conversion rates.
- Competitive Advantage: A customized website sets you apart from competitors and positions you as a leader in your industry, attracting and retaining customers.

Chapter 2: Elements of Website Customization

In this chapter, we'll explore the various elements of website customization that you can leverage to personalize your website and create a compelling user experience.

Section 2.1: Design Customization

- Discuss design customization options, including:

- Color Scheme: Choose colors that reflect your brand personality and evoke the desired emotions in your audience.
- Typography: Select fonts that enhance readability and convey your brand voice effectively.

- Layout: Arrange content and design elements in a way that optimizes usability and visual appeal.
- Images and Graphics: Use high-quality images and graphics that complement your content and reinforce your brand message.

Section 2.2: Content Customization

- Explore content customization options, including:

- Written Content: Craft compelling copy that resonates with your target audience and communicates your brand message effectively.
- Multimedia Content: Incorporate videos, images, infographics, and other multimedia elements to enrich your content and engage users.
- Personalization: Tailor content to individual users' preferences and behavior, such as recommending relevant products or content based on their past interactions.

Section 2.3: Functionality Customization

- Discuss functionality customization options, including:

- Navigation: Design intuitive navigation menus and site structure to help users find the information they need quickly and easily.
- Forms and Interactivity: Implement interactive elements such as contact forms, surveys, quizzes, and live chat to facilitate user engagement and communication.
- E-Commerce Features: Customize e-commerce functionality, such as product listings, shopping carts, and checkout processes, to streamline the online shopping experience for customers.

Chapter 3: Customization Tools and Techniques

Now that we understand the elements of website customization, let's explore the tools and techniques you can use to customize your website effectively.

Section 3.1: Wix Editor

- Introduce the Wix Editor as a powerful tool for customizing websites without coding knowledge.
- Explore the features and capabilities of the Wix Editor, including:

- Drag-and-Drop Interface: Easily add, remove, and rearrange design elements on your website.
- Design Tools: Customize colors, fonts, backgrounds, and other design elements to match your brand identity.
- App Integrations: Enhance functionality with apps and integrations from the Wix App Market, such as e-commerce, social media, and marketing tools.

Section 3.2: Wix Code

- Discuss Wix Code as an advanced tool for adding custom functionality and interactivity to your website using JavaScript and APIs.
- Explore the capabilities of Wix Code, including:

- Database Collections: Store and manage dynamic content such as user data, product listings, and blog posts.
- Dynamic Pages: Create dynamic pages that display content based on user input or database queries.
- User Input Forms: Collect and process user input through customizable forms and input fields.

Section 3.3: Third-Party Integrations

- Discuss the availability of third-party integrations and plugins that extend the functionality of your website.
- Explore popular third-party integrations for Wix websites, including:

- Payment Gateways: Accept payments online through secure payment gateways such as PayPal, Stripe, or Square.
- Marketing Tools: Integrate email marketing, social media, and analytics tools to track user behavior and optimize marketing campaigns.
- CRM Systems: Sync customer data and manage customer relationships more effectively with CRM integrations like Salesforce or HubSpot.

Chapter 4: Best Practices for Website Customization

In this chapter, we'll discuss best practices for website customization to help you create a cohesive, user-friendly, and effective online presence.

Section 4.1: Maintain Consistency

- Emphasize the importance of maintaining consistency in design, branding, and user experience across your website.
- Use consistent colors, fonts, imagery, and messaging to reinforce your brand identity and build trust with users.

Section 4.2: Prioritize Usability

- Prioritize usability and user experience when customizing your website.
- Design intuitive navigation, clear calls-to-action, and accessible content to ensure users can easily find what they're looking for and complete desired actions.

Section 4.3: Optimize for Mobile

- Optimize your website for mobile devices to accommodate users who access your site on smartphones and tablets.
- Use responsive design techniques to ensure your website displays properly and functions seamlessly across a range of screen sizes and devices.

Section 4.4: Test and Iterate

- Test your website regularly to identify areas for improvement and optimization.
- Use tools such as A/B testing, heatmaps, and user feedback to gather insights and make data-driven decisions about customization changes.

Chapter 5: Conclusion and Next Steps

In conclusion, website customization is a powerful tool for creating a unique and engaging online presence that resonates with your audience and achieves your business goals. By leveraging design, content, and functionality customization options, along with the right tools and techniques, you can create a website that stands out from the competition and delivers an exceptional user experience.

Introduction to Adding Pages

Adding pages to your website is essential for organizing content, providing navigation pathways for users, and expanding the scope of your online presence. In this chapter, we'll explore the importance of adding pages to your website, the types of pages you can create, and best practices for structuring and organizing your site's content.

Section 1.1: Importance of Adding Pages

- Discuss the significance of adding pages to your website in providing a comprehensive and user-friendly experience for visitors.
- Highlight how adding pages allows you to organize and present your content effectively, making it easier for users to find information and navigate your site.
- Explain how adding pages enables you to expand the scope and depth of your website, covering a wider range of topics, products, or services.

Section 1.2: Types of Pages

- Explore the various types of pages commonly found on websites, including:

- Home Page: The main entry point to your website, providing an overview of your brand, offerings, and key features.
- About Us Page: Introduces your brand, mission, team, and history to visitors, helping build trust and credibility.
- Products/Services Pages: Showcase your offerings in detail, providing information, images, pricing, and purchase options.
- Contact Page: Provides contact information, such as email addresses, phone numbers, and physical addresses, allowing visitors to get in touch with you.
- Blog Pages: Host blog posts, articles, and other dynamic content to engage visitors and drive traffic to your site.
- Portfolio/Gallery Pages: Display examples of your work, projects, or achievements to showcase your skills and expertise.
- FAQ Page: Address common questions and concerns from visitors, providing answers and solutions to help them make informed decisions.

Section 1.3: Benefits of Well-Structured Pages

- Discuss the benefits of structuring and organizing your website's pages effectively, including:

- Improved Navigation: Well-structured pages make it easier for users to navigate your site and find the information they're looking for.
- Enhanced User Experience: Clear page organization and hierarchy improve user experience by reducing confusion and frustration.

- SEO Benefits: Organized pages with relevant content help search engines understand and index your site more effectively, improving your search rankings.
- Increased Engagement: Pages that provide valuable and relevant content encourage visitors to stay on your site longer and engage more deeply with your brand.

Chapter 2: Creating and Adding Pages

In this chapter, we'll delve into the process of creating and adding pages to your website, covering the steps involved and best practices for page creation and management.

Section 2.1: Planning Your Pages

- Discuss the importance of planning your website's pages before creating them, including defining their purpose, content, and structure.
- Outline steps for page planning, such as conducting audience research, identifying key topics or categories, and creating a site map or wireframe to visualize page hierarchy and navigation pathways.

Section 2.2: Using the Wix Editor to Add Pages

- Introduce the Wix Editor as a user-friendly tool for creating and managing pages on your website.
- Walk through the steps of adding pages to your website using the Wix Editor, including:

- Accessing the Pages menu in the Wix Editor.
- Clicking on the "Add Page" button to create a new page.
- Choosing a page template or starting from scratch.
- Customizing the page layout, design, and content using the Wix Editor's drag-and-drop interface.
- Saving and publishing the new page to make it live on your website.

Section 2.3: Naming and Categorizing Pages

- Discuss best practices for naming and categorizing pages on your website to improve usability and SEO.
- Provide tips for choosing descriptive and intuitive page names that accurately reflect the page's content and purpose.
- Explore options for organizing pages into categories or sections to facilitate navigation and help users find related content more easily.

Section 2.4: Adding Content to Pages

- Explore options for adding content to your website's pages, including text, images, videos, and interactive elements.

- Provide guidance on structuring and formatting page content for readability and visual appeal.
- Discuss best practices for optimizing content for SEO, such as using relevant keywords, headings, and meta tags.

Chapter 3: Managing and Organizing Pages

In this chapter, we'll explore strategies for managing and organizing your website's pages effectively to maintain a cohesive and user-friendly experience.

Section 3.1: Page Hierarchy and Navigation

- Discuss the importance of establishing a clear page hierarchy and navigation structure to help users navigate your website intuitively.
- Provide guidance on organizing pages into primary and secondary navigation menus, dropdown menus, or nested categories to accommodate different levels of content depth.

Section 3.2: Linking Between Pages

- Explore strategies for linking between pages on your website to create logical pathways for users to navigate.
- Discuss the use of internal links within page content, navigation menus, footer links, and call-to-action buttons to guide users to relevant pages and encourage exploration.

Section 3.3: Updating and Maintaining Pages

- Highlight the importance of regularly updating and maintaining your website's pages to keep content fresh, accurate, and relevant.
- Discuss strategies for monitoring page performance, tracking user engagement, and analyzing metrics to identify areas for improvement.
- Provide tips for conducting regular audits of your website's pages to identify outdated or redundant content and make necessary updates or revisions.

Chapter 4: Conclusion and Next Steps

In conclusion, adding pages to your website is essential for providing a comprehensive and engaging online experience for visitors. By understanding the importance of page structure, organization, and content, and leveraging the tools and techniques available, you can create a website that effectively communicates your brand message, showcases your offerings, and meets the needs of your target audience.

Introduction to Navigation Menus

Navigation menus play a crucial role in guiding visitors through your website, helping them find the information they need quickly and easily. In this chapter, we'll explore the importance of navigation menus, the elements of an effective menu, and best practices for creating a user-friendly navigation experience.

Section 1.1: Importance of Navigation Menus

- Discuss the significance of navigation menus in website design and user experience.
- Highlight how navigation menus serve as roadmaps for visitors, helping them navigate your site's content and find relevant information.
- Explain how well-designed navigation menus can improve usability, engagement, and overall satisfaction for website visitors.

Section 1.2: Elements of an Effective Navigation Menu

- Explore the key elements of an effective navigation menu, including:

- Clear Labels: Use descriptive and intuitive labels that accurately represent the content of each page or section.
- Logical Hierarchy: Organize menu items in a logical hierarchy that reflects the structure and organization of your website's content.
- Consistent Placement: Place the navigation menu in a consistent location across all pages of your website, such as the top header or sidebar.
- Accessibility: Ensure that navigation menus are accessible to all users, including those using screen readers or assistive technologies.
- Mobile Responsiveness: Optimize navigation menus for mobile devices by using responsive design techniques and mobile-friendly layouts.

Section 1.3: Types of Navigation Menus

- Explore different types of navigation menus commonly used in website design, including:

- Horizontal Menus: Displayed horizontally across the top of the webpage, typically used for primary navigation.
- Vertical Menus: Positioned vertically along the side of the webpage, often used for secondary navigation or sub-menus.
- Dropdown Menus: Expandable menus that display additional options when users hover or click on a menu item.
- Hamburger Menus: Icon-based menus that collapse into a compact icon (usually a hamburger icon) on smaller screens, conserving space and improving mobile usability.

Chapter 2: Designing Your Navigation Menu

In this chapter, we'll delve into the process of designing your navigation menu, covering best practices for menu layout, styling, and functionality.

Section 2.1: Planning Your Menu Structure

- Discuss the importance of planning your menu structure before designing your navigation menu.
- Outline steps for menu planning, such as conducting a content audit, identifying key pages or sections, and prioritizing menu items based on user needs and goals.

Section 2.2: Choosing Menu Placement and Layout

- Explore options for menu placement and layout based on your website's design and user experience goals.
- Discuss the pros and cons of different menu placements, such as top header, sidebar, footer, or sticky/fixed menus.
- Provide guidance on selecting a menu layout that balances visual appeal with usability and accessibility considerations.

Section 2.3: Styling Your Menu

- Discuss best practices for styling your navigation menu to align with your website's branding and design aesthetics.
- Explore options for customizing menu appearance, including:

- Color and Typography: Choose colors and fonts that complement your website's overall design scheme and enhance readability.
- Size and Spacing: Adjust menu item size, spacing, and alignment to ensure visual balance and clarity.
- Hover Effects: Add hover effects or animations to indicate interactivity and improve user engagement.
- Icons and Symbols: Incorporate icons or symbols alongside menu items to provide visual cues and enhance navigation clarity.

Section 2.4: Implementing Menu Functionality

- Discuss considerations for implementing menu functionality to ensure a seamless and intuitive user experience.
- Explore options for adding interactivity to your navigation menu, such as dropdowns, mega menus, sticky/fixed menus, and smooth scrolling.
- Provide guidance on testing menu functionality across different devices and screen sizes to ensure responsiveness and usability.

Chapter 3: Building Your Navigation Menu with Wix

In this chapter, we'll walk through the process of building your navigation menu using the Wix platform, leveraging its intuitive tools and features.

Section 3.1: Accessing the Wix Editor

- Explain how to access the Wix Editor and navigate to the website editor dashboard.
- Discuss options for accessing the navigation menu editor within the Wix Editor interface.

Section 3.2: Adding Menu Items

- Walk through the steps of adding menu items to your navigation menu using the Wix Editor.
- Explain how to add new pages, sections, or external links to your menu, and customize the labels and URLs for each menu item.

Section 3.3: Customizing Menu Appearance

- Explore options for customizing the appearance of your navigation menu using the Wix Editor.
- Discuss how to adjust menu styling, such as colors, fonts, size, spacing, and hover effects, using the design tools available in the Wix Editor.

Section 3.4: Configuring Menu Behavior

- Provide guidance on configuring menu behavior and functionality to enhance user experience.
- Discuss options for configuring dropdown menus, sticky/fixed menus, mobile responsiveness, and other interactive features using the Wix Editor.

Chapter 4: Best Practices for Navigation Menu Design

In this chapter, we'll discuss best practices for navigation menu design to ensure a seamless and user-friendly navigation experience for your website visitors.

Section 4.1: Keep It Simple

- Emphasize the importance of keeping your navigation menu simple and streamlined to avoid overwhelming users with too many options.
- Limit the number of menu items to essential pages or sections, prioritizing the most important content for easy access.

Section 4.2: Prioritize Accessibility

- Discuss the importance of prioritizing accessibility in navigation menu design to ensure all users can navigate your website effectively.
- Provide guidance on implementing accessible design practices, such as using descriptive link labels, providing alternative text for images, and ensuring keyboard navigation.

Section 4.3: Test and Iterate

- Highlight the importance of testing your navigation menu across different devices, browsers, and user scenarios to identify and address any usability issues.
- Encourage iterative design and optimization based on user feedback, analytics data, and usability testing results to continuously improve navigation menu performance.

Chapter 5: Conclusion and Next Steps

In conclusion, creating a user-friendly navigation menu is essential for guiding visitors through your website and helping them find the information they need efficiently. By understanding the principles of navigation menu design and leveraging the tools and techniques available, you can create a navigation experience that enhances usability, engagement, and overall satisfaction for your website visitors.

Introduction to Mobile Optimization

Mobile optimization is essential in today's digital landscape, where an increasing number of users access websites and applications on smartphones and tablets. In this chapter, we'll explore the importance of mobile optimization, the challenges it presents, and strategies for ensuring a seamless user experience across mobile devices.

Section 1.1: Importance of Mobile Optimization

- Discuss the significance of mobile optimization in providing a user-friendly experience for mobile users.
- Highlight the growing trend of mobile device usage for internet browsing and online activities.
- Explain how mobile optimization improves user engagement, retention, and conversion rates for websites and applications.

Section 1.2: Challenges of Mobile Optimization

- Explore the challenges and considerations involved in optimizing websites and applications for mobile devices.
- Discuss factors such as varying screen sizes, resolutions, and input methods that impact mobile usability.
- Highlight the importance of responsive design, performance optimization, and usability testing in overcoming mobile optimization challenges.

Section 1.3: Benefits of Mobile Optimization

- Explore the benefits that mobile optimization offers, including:

- Improved User Experience: Mobile-optimized websites and applications provide a seamless and intuitive experience for mobile users, leading to higher satisfaction and engagement.
- Higher Search Rankings: Search engines prioritize mobile-friendly websites in search results, leading to increased visibility and organic traffic.
- Increased Conversions: Mobile optimization reduces friction in the user journey, making it easier for users to complete desired actions such as making purchases or submitting forms.

Chapter 2: Principles of Mobile Optimization

In this chapter, we'll delve into the principles of mobile optimization and explore strategies for designing and optimizing websites and applications for mobile devices.

Section 2.1: Responsive Design

- Discuss responsive design as a key principle of mobile optimization, allowing websites and applications to adapt to different screen sizes and resolutions.

- Explore techniques for implementing responsive design, such as fluid layouts, flexible images, and media queries.
- Provide guidance on testing and optimizing responsive designs across a range of devices and viewport sizes.

Section 2.2: Performance Optimization

- Highlight the importance of performance optimization in mobile optimization, as mobile users expect fast-loading and responsive experiences.
- Discuss strategies for optimizing website and application performance on mobile devices, including:

- Minimizing HTTP requests: Reduce the number of server requests by combining files, using CSS sprites, and optimizing images.
- Implementing browser caching: Leverage browser caching to store static assets locally and reduce loading times for returning visitors.
- Compressing resources: Minify and compress CSS, JavaScript, and HTML files to reduce file sizes and improve load times.
- Prioritizing content: Optimize critical rendering paths to ensure that essential content loads quickly and is visible to users as soon as possible.

Section 2.3: User Experience Optimization

- Explore strategies for optimizing user experience on mobile devices, considering factors such as touch input, screen size, and navigation patterns.
- Discuss best practices for designing intuitive user interfaces (UI) and user experiences (UX) for mobile users, including:

- Large, tappable buttons: Use touch-friendly button sizes and spacing to accommodate users' fingers and minimize accidental clicks.
- Clear, concise content: Streamline content and navigation to prioritize essential information and reduce cognitive load for mobile users.
- Gestural navigation: Implement intuitive gestures such as swipe, pinch-to-zoom, and tap-and-hold to enhance navigation and interaction on touch screens.

Chapter 3: Mobile Optimization Techniques

In this chapter, we'll explore specific techniques and tools for optimizing websites and applications for mobile devices, including both design and development considerations.

Section 3.1: Mobile-Friendly Design Patterns

- Discuss mobile-friendly design patterns and techniques that improve usability and engagement for mobile users.
- Explore design patterns such as:

- Scannable content: Use concise headings, bullet points, and short paragraphs to make content easy to scan and digest on small screens.
- Sticky/fixed elements: Keep important elements such as navigation menus, headers, or calls-to-action fixed at the top or bottom of the screen for easy access.
- Progressive disclosure: Present information progressively, revealing additional details or options as users interact with the interface to prevent overload and maintain focus.

Section 3.2: Mobile Optimization Tools

- Introduce tools and resources for mobile optimization that assist in testing, monitoring, and improving mobile performance and user experience.
- Discuss tools such as:

- Google's Mobile-Friendly Test: Test your website's mobile-friendliness and receive recommendations for improvement from Google.
- PageSpeed Insights: Analyze your website's performance on mobile devices and receive optimization suggestions to improve loading times.
- Mobile Emulators: Use mobile emulators or device simulators to preview and test your website on different devices and screen sizes.

Section 3.3: Mobile SEO Optimization

- Explore strategies for optimizing websites for mobile search engines to improve visibility and ranking in mobile search results.
- Discuss mobile SEO best practices such as:

- Mobile-friendly design: Ensure your website is responsive and mobile-friendly to meet Google's mobile-first indexing criteria.
- Fast loading times: Optimize your website's performance to improve loading times on mobile devices, as page speed is a ranking factor for mobile search.
- Local SEO optimization: Optimize your website for local search queries by including location-based keywords, creating a Google My Business listing, and obtaining local citations.

Chapter 4: Testing and Iteration

In this chapter, we'll discuss the importance of testing and iteration in mobile optimization and explore strategies for identifying and addressing issues to improve mobile performance and user experience.

Section 4.1: Usability Testing

- Discuss the importance of usability testing in evaluating the effectiveness of mobile optimization strategies and identifying areas for improvement.
- Explore methods for conducting usability testing on mobile devices, such as:

- Remote usability testing: Use remote testing tools to gather feedback from users across different locations and devices.
- In-person testing: Conduct in-person usability tests with participants using mobile devices to observe their interactions and gather insights in real-time.

Section 4.2: A/B Testing

- Introduce A/B testing as a method for comparing different versions of a website or application to determine which performs better in terms of mobile optimization metrics.
- Discuss how to set up and conduct A/B tests for mobile optimization, including defining test hypotheses, selecting test variables, and measuring key performance indicators (KPIs).

Section 4.3: Continuous Improvement

- Emphasize the importance of continuous improvement in mobile optimization, as mobile technology and user behavior evolve over time.
- Discuss strategies for ongoing monitoring, analysis, and iteration to identify emerging trends, address performance issues, and implement new optimization techniques.

Chapter 5: Conclusion and Next Steps

In conclusion, mobile optimization is essential for providing a seamless and engaging user experience for mobile users. By understanding the principles of mobile optimization, leveraging optimization techniques and tools, and continuously testing and iterating, you can create websites and applications that meet the needs and expectations of mobile users and drive success in the mobile-first era.

Introduction to Previewing and Publishing

Previewing and publishing your website are crucial steps in the website development process, allowing you to review your work and make it accessible to the public. In this chapter, we'll explore the importance of previewing and publishing, the steps involved in each process, and best practices for ensuring a successful launch.

Section 1.1: Importance of Previewing and Publishing

- Discuss the significance of previewing and publishing your website in making it accessible to visitors and achieving your goals.
- Highlight the role of previewing in reviewing and testing your website's design, functionality, and content before making it live.
- Explain how publishing your website enables you to share your work with the world, attract visitors, and achieve your desired outcomes, such as generating leads, making sales, or sharing information.

Section 1.2: Benefits of Previewing and Testing

- Explore the benefits of previewing and testing your website before publishing, including:

- Identifying Errors: Previewing allows you to catch and fix errors such as broken links, layout issues, and typos before they impact user experience.
- Ensuring Consistency: Previewing helps ensure that your website displays consistently across different devices, browsers, and screen sizes.
- Improving User Experience: Testing allows you to evaluate usability, navigation, and performance to optimize user experience before launching your site.

Section 1.3: Benefits of Publishing

- Discuss the benefits of publishing your website and making it accessible to the public, including:

- Increased Visibility: Publishing your website makes it discoverable to search engines and users, increasing visibility and potential traffic.
- Establishing Credibility: A published website conveys professionalism and credibility, building trust with visitors and stakeholders.
- Achieving Goals: Publishing your website enables you to achieve your desired outcomes, such as attracting customers, sharing information, or promoting your brand.

Chapter 2: Previewing Your Website

In this chapter, we'll explore the process of previewing your website to review and test its design, functionality, and content before publishing.

Section 2.1: Using Preview Modes

- Introduce preview modes available in website builders such as Wix, allowing you to preview your website in different contexts, such as desktop, mobile, and tablet.
- Discuss how preview modes help you evaluate how your website will appear and function across different devices and screen sizes.

Section 2.2: Reviewing Design and Layout

- Explore strategies for reviewing the design and layout of your website during the preview process.
- Discuss considerations such as color schemes, typography, spacing, and alignment, ensuring visual consistency and appeal across pages.

Section 2.3: Testing Functionality and Interactivity

- Discuss the importance of testing functionality and interactivity during the preview process.
- Explore techniques for testing features such as navigation menus, forms, buttons, links, and multimedia content to ensure they work as intended.

Section 2.4: Proofreading and Editing Content

- Highlight the importance of proofreading and editing content during the preview process to ensure accuracy, clarity, and professionalism.
- Discuss strategies for reviewing written content, images, videos, and other media to identify and correct errors, typos, and inconsistencies.

Chapter 3: Publishing Your Website

In this chapter, we'll explore the process of publishing your website and making it accessible to the public.

Section 3.1: Configuring Publishing Settings

- Discuss the publishing settings available in website builders such as Wix, allowing you to customize how your website is published and accessed.
- Explore options for configuring domain settings, SEO settings, privacy settings, and access permissions before publishing.

Section 3.2: Choosing a Domain

- Discuss considerations for choosing a domain name for your website, such as relevance, memorability, and availability.
- Explore options for registering a new domain or connecting an existing domain to your website builder platform.

Section 3.3: Publishing Your Website

- Walk through the steps of publishing your website using website builder platforms such as Wix.
- Discuss how to initiate the publishing process, review final settings and configurations, and confirm the publication of your website to make it live.

Section 3.4: Post-Publishing Considerations

- Discuss considerations for post-publishing, including:

- Monitoring Performance: Use analytics tools to monitor website performance, track visitor behavior, and measure key metrics such as traffic, engagement, and conversions.
- Regular Updates: Schedule regular updates and maintenance to keep your website content fresh, relevant, and accurate.
- Marketing and Promotion: Implement marketing and promotion strategies to attract visitors, such as search engine optimization (SEO), social media marketing, and email campaigns.

Chapter 4: Best Practices for Previewing and Publishing

In this chapter, we'll discuss best practices for previewing and publishing your website to ensure a successful launch and ongoing success.

Section 4.1: Test Across Devices and Browsers

- Emphasize the importance of testing your website across different devices, browsers, and screen sizes to ensure compatibility and consistency.
- Discuss the use of testing tools and emulators to simulate various user scenarios and identify potential issues before publishing.

Section 4.2: Collaborate and Gather Feedback

- Encourage collaboration and feedback from stakeholders, colleagues, and target audience members during the previewing and testing process.
- Discuss strategies for gathering feedback, such as usability testing, peer reviews, and surveys, to identify areas for improvement and refinement.

Section 4.3: Monitor and Iterate

- Highlight the importance of monitoring website performance and user feedback after publishing to identify opportunities for optimization and improvement.
- Discuss strategies for iterative development, such as A/B testing, data analysis, and user feedback integration, to continuously enhance your website over time.

Chapter 5: Conclusion and Next Steps

In conclusion, previewing and publishing your website are critical steps in the website development process, enabling you to review, test, and share your work with the world. By following best practices, leveraging available tools and resources, and continuously monitoring and iterating, you can ensure a successful launch and ongoing success for your website.

Introduction to Domain Names

Choosing a domain name is a critical step in establishing an online presence, as it serves as the foundation of your website's identity and branding. In this chapter, we'll explore the importance of domain names, factors to consider when choosing one, and best practices for selecting a domain name that aligns with your goals and objectives.

Section 1.1: Importance of Domain Names

- Discuss the significance of domain names in the context of website identity and branding.
- Highlight how domain names act as the gateway for users to access your website and serve as a memorable identifier for your brand or business.
- Explain how domain names contribute to search engine optimization (SEO) efforts by influencing search rankings and visibility.

Section 1.2: Branding Considerations

- Explore the role of domain names in branding and brand identity.
- Discuss how domain names should reflect your brand's personality, values, and offerings to resonate with your target audience.
- Highlight the importance of choosing a domain name that is memorable, distinctive, and easy to spell and pronounce.

Section 1.3: SEO Implications

- Discuss the impact of domain names on search engine optimization (SEO) efforts.
- Explore factors such as keyword relevance, domain age, and domain authority that influence search engine rankings.
- Provide guidance on selecting a domain name that incorporates relevant keywords or phrases to improve SEO performance.

Chapter 2: Factors to Consider When Choosing a Domain Name

In this chapter, we'll delve into the factors you should consider when choosing a domain name for your website, covering both practical and strategic considerations.

Section 2.1: Relevance to Your Brand or Niche

- Discuss the importance of choosing a domain name that is relevant to your brand, business, or niche.
- Explore strategies for incorporating brand names, product names, or industry keywords into your domain name to communicate your focus and expertise.

Section 2.2: Memorability and Brand Recall

- Highlight the importance of selecting a domain name that is memorable and easy to recall.
- Discuss techniques for creating memorable domain names, such as using short, catchy words, avoiding hyphens or numbers, and using unique or creative combinations.

Section 2.3: Brand Consistency Across Platforms

- Discuss the importance of maintaining brand consistency across different online platforms and channels.
- Explore considerations for selecting a domain name that aligns with your existing branding elements, such as company name, logo, tagline, and social media handles.

Section 2.4: Domain Extension (TLD) Selection

- Explore the different types of domain extensions (Top-Level Domains or TLDs) available, such as .com, .net, .org, and country-code TLDs (ccTLDs).
- Discuss factors to consider when selecting a domain extension, including availability, relevance, and audience perception.

Section 2.5: Avoiding Trademark and Copyright Issues

- Discuss the importance of conducting thorough research to avoid trademark and copyright issues when selecting a domain name.
- Provide guidance on performing trademark searches and legal checks to ensure your chosen domain name does not infringe on existing trademarks or copyrights.

Chapter 3: Best Practices for Choosing a Domain Name

In this chapter, we'll discuss best practices and strategies for choosing a domain name that aligns with your goals and objectives.

Section 3.1: Conducting Research and Brainstorming

- Discuss the importance of conducting research and brainstorming sessions to generate potential domain name ideas.
- Explore techniques for brainstorming domain names, such as using keyword research tools, mind mapping, and word association exercises.

Section 3.2: Checking Domain Availability

- Explain the process of checking domain name availability and registering a domain name for your website.
- Discuss domain registrar platforms and tools for searching and registering available domain names, such as GoDaddy, Namecheap, and Google Domains.

Section 3.3: Securing Alternative Domain Extensions

- Discuss the importance of securing alternative domain extensions (TLDs) to protect your brand and prevent domain squatting.
- Explore options for registering multiple domain extensions (.com, .net, .org, etc.) to maintain brand consistency and prevent competitors from acquiring similar domain names.

Section 3.4: Seeking Feedback and Validation

- Encourage seeking feedback and validation from peers, colleagues, and target audience members when finalizing domain name choices.
- Discuss the importance of testing domain names for readability, memorability, and brand association to ensure they resonate with your target audience.

Chapter 4: Registering Your Domain Name

In this chapter, we'll explore the process of registering your chosen domain name and securing it for your website.

Section 4.1: Choosing a Domain Registrar

- Discuss factors to consider when selecting a domain registrar for registering your domain name, such as pricing, customer support, and additional services.
- Explore popular domain registrars and their features, such as domain privacy protection, DNS management, and website hosting options.

Section 4.2: Completing the Registration Process

- Walk through the steps of completing the domain registration process with your chosen registrar.
- Discuss the required information for domain registration, such as contact details, payment information, and domain configuration settings.

Section 4.3: Managing Domain Settings

- Provide guidance on managing domain settings and configurations after registering your domain name.
- Discuss options for configuring DNS settings, setting up domain forwarding or redirection, and enabling domain privacy protection to protect your personal information.

Chapter 5: Conclusion and Next Steps

In conclusion, choosing a domain name is a critical step in establishing your online presence and building your brand identity. By considering factors such as relevance, memorability, brand consistency, and legal considerations, and following best practices for research, brainstorming, and validation, you can select a domain name that resonates with your target audience and supports your goals and objectives.

Introduction to SEO Optimization

Search Engine Optimization (SEO) is a critical aspect of online marketing, aiming to improve a website's visibility and ranking in search engine results pages (SERPs). In this chapter, we'll explore the importance of SEO optimization, its key components, and strategies for maximizing your website's search engine performance.

Section 1.1: Importance of SEO Optimization

- Discuss the significance of SEO optimization in driving organic traffic to websites and increasing visibility.
- Highlight how higher search engine rankings lead to increased website traffic, user engagement, and conversions.
- Explain the long-term benefits of SEO optimization in establishing authority, credibility, and brand awareness.

Section 1.2: Key Components of SEO Optimization

- Explore the key components of SEO optimization, including:

- On-Page SEO: Optimizing individual web pages for target keywords, meta tags, headings, and content quality.
- Off-Page SEO: Building backlinks from reputable websites, social media engagement, and online reputation management.
- Technical SEO: Improving website performance, crawlability, and indexability through site structure, speed optimization, and mobile responsiveness.

Section 1.3: SEO Best Practices and Guidelines

- Discuss SEO best practices and guidelines recommended by search engines such as Google, Bing, and Yahoo.
- Explore white hat SEO techniques that adhere to search engine guidelines and avoid black hat tactics such as keyword stuffing, cloaking, and link manipulation.

Chapter 2: On-Page SEO Optimization

In this chapter, we'll delve into the strategies and techniques for optimizing individual web pages for search engines through on-page SEO.

Section 2.1: Keyword Research and Analysis

- Discuss the importance of keyword research in identifying relevant search terms and phrases used by your target audience.
- Explore keyword research tools and techniques for identifying high-value keywords with high search volume, low competition, and relevance to your content.

Section 2.2: Optimizing Meta Tags and Headings

- Provide guidance on optimizing meta tags, including title tags, meta descriptions, and header tags (H1, H2, H3, etc.).
- Discuss best practices for writing compelling and descriptive meta tags that accurately reflect the page content and encourage click-throughs in search results.

Section 2.3: Content Optimization

- Explore strategies for optimizing on-page content for search engines and users.
- Discuss techniques such as incorporating target keywords naturally into content, writing high-quality and engaging copy, and structuring content with headings, bullet points, and multimedia elements.

Section 2.4: Image Optimization

- Highlight the importance of image optimization for SEO and user experience.
- Discuss techniques for optimizing images for search engines, including using descriptive file names, alt tags, and captions, and reducing file sizes for faster loading times.

Chapter 3: Off-Page SEO Optimization

In this chapter, we'll explore strategies for improving off-page SEO through link building, social media engagement, and online reputation management.

Section 3.1: Link Building Strategies

- Discuss the importance of backlinks in off-page SEO and their impact on search engine rankings.
- Explore link building strategies such as guest blogging, directory submissions, influencer outreach, and content promotion to acquire high-quality backlinks from authoritative websites.

Section 3.2: Social Media Engagement

- Discuss the role of social media in off-page SEO and its impact on brand visibility and reputation.
- Explore strategies for engaging with your audience on social media platforms, sharing content, and building relationships with influencers and industry leaders to increase social signals and referral traffic.

Section 3.3: Online Reputation Management

- Highlight the importance of online reputation management in off-page SEO and brand perception.
- Discuss strategies for monitoring and managing online reviews, responding to customer feedback and inquiries, and building a positive online reputation through transparency and authenticity.

Chapter 4: Technical SEO Optimization

In this chapter, we'll explore technical SEO optimization techniques for improving website performance, crawlability, and indexability.

Section 4.1: Site Structure and Navigation

- Discuss the importance of site structure and navigation in technical SEO and user experience.
- Explore strategies for organizing website content hierarchically, optimizing internal linking structure, and creating XML sitemaps to facilitate search engine crawling and indexing.

Section 4.2: Website Speed Optimization

- Highlight the importance of website speed in technical SEO and user experience.
- Discuss techniques for optimizing website speed, such as minimizing HTTP requests, leveraging browser caching, compressing images, and reducing server response times.

Section 4.3: Mobile Responsiveness

- Discuss the importance of mobile responsiveness in technical SEO and user experience, especially with the increasing use of mobile devices for internet browsing.
- Explore techniques for optimizing websites for mobile devices, such as using responsive design, optimizing page load times, and implementing mobile-friendly navigation and layouts.

Chapter 5: SEO Tools and Analytics

In this chapter, we'll explore tools and analytics for monitoring and measuring SEO performance, tracking key metrics, and optimizing your SEO strategies.

Section 5.1: SEO Tools

- Introduce popular SEO tools and software for keyword research, on-page optimization, link building, and performance tracking.
- Discuss the features and functionalities of SEO tools such as Google Analytics, Google Search Console, SEMrush, Moz, and Ahrefs.

Section 5.2: SEO Analytics

- Discuss key metrics and KPIs for measuring SEO performance and effectiveness.
- Explore metrics such as organic traffic, keyword rankings, backlink profile, click-through rates (CTR), and conversion rates, and discuss how to interpret and analyze these metrics to optimize SEO strategies.

Chapter 6: Local SEO Optimization

In this chapter, we'll explore strategies for optimizing websites for local search, targeting geo-specific keywords, and improving visibility in local search results.

Section 6.1: Local Keyword Research

- Discuss the importance of local keyword research in targeting geo-specific search terms and phrases.
- Explore techniques for identifying local keywords, such as incorporating location modifiers (city names, ZIP codes) into keyword research tools and analyzing local search trends and user intent.

Section 6.2: Google My Business Optimization

- Highlight the importance of Google My Business (GMB) optimization in local SEO and Google Maps visibility.
- Discuss strategies for optimizing GMB profiles, including completing all profile sections, verifying location information, and regularly updating business hours, services, and customer reviews.

Section 6.3: Local Citations and NAP Consistency

- Discuss the significance of local citations (mentions of your business name, address, and phone number) in local SEO and online visibility.
- Explore strategies for building local citations on reputable directories, review websites, and local business listings, and ensuring consistency and accuracy of NAP (Name, Address, Phone Number) information across all citations.

Chapter 7: Voice Search Optimization

In this chapter, we'll explore strategies for optimizing websites for voice search, considering the increasing prevalence of voice-activated digital assistants and smart speakers.

Section 7.1: Understanding Voice Search Trends

- Discuss the rising popularity of voice search and its impact on SEO strategies.
- Explore voice search trends, user behaviors, and search queries, and discuss how voice search differs from traditional text-based search.

Section 7.2: Optimizing Content for Voice Search

- Explore techniques for optimizing website content for voice search queries.
- Discuss strategies such as answering user questions directly, using natural language and conversational tone, and optimizing for long-tail keywords and semantic search.

Section 7.3: Local Voice Search Optimization

- Discuss strategies for optimizing websites for local voice search queries.

- Explore techniques such as incorporating location-based keywords, providing relevant and accurate business information, and optimizing for "near me" searches to improve visibility in local voice search results.

Chapter 8: Conclusion and Next Steps

In conclusion, SEO optimization is essential for improving website visibility, attracting organic traffic, and achieving business objectives. By understanding the key components of SEO, implementing best practices, leveraging tools and analytics, and staying updated on emerging trends, you can develop effective SEO strategies to enhance your online presence and drive success in the digital landscape.

Introduction to Analytics

Analytics play a crucial role in understanding user behavior, measuring website performance, and optimizing digital marketing strategies. In this chapter, we'll explore the importance of analytics, key metrics to track, and strategies for leveraging analytics data to drive informed decisions.

Section 1.1: Importance of Analytics

- Discuss the significance of analytics in digital marketing and website management.
- Highlight how analytics provide insights into user behavior, traffic sources, conversion rates, and other key performance indicators (KPIs) essential for business growth.
- Explain how analytics help in identifying strengths and weaknesses in marketing campaigns, website design, and content strategy, enabling continuous improvement and optimization.

Section 1.2: Key Metrics to Track

- Explore essential metrics and KPIs to track in website analytics, including:

- Traffic Metrics: such as sessions, users, pageviews, and bounce rate, to measure website engagement and popularity.
- Conversion Metrics: such as conversion rate, goal completions, and revenue, to measure the effectiveness of marketing campaigns and website performance in driving desired actions.
- Engagement Metrics: such as average session duration, pages per session, and time on page, to gauge user interaction and content relevance.
- Acquisition Metrics: such as traffic sources, referral sources, and campaign performance, to assess the effectiveness of marketing channels in driving traffic and conversions.

Section 1.3: Goals and Objectives

- Discuss the importance of defining clear goals and objectives for analytics tracking.
- Explore how setting specific goals, such as increasing website traffic, improving conversion rates, or enhancing user engagement, helps in aligning analytics efforts with business objectives and measuring success.

Chapter 2: Website Analytics

In this chapter, we'll delve into website analytics and explore tools, techniques, and best practices for tracking and analyzing website performance.

Section 2.1: Introduction to Website Analytics Tools

- Introduce popular website analytics tools such as Google Analytics, Adobe Analytics, and Matomo (formerly Piwik).
- Discuss the features, capabilities, and benefits of each analytics platform, including tracking options, reporting capabilities, and integration with other marketing tools.

Section 2.2: Setting Up Analytics Tracking

- Walk through the process of setting up analytics tracking for a website using Google Analytics as an example.
- Discuss steps such as creating an analytics account, generating tracking code, and implementing tracking code on website pages to start collecting data.

Section 2.3: Customizing Analytics Reports

- Explore customization options available in website analytics platforms for creating custom reports and dashboards.
- Discuss how to tailor reports to focus on specific metrics, segments, or goals relevant to business objectives, and how to schedule automated report delivery.

Section 2.4: Analyzing Website Performance

- Discuss strategies for analyzing website performance using analytics data.
- Explore techniques for identifying trends, patterns, and insights in website traffic, user behavior, and conversion funnels, and discuss how to interpret analytics metrics to uncover actionable insights.

Chapter 3: Social Media Analytics

In this chapter, we'll explore social media analytics and strategies for tracking and measuring the effectiveness of social media marketing efforts.

Section 3.1: Introduction to Social Media Analytics Tools

- Introduce social media analytics tools such as Facebook Insights, Twitter Analytics, and LinkedIn Analytics.
- Discuss the features and capabilities of each social media analytics platform, including audience demographics, engagement metrics, and content performance insights.

Section 3.2: Tracking Social Media Metrics

- Explore key metrics to track in social media analytics, including:

- Audience Metrics: such as followers, reach, and demographics, to understand the composition and interests of your social media audience.
- Engagement Metrics: such as likes, shares, comments, and click-through rates, to measure user interaction and content effectiveness.

- Conversion Metrics: such as conversion rate, lead generation, and revenue generated from social media channels, to assess the impact of social media marketing on business goals.

Section 3.3: Analyzing Social Media Performance

- Discuss strategies for analyzing social media performance using analytics data.
- Explore techniques for evaluating the effectiveness of social media campaigns, identifying top-performing content, and optimizing social media strategy based on audience insights and engagement metrics.

Chapter 4: Email Marketing Analytics

In this chapter, we'll explore email marketing analytics and techniques for tracking and measuring the effectiveness of email campaigns.

Section 4.1: Introduction to Email Marketing Analytics Tools

- Introduce email marketing analytics tools such as Mailchimp, Constant Contact, and Campaign Monitor.
- Discuss the features and capabilities of each email marketing analytics platform, including open rates, click-through rates, and conversion tracking.

Section 4.2: Tracking Email Metrics

- Explore key metrics to track in email marketing analytics, including:

- Open Rate: Percentage of recipients who open an email.
- Click-Through Rate (CTR): Percentage of recipients who click on links within an email.
- Conversion Rate: Percentage of recipients who take a desired action, such as making a purchase or filling out a form, after clicking on a link in an email.

Section 4.3: Analyzing Email Campaign Performance

- Discuss strategies for analyzing email campaign performance using analytics data.
- Explore techniques for assessing the effectiveness of email subject lines, content, design, and timing, and discuss how to use analytics insights to optimize future email campaigns for better results.

Chapter 5: E-commerce Analytics

In this chapter, we'll explore e-commerce analytics and strategies for tracking and optimizing online sales performance.

Section 5.1: Introduction to E-commerce Analytics Tools

- Introduce e-commerce analytics tools such as Google Analytics Enhanced E-commerce, Shopify Analytics, and WooCommerce Analytics.

- Discuss the features and capabilities of each e-commerce analytics platform, including sales tracking, product performance, and cart abandonment analysis.

Section 5.2: Tracking E-commerce Metrics

- Explore key metrics to track in e-commerce analytics, including:

- Sales Performance: Total revenue, average order value, and conversion rate.
- Product Performance: Best-selling products, revenue by product category, and product attribution.
- Cart Abandonment Rate: Percentage of users who add items to their cart but do not complete the purchase.

Section 5.3: Analyzing E-commerce Performance

- Discuss strategies for analyzing e-commerce performance using analytics data.
- Explore techniques for identifying sales trends, understanding user behavior in the purchase funnel, and optimizing product pages, checkout process, and marketing campaigns to increase e-commerce sales.

Chapter 6: Data Visualization and Reporting

In this chapter, we'll explore techniques for visualizing analytics data and creating actionable reports to communicate insights effectively.

Section 6.1: Data Visualization Tools

- Introduce data visualization tools such as Google Data Studio, Tableau, and Microsoft Power BI.
- Discuss the features and capabilities of each data visualization platform, including drag-and-drop interfaces, customizable dashboards, and interactive data exploration.

Section 6.2: Creating Actionable Reports

- Discuss best practices for creating actionable reports that communicate insights and recommendations effectively.
- Explore techniques for structuring reports, selecting relevant metrics, visualizing data effectively, and providing context and analysis to guide decision-making.

Section 6.3: Sharing and Presenting Insights

- Discuss strategies for sharing and presenting analytics insights with stakeholders, clients, or team members.
- Explore options for sharing reports via email, sharing links, embedding reports in presentations, and conducting live presentations to facilitate discussion and decision-making.

Chapter 7: Advanced Analytics Techniques

In this chapter, we'll explore advanced analytics techniques and strategies for leveraging data science and machine learning to gain deeper insights and drive more informed decisions.

Section 7.1: Predictive Analytics

- Introduce predictive analytics techniques for forecasting future trends and outcomes based on historical data.
- Discuss predictive modeling methods such as regression analysis, time series forecasting, and machine learning algorithms, and explore use cases in marketing, sales, and customer behavior prediction.

Section 7.2: Customer Segmentation and Personalization

- Discuss the importance of customer segmentation and personalization in marketing and customer experience.
- Explore techniques for segmenting customers based on demographics, behavior, and preferences, and discuss how to use segmentation to deliver targeted messaging and personalized experiences.

Section 7.3: A/B Testing and Experimentation

- Discuss the importance of A/B testing and experimentation in optimizing marketing campaigns and website performance.
- Explore techniques for designing and conducting A/B tests, analyzing results, and using experimentation to iterate and improve marketing strategies and user experiences.

Chapter 8: Ethics and Privacy in Analytics

In this chapter, we'll explore ethical considerations and privacy implications in analytics, and discuss best practices for responsible data usage and protection.

Section 8.1: Data Privacy and Compliance

- Discuss the importance of data privacy and compliance with regulations such as GDPR (General Data Protection Regulation) and CCPA (California Consumer Privacy Act).
- Explore best practices for collecting, storing, and processing user data responsibly, including obtaining consent, anonymizing data, and implementing security measures to protect sensitive information.

Section 8.2: Ethical Data Usage

- Discuss ethical considerations in data usage and analysis, such as transparency, fairness, and accountability.
- Explore ethical frameworks and guidelines for responsible data practices, and discuss the role of data ethics in building trust with customers and stakeholders.

Chapter 9: Conclusion and Next Steps

In conclusion, analytics provide invaluable insights into user behavior, marketing performance, and business outcomes, enabling data-driven decision-making and continuous improvement. By leveraging analytics tools, tracking key metrics, and analyzing data effectively, businesses can optimize their digital marketing efforts, enhance customer experiences, and achieve their goals and objectives in the dynamic digital landscape.

Introduction to Advanced Editing Tools

Advanced editing tools are essential for professionals and enthusiasts alike who require precise control and creative freedom over their digital content. In this chapter, we'll explore the importance of advanced editing tools, their functionalities, and how they contribute to enhancing the quality and aesthetics of digital media.

Section 1.1: Importance of Advanced Editing Tools

- Discuss the significance of advanced editing tools in the creative process for various digital media, including photography, videography, graphic design, and audio production.
- Highlight how advanced editing tools enable professionals to achieve sophisticated effects, refine details, and express their artistic vision with precision and versatility.
- Explore how advanced editing tools empower creators to push the boundaries of creativity and produce content that captivates audiences and stands out in a competitive landscape.

Section 1.2: Key Features and Functionalities

- Introduce the key features and functionalities commonly found in advanced editing tools across different disciplines.
- Discuss functionalities such as layer-based editing, non-destructive editing, advanced color correction and grading, masking and selection tools, and special effects and filters.
- Explore how these features enable users to manipulate and enhance digital media with precision, control, and efficiency, resulting in professional-quality output.

Section 1.3: Evolution of Editing Tools

- Trace the evolution of editing tools from traditional analog methods to modern digital software and applications.
- Discuss milestones in the development of editing tools, such as the transition from darkroom techniques to digital photo editing software, and the emergence of non-linear video editing systems.
- Explore how advancements in technology, computing power, and user interfaces have shaped the capabilities and usability of editing tools over time.

Chapter 2: Advanced Photo Editing Tools

In this chapter, we'll explore advanced photo editing tools and techniques for enhancing and manipulating digital photographs.

Section 2.1: Layer-Based Editing

- Discuss the concept of layer-based editing and its significance in photo manipulation and compositing.
- Explore how layer-based editing allows users to work with multiple elements, adjustments, and effects independently, facilitating non-destructive editing and creative experimentation.

Section 2.2: Selection and Masking Tools

- Introduce advanced selection and masking tools for isolating and manipulating specific areas of an image.
- Discuss techniques for precise selection and masking, including the use of selection tools such as the Magic Wand, Quick Selection, and Pen Tool, and advanced masking techniques such as luminosity masking and channel-based masking.

Section 2.3: Advanced Color Correction and Grading

- Explore advanced color correction and grading techniques for enhancing the color and tonal balance of photographs.
- Discuss tools and workflows for adjusting exposure, contrast, white balance, and color saturation, as well as techniques for creating stylistic color grades and effects.

Section 2.4: Retouching and Restoration

- Discuss retouching and restoration techniques for repairing and enhancing digital photographs.
- Explore tools and methods for removing blemishes, wrinkles, and imperfections, as well as restoring old or damaged photographs using cloning, healing, and content-aware fill tools.

Section 2.5: Special Effects and Filters

- Introduce special effects and filters for adding creative elements and visual enhancements to photographs.
- Discuss techniques for applying effects such as blurs, glows, vignettes, and textures, as well as using filter presets and plugins to achieve specific looks and styles.

Chapter 3: Advanced Video Editing Tools

In this chapter, we'll explore advanced video editing tools and techniques for editing and enhancing digital video content.

Section 3.1: Non-Linear Editing Systems (NLEs)

- Discuss the concept of non-linear editing systems (NLEs) and their advantages over linear editing methods.

- Explore popular NLE software platforms such as Adobe Premiere Pro, Final Cut Pro, and DaVinci Resolve, and discuss their features, workflows, and capabilities for editing video.

Section 3.2: Timeline Editing and Multicam Support

- Explore timeline editing techniques for organizing and arranging video clips, audio tracks, and visual effects on a non-linear timeline.
- Discuss multicam editing features and workflows for synchronizing and switching between multiple camera angles or sources in a single project.

Section 3.3: Color Correction and Grading

- Discuss color correction and grading techniques for adjusting and enhancing the color and tone of video footage.
- Explore tools and workflows for correcting exposure, white balance, and color balance, as well as creating cinematic looks and stylized color grades.

Section 3.4: Motion Graphics and Visual Effects

- Introduce motion graphics and visual effects tools for adding animated elements, text overlays, and visual enhancements to video projects.
- Discuss techniques for creating titles, lower thirds, transitions, and other graphic elements using built-in tools or third-party plugins and templates.

Section 3.5: Audio Editing and Mixing

- Explore audio editing and mixing techniques for enhancing the sound quality and mixing audio tracks in video projects.
- Discuss tools and workflows for adjusting volume levels, adding effects and filters, synchronizing audio with video, and creating immersive soundscapes.

Chapter 4: Advanced Graphic Design Tools

In this chapter, we'll explore advanced graphic design tools and techniques for creating and manipulating digital artwork and illustrations.

Section 4.1: Vector Graphics Editing

- Discuss vector graphics editing tools and techniques for creating scalable and resolution-independent artwork.
- Explore vector drawing tools such as the Pen Tool, Shape Tools, and Path Selection tools, as well as techniques for creating complex shapes, paths, and illustrations.

Section 4.2: Typography and Text Effects

- Explore typography and text effects tools for creating custom lettering, typographic compositions, and text-based designs.
- Discuss techniques for applying text effects such as shadows, gradients, outlines, and textures, as well as working with typefaces, fonts, and kerning.

Section 4.3: Image Trace and Vectorization

- Discuss image trace and vectorization techniques for converting raster images into editable vector artwork.
- Explore tools and workflows for tracing and converting bitmap images into vector graphics, as well as optimizing vector artwork for scalability and editability.

Section 4.4: 3D Modeling and Rendering

- Introduce 3D modeling and rendering tools for creating three-dimensional digital objects and scenes.
- Discuss techniques for modeling objects using polygonal modeling, nurbs modeling, and sculpting tools, as well as rendering techniques for creating realistic lighting, shading, and textures.

Chapter 5: Advanced Audio Editing Tools

In this chapter, we'll explore advanced audio editing tools and techniques for recording, editing, and mixing digital audio content.

Section 5.1: Digital Audio Workstations (DAWs)

- Discuss the concept of digital audio workstations (DAWs) and their role in audio production and editing.
- Explore popular DAW software platforms such as Pro Tools, Logic Pro, and Ableton Live, and discuss their features, workflows, and capabilities for audio editing and mixing.

Section 5.2: Audio Editing and Processing

- Explore audio editing and processing techniques for editing and enhancing digital audio recordings.
- Discuss tools and workflows for cutting, trimming, and arranging audio clips, as well as applying effects such as EQ, compression, reverb, and delay.

Section 5.3: MIDI Sequencing and Virtual Instruments

- Introduce MIDI sequencing and virtual instrument tools for creating and editing musical compositions and arrangements.
- Discuss techniques for recording and editing MIDI data, as well as using virtual instruments and software synthesizers to create realistic or synthesized sounds.

Section 5.4: Audio Mixing and Mastering

- Explore audio mixing and mastering techniques for balancing, blending, and finalizing audio tracks.
- Discuss techniques for adjusting volume levels, panning, and spatial positioning, as well as mastering techniques for optimizing audio quality, dynamics, and loudness for distribution.

Chapter 6: Advanced Editing Workflows and Best Practices

In this chapter, we'll explore advanced editing workflows and best practices for maximizing efficiency, creativity, and quality in digital content creation.

Section 6.1: Workflow Optimization

- Discuss workflow optimization strategies for streamlining editing processes and increasing productivity.
- Explore techniques for organizing files and assets, creating reusable templates and presets, and automating repetitive tasks to save time and effort.

Section 6.2: Collaboration and Version Control

- Discuss collaboration and version control strategies for working on editing projects with multiple team members or collaborators.
- Explore tools and workflows for sharing files, providing feedback, and managing revisions and changes, as well as best practices for maintaining project integrity and consistency.

Section 6.3: Creative Experimentation and Iteration

- Encourage creative experimentation and iteration as essential components of the editing process.
- Discuss techniques for exploring different ideas, styles, and approaches, as well as embracing experimentation, feedback, and iteration to refine and improve creative output.

Chapter 7: Conclusion and Next Steps

In conclusion, advanced editing tools empower creators to push the boundaries of creativity and produce high-quality digital content across various mediums. By mastering advanced editing techniques, exploring innovative workflows, and embracing creative experimentation, professionals and enthusiasts can elevate their craft and achieve their artistic vision in the dynamic digital landscape.

Lesson 2: Adding Custom Elements to Your Website

In the digital landscape, having a unique and visually appealing website is crucial for capturing the attention of your audience and conveying your brand's identity effectively. While website templates provide a solid foundation, adding custom elements allows you to personalize your site further and differentiate it from the competition. In this chapter, we'll explore the process of adding custom elements to your website, including the importance of customization, different types of custom elements, and best practices for implementation.

Section 1: The Importance of Customization

Customization is the key to making your website stand out in a sea of online content. It allows you to tailor your site to your specific needs, audience preferences, and branding requirements. By adding custom elements, you can create a unique and memorable user experience that resonates with your visitors and helps you achieve your business goals. Whether it's incorporating custom graphics, animations, or interactive features, customization enables you to showcase your creativity and personality while effectively communicating your message to your audience.

Section 2: Types of Custom Elements

2.1: Custom Graphics and Images

Graphics and images play a crucial role in visually communicating your brand's message and capturing the attention of your audience. In this section, we'll explore techniques for creating custom graphics and images, including graphic design principles, tools, and best practices for optimizing images for the web. Additionally, we'll discuss the importance of using high-quality visuals that align with your brand's aesthetics and messaging.

2.2: Custom Typography

Typography is a powerful tool for conveying tone, personality, and hierarchy on your website. In this section, we'll explore the world of custom typography, including techniques for selecting and pairing fonts, customizing font styles, sizes, and weights, and incorporating custom fonts using web font services or self-hosting options. We'll also discuss accessibility considerations and best practices for ensuring readability and legibility across different devices and screen sizes.

2.3: Custom Layouts and Structures

The layout and structure of your website play a significant role in guiding users through your content and creating a seamless browsing experience. In this section, we'll explore techniques for designing custom layouts and structures, including grid systems, responsive design principles, and CSS frameworks. We'll also discuss the importance of mobile responsiveness and accessibility in modern web design and provide tips for creating flexible and adaptive layouts that work across devices.

2.4: Custom Navigation Menus

Navigation menus are the backbone of any website, allowing users to navigate between different pages and sections effortlessly. In this section, we'll explore techniques for creating custom navigation menus, including menu design principles, dropdown menus, mega menus, and sticky navigation bars. We'll also discuss best practices for organizing menu items, optimizing navigation for mobile devices, and enhancing user experience through intuitive navigation design.

2.5: Custom Interactive Elements

Interactive elements such as sliders, carousels, accordions, and interactive forms add dynamism and engagement to your website. In this section, we'll explore techniques for creating custom interactive elements using HTML, CSS, and JavaScript. We'll discuss how to design interactive elements that are both visually appealing and user-friendly, as well as best practices for optimizing performance and accessibility.

Section 3: Best Practices for Implementation

3.1: Maintain Consistency

Consistency is key to creating a cohesive and professional-looking website. Ensure that your custom elements align with your overall design aesthetic, brand guidelines, and user experience standards. Use consistent colors, fonts, and styles across different elements to create a unified visual identity.

3.2: Prioritize Performance

Optimize your custom elements for performance to ensure fast loading times and smooth user interactions. Use efficient coding practices, optimize image and file sizes, and minimize the use of external dependencies to reduce page load times and improve overall performance.

3.3: Test Across Devices and Browsers

Test your custom elements across various devices, screen sizes, and browsers to ensure compatibility and consistency. Use responsive design techniques to adapt your custom elements to different viewport sizes, and conduct thorough testing to identify and fix any layout or functionality issues.

3.4: Stay Up-to-Date with Trends

Keep abreast of current design trends and technological advancements in web development to stay ahead of the curve. Experiment with new techniques, tools, and design patterns to keep your website fresh and engaging. However, ensure that trendy elements align with your brand identity and serve a functional purpose for your audience.

Section 4: Case Studies and Examples

In this section, we'll showcase real-world examples of websites that have successfully incorporated custom elements to enhance their design and user experience. We'll analyze the design choices, functionality, and impact of custom elements on each website, providing inspiration and insights for your own projects.

Section 5: Conclusion

In conclusion, adding custom elements to your website allows you to create a unique and memorable online presence that sets you apart from the competition. By leveraging custom graphics, typography, layouts, navigation menus, and interactive elements, you can create a visually stunning and user-friendly website that effectively communicates your brand's message and captivates your audience. Follow best practices for implementation, stay abreast of design trends, and continuously iterate and improve your custom elements to create a truly exceptional web experience.

Title: Lesson 3: Integrating Apps and Widgets into Your Website

In today's digital landscape, websites serve as more than just static pages. They have evolved into dynamic platforms that offer interactive features and functionalities to engage users and enhance their browsing experience. Integrating apps and widgets into your website allows you to extend its capabilities, provide valuable tools and resources, and drive user engagement and retention. In this chapter, we'll explore the process of integrating apps and widgets into your website, including the types of apps and widgets available, integration methods, and best practices for implementation.

Section 1: Understanding Apps and Widgets

1.1: Definition and Types

Apps and widgets are interactive elements that can be embedded into websites to provide additional functionality and content. In this section, we'll define what apps and widgets are and differentiate between the various types available. We'll explore the differences between native apps, web apps, and widgets, as well as examples of common apps and widgets used on websites.

1.2: Benefits of Integration

Integrating apps and widgets into your website offers numerous benefits, both for you as a website owner and for your users. We'll discuss the advantages of integrating apps and widgets, including enhanced functionality, improved user experience, increased engagement and interactivity, and the ability to provide valuable resources and tools to your audience.

Section 2: Types of Apps and Widgets

2.1: Social Media Integration

Social media apps and widgets allow you to connect your website with popular social media platforms such as Facebook, Twitter, Instagram, and LinkedIn. We'll explore different integration options, including social media sharing buttons, embedded feeds, follow buttons, and social login functionality, and discuss how they can enhance user engagement and help grow your social media presence.

2.2: Content Syndication and Aggregation

Content syndication and aggregation apps and widgets enable you to curate and display external content from sources such as news websites, blogs, and RSS feeds on your website. We'll discuss how to integrate content syndication and aggregation tools, customize the display of syndicated content, and leverage curated content to provide value to your audience and keep them engaged.

2.3: E-commerce Integration

E-commerce apps and widgets allow you to add online shopping functionality to your website, enabling users to browse products, make purchases, and complete transactions without leaving your site. We'll explore different e-commerce integration options, including shopping carts, product catalogs, payment gateways, and inventory management systems, and discuss best practices for setting up and managing an e-commerce storefront.

2.4: Productivity Tools

Productivity apps and widgets provide users with tools and resources to streamline their workflow, organize their tasks, and boost their productivity. We'll discuss popular productivity tools such as calendars, to-do lists, project management platforms, and collaboration tools, and explore how to integrate them into your website to help users stay organized and efficient.

2.5: Custom Forms and Surveys

Custom forms and surveys allow you to collect valuable feedback, information, and data from your website visitors. We'll explore different types of forms and surveys, including contact forms, feedback forms, registration forms, and online surveys, and discuss how to integrate them into your website using form builders, survey tools, and third-party platforms.

Section 3: Integration Methods

3.1: Embedding Code Snippets

One common method of integrating apps and widgets into a website is by embedding code snippets provided by the app or widget provider. In this section, we'll discuss how to embed code snippets into your website's HTML code, including best practices for placement, customization options, and troubleshooting common issues.

3.2: Using Plugins and Extensions

Many content management systems (CMS) and website builders offer plugins and extensions that allow you to easily integrate apps and widgets into your website without the need for coding. We'll explore how to find and install plugins and extensions for popular CMS platforms such as WordPress, Joomla, and Drupal, and discuss considerations for choosing and configuring plugins.

3.3: API Integration

For more advanced integration scenarios, you may need to use application programming interfaces (APIs) provided by app and widget providers. We'll discuss how to use APIs to integrate apps and widgets into your website, including authentication, data retrieval, and interaction with external services. We'll also explore considerations for security, rate limiting, and versioning when working with APIs.

Section 4: Best Practices for Implementation

4.1: Choose Quality Apps and Widgets

When selecting apps and widgets to integrate into your website, it's essential to choose quality solutions from reputable providers. We'll discuss considerations for evaluating apps and widgets, including functionality, reliability, compatibility, and support options, to ensure that you're integrating the best tools for your website and audience.

4.2: Consider User Experience

User experience (UX) is paramount when integrating apps and widgets into your website. We'll discuss best practices for designing and implementing app and widget integrations that enhance rather than detract from the overall user experience. This includes considerations for placement, design, functionality, and performance optimization to ensure a seamless and intuitive user experience.

4.3: Test and Monitor Performance

Before deploying apps and widgets on your live website, it's crucial to thoroughly test their functionality and performance. We'll discuss strategies for testing app and widget integrations, including functional testing, compatibility testing, and performance testing, to identify and resolve any issues before they impact your users. Additionally, we'll explore tools and techniques for monitoring the performance of integrated apps and widgets over time to ensure ongoing reliability and optimal user experience.

Section 5: Case Studies and Examples

In this section, we'll showcase real-world examples of websites that have successfully integrated apps and widgets to enhance their functionality and user experience. We'll analyze the design choices, implementation methods, and impact of app and widget integrations on each website, providing inspiration and insights for your own projects.

Section 6: Conclusion

In conclusion, integrating apps and widgets into your website is a powerful way to enhance its functionality, engage your audience, and provide value to your users. By understanding the types of apps and widgets available, choosing the right integration methods, and following best practices for implementation, you can create a dynamic and compelling website that meets the needs of your audience and achieves your business goals. Whether you're adding social media integration, e-commerce functionality, productivity tools, or custom forms, the possibilities for enhancing your website with apps and widgets are endless.

Title: Lesson 4: Creating Interactive Features for Your Website

In today's digital era, static websites are a thing of the past. Users now expect dynamic and engaging online experiences that captivate their attention and encourage interaction. Creating interactive features for your website is essential for enhancing user engagement, providing value to your audience, and achieving your business objectives. In this chapter, we'll explore the process of creating interactive features for your website, including the types of interactive elements available, design considerations, implementation methods, and best practices for creating compelling user experiences.

Section 1: Understanding Interactive Features

1.1: Definition and Importance

Interactive features are elements on a website that allow users to engage with content, manipulate elements, and participate in a two-way communication. In this section, we'll define what interactive features are and discuss their importance in creating engaging and memorable user experiences. We'll explore how interactive features can enhance user engagement, increase time spent on site, and drive conversions and actions.

1.2: Types of Interactive Features

There are various types of interactive features that you can incorporate into your website to engage users and enhance their experience. We'll explore different categories of interactive features, including:

- **User-Generated Content: Allow users to contribute content such as comments, reviews, and ratings.**
- **Quizzes and Surveys: Engage users with interactive quizzes, polls, and surveys to gather feedback or data.**
- **Interactive Maps: Provide interactive maps with location-based features such as search, directions, and points of interest.**
- **Scroll-Triggered Animations: Add animations and effects that respond to user scrolling to create a dynamic browsing experience.**
- **Interactive Forms: Create forms with interactive elements such as conditional logic, autocomplete suggestions, and real-time validation.**

Section 2: Design Considerations for Interactive Features

2.1: User-Centric Design

When designing interactive features for your website, it's essential to prioritize user experience (UX) and ensure that your designs are user-centric. We'll discuss best practices for user-centered design, including conducting user research, creating personas, and designing intuitive and accessible interfaces that cater to your target audience's needs and preferences.

2.2: Visual Hierarchy and Feedback

Visual hierarchy and feedback play a crucial role in guiding users' attention and interactions with interactive features. We'll explore techniques for establishing clear visual hierarchy, using visual cues such as color, typography, and spacing to indicate interactive elements, and providing feedback to users to confirm their actions and reassure them of their progress.

2.3: Responsiveness and Compatibility

With the proliferation of devices and screen sizes, it's essential to ensure that your interactive features are responsive and compatible across different platforms and devices. We'll discuss the principles of responsive design, including fluid layouts, flexible images, and media queries, and explore strategies for testing and optimizing interactive features for compatibility with various browsers and devices.

Section 3: Implementation Methods for Interactive Features

3.1: HTML, CSS, and JavaScript

Many interactive features can be implemented using standard web technologies such as HTML, CSS, and JavaScript. We'll discuss the basics of each technology and explore examples of how they can be used to create interactive elements such as buttons, forms, animations, and effects. We'll also provide tips and resources for learning and mastering these technologies for creating custom interactive features.

3.2: Content Management Systems (CMS)

Content management systems (CMS) such as WordPress, Joomla, and Drupal offer plugins and extensions that allow you to add interactive features to your website without writing code. We'll explore popular CMS plugins for creating interactive forms, quizzes, surveys, and other dynamic content, and discuss considerations for choosing and configuring plugins to meet your needs.

3.3: Third-Party Tools and Services

There are numerous third-party tools and services available that offer pre-built interactive features and widgets that you can easily integrate into your website. We'll explore popular tools and platforms for creating interactive maps, forms, quizzes, and more, and discuss the benefits and limitations of using third-party solutions compared to custom development or CMS plugins.

Section 4: Best Practices for Creating Interactive Features

4.1: Keep It Simple and Intuitive

When designing interactive features, simplicity and intuitiveness are key. Avoid overwhelming users with too many options or complex interactions. Instead, focus on creating clear, concise, and intuitive interfaces that guide users through the interaction process seamlessly.

4.2: Test and Iterate

Before deploying interactive features on your live website, it's essential to test them thoroughly to ensure functionality, usability, and compatibility. Conduct usability testing with real users to gather feedback and identify areas for improvement. Iterate on your designs based on user feedback and testing results to create a polished and user-friendly experience.

4.3: Monitor Performance and Analytics

Once your interactive features are live, monitor their performance and track user engagement metrics using web analytics tools. Analyze data such as click-through rates, completion rates, and time spent on interactive elements to gauge their effectiveness and identify opportunities for optimization and refinement.

Section 5: Case Studies and Examples

In this section, we'll showcase real-world examples of websites that have successfully implemented interactive features to enhance user engagement and drive conversions. We'll analyze the design choices, functionality, and impact of interactive features on each website, providing inspiration and insights for your own projects.

Section 6: Conclusion

In conclusion, creating interactive features for your website is essential for engaging users, enhancing their experience, and achieving your business goals. By understanding the types of interactive features available,

Title: Lesson 5: Customizing Your Mobile Site for Enhanced User Experience

In today's mobile-centric world, ensuring that your website is optimized for mobile devices is no longer optional—it's essential. With an increasing number of users accessing the web via smartphones and tablets, providing a seamless and enjoyable mobile experience is critical for retaining visitors, driving conversions, and maintaining a competitive edge. In this chapter, we'll explore the process of customizing your mobile site to enhance user experience, including the importance of mobile optimization, key considerations, design principles, implementation methods, and best practices.

Section 1: Understanding the Importance of Mobile Optimization

1.1: Mobile Usage Trends

Start by examining the current landscape of mobile usage trends, including statistics on the rising prevalence of mobile devices and the proportion of website traffic coming from mobile users. Understanding these trends underscores the importance of prioritizing mobile optimization for your website.

1.2: Impact on User Experience and Engagement

Discuss the impact of mobile optimization on user experience and engagement. Highlight how a well-optimized mobile site can improve usability, reduce bounce rates, increase time spent on site, and ultimately lead to higher conversions and customer satisfaction.

Section 2: Key Considerations for Mobile Optimization

2.1: Responsive Design vs. Mobile-Friendly Design

Differentiate between responsive design and mobile-friendly design approaches. Explain the benefits and drawbacks of each approach and help readers choose the most suitable option based on their website's goals, content, and target audience.

2.2: Content Prioritization

Explore strategies for prioritizing content on mobile devices. Emphasize the importance of concise, scannable content and discuss techniques for condensing and organizing content to ensure a seamless mobile browsing experience.

2.3: Touch-Friendly Navigation

Discuss the significance of touch-friendly navigation elements for mobile sites. Provide examples of intuitive navigation patterns such as hamburger menus, swipe gestures, and large, tappable buttons, and explain how these elements contribute to a smoother user experience on touchscreens.

2.4: Page Speed Optimization

Highlight the critical role of page speed in mobile optimization. Offer tips and techniques for optimizing page load times on mobile devices, including image optimization, minification of CSS and JavaScript, and leveraging browser caching.

Section 3: Design Principles for Mobile Optimization

3.1: Simplified Design

Advocate for a simplified design approach for mobile sites. Discuss the importance of clean layouts, ample white space, and minimalist aesthetics to reduce clutter and enhance readability on smaller screens.

3.2: Consistent Branding

Stress the importance of maintaining consistent branding across desktop and mobile versions of the website. Provide guidelines for adapting brand elements such as logos, color schemes, and typography to ensure visual coherence across platforms.

3.3: Adaptive Images and Media

Explain the concept of adaptive images and media and their role in mobile optimization. Introduce techniques such as responsive images, scalable vector graphics (SVG), and lazy loading to ensure that images and media assets adapt seamlessly to various screen sizes and resolutions.

Section 4: Implementation Methods for Mobile Optimization

4.1: Responsive Web Design

Delve into the principles of responsive web design (RWD) and its implementation using CSS media queries, flexible grids, and fluid layouts. Provide step-by-step instructions for creating a responsive design that adapts to different screen sizes and orientations.

4.2: Mobile-Friendly Frameworks

Introduce popular mobile-friendly frameworks such as Bootstrap, Foundation, and Materialize CSS. Discuss the features and benefits of each framework and demonstrate how to use them to quickly build mobile-optimized websites with pre-designed components and responsive layouts.

4.3: Device Detection and User Agent Redirection

Explain the concept of device detection and user agent redirection as a method for delivering optimized experiences to mobile users. Discuss the pros and cons of server-side and client-side detection techniques and provide guidance on implementing device-specific redirects using JavaScript or server-side scripts.

Section 5: Best Practices for Mobile Optimization

5.1: Test Across Multiple Devices and Browsers

Emphasize the importance of testing mobile optimization across a wide range of devices, screen sizes, and browsers. Encourage readers to use device emulators, remote testing services, and real devices to ensure compatibility and consistency across platforms.

5.2: Monitor Performance and Analytics

Highlight the value of monitoring performance metrics and user analytics to track the effectiveness of mobile optimization efforts. Discuss key metrics such as bounce rate, page views, and conversion rates and provide recommendations for using analytics tools to identify areas for improvement.

5.3: Continuous Iteration and Improvement

Encourage a mindset of continuous iteration and improvement in mobile optimization. Suggest techniques such as A/B testing, user feedback surveys, and heuristic evaluations to gather insights and refine the mobile user experience over time.

Section 6: Case Studies and Examples

In this section, showcase real-world examples of websites that have successfully implemented mobile optimization strategies. Analyze the design choices, navigation patterns, and performance improvements of each example to provide inspiration and practical insights for readers.

Section 7: Conclusion

Summarize the key takeaways from the chapter and reinforce the importance of mobile optimization for providing a seamless and engaging user experience. Encourage readers to apply the principles, strategies, and best practices discussed to their own websites to ensure they remain competitive in an increasingly mobile-driven digital landscape.

Lesson 6: Implementing Advanced SEO Strategies for Maximum Online Visibility

In today's competitive online landscape, having a strong search engine optimization (SEO) strategy is crucial for improving your website's visibility, driving organic traffic, and staying ahead of the competition. While basic SEO techniques are essential, implementing advanced SEO strategies can take your website to the next level and help you achieve higher rankings, increased traffic, and improved user engagement. In this chapter, we'll delve into advanced SEO strategies, including technical optimization, content optimization, off-page optimization, and analytics, to help you maximize your online presence and achieve your business goals.

Section 1: Technical SEO Optimization

1.1: Website Architecture and Navigation

Discuss the importance of a well-structured website architecture and navigation for SEO. Explore best practices for organizing site content, optimizing internal linking structures, and creating user-friendly navigation menus to improve crawlability, indexability, and user experience.

1.2: Page Speed and Performance

Explain the significance of page speed and performance for SEO and user experience. Provide tips and techniques for optimizing website performance, including image optimization, minification of CSS and JavaScript, leveraging browser caching, and implementing content delivery networks (CDNs) to reduce load times and improve site speed.

1.3: Mobile Optimization

Highlight the importance of mobile optimization for SEO in light of Google's mobile-first indexing. Discuss strategies for creating mobile-friendly websites, including responsive design, mobile-friendly navigation, and optimizing page load times for mobile devices, to ensure optimal performance on smartphones and tablets.

1.4: Schema Markup and Structured Data

Introduce schema markup and structured data markup as advanced techniques for enhancing search engine visibility and generating rich snippets in search results. Discuss the benefits of implementing schema markup, provide examples of schema types relevant to different industries, and explain how to add structured data to your website using JSON-LD or microdata.

Section 2: Content Optimization Strategies

2.1: Semantic SEO and Natural Language Processing (NLP)

Explore the concept of semantic SEO and how search engines use natural language processing (NLP) to understand user intent and context. Discuss advanced content optimization techniques such as semantic keyword research, latent semantic indexing (LSI), and optimizing for entities and concepts rather than just keywords to improve relevancy and rank for a broader range of search queries.

2.2: Content Depth and Authority

Discuss the importance of creating in-depth, comprehensive content that demonstrates expertise, authority, and trustworthiness (E-A-T) in your niche or industry. Provide strategies for conducting thorough research, creating long-form content, incorporating multimedia elements, and citing authoritative sources to establish credibility and authority in the eyes of search engines and users.

2.3: Content Optimization for Voice Search

Explain the growing importance of optimizing content for voice search as voice-enabled devices and virtual assistants become increasingly prevalent. Discuss best practices for optimizing content for voice search queries, including using natural language, answering specific questions, and targeting conversational keywords to align with user search behavior.

2.4: User Experience (UX) and Engagement Signals

Explore how user experience (UX) and engagement signals impact search rankings and organic visibility. Discuss advanced techniques for improving UX and engagement metrics such as dwell time, click-through rate (CTR), and bounce rate, including optimizing page layout, enhancing readability, and providing interactive elements to encourage user interaction and exploration.

Section 3: Off-Page SEO Strategies

3.1: Advanced Link Building Techniques

Delve into advanced link building strategies for acquiring high-quality backlinks and improving domain authority. Discuss techniques such as broken link building, skyscraper content outreach, guest blogging, and leveraging influencer relationships to earn authoritative backlinks and boost organic rankings.

3.2: Brand Mentions and Unlinked Brand Citations

Discuss the importance of brand mentions and unlinked brand citations for SEO and online reputation management. Provide strategies for monitoring brand mentions, reclaiming unlinked brand citations, and leveraging brand authority signals to improve search visibility and brand awareness.

3.3: Social Signals and Social Media Optimization (SMO)

Explain the relationship between social signals and SEO and how social media optimization (SMO) can indirectly impact search rankings. Discuss strategies for optimizing social profiles, generating social engagement, and leveraging social sharing to increase brand visibility and drive referral traffic, thereby enhancing overall SEO performance.

Section 4: Advanced Analytics and Measurement

4.1: Advanced Keyword Research and Analysis

Explore advanced keyword research techniques for identifying high-value keywords, analyzing keyword intent, and uncovering content gaps. Discuss tools and methodologies for conducting competitive keyword analysis, semantic keyword research, and long-tail keyword optimization to inform content strategy and drive targeted organic traffic.

4.2: Advanced SEO Audits and Technical Analysis

Discuss advanced techniques for conducting comprehensive SEO audits and technical analysis to identify and address issues that may impact search visibility. Explore tools and methodologies for analyzing crawlability, indexability, site structure, and technical SEO factors such as canonicalization, hreflang tags, and XML sitemaps to ensure optimal website performance in search results.

4.3: Advanced Reporting and Performance Tracking

Examine advanced reporting and performance tracking techniques for monitoring SEO metrics, tracking key performance indicators (KPIs), and measuring the impact of SEO efforts on website traffic, rankings, and conversions. Discuss the use of advanced analytics platforms, custom dashboards, and attribution modeling to gain actionable insights and refine SEO strategies for maximum effectiveness.

Section 5: Case Studies and Examples

In this section, present real-world case studies and examples of websites that have successfully implemented advanced SEO strategies to achieve significant improvements in search visibility, organic traffic, and business outcomes. Analyze the strategies, tactics, and outcomes of each case study to provide actionable insights and inspiration for readers.

Section 6: Conclusion

Summarize the key takeaways from the chapter and emphasize the importance of implementing advanced SEO strategies to achieve sustainable long-term success in organic search. Encourage readers to leverage the techniques and best practices discussed to optimize their websites for maximum visibility, traffic, and business growth in today's competitive online environment

Title: Lesson 7: Exploring Current Design Trends for Modern Websites

In the ever-evolving landscape of web design, staying updated with the latest trends is essential for creating visually appealing, engaging, and user-friendly websites. Design trends not only reflect aesthetic preferences but also respond to technological advancements, user behaviors, and cultural influences. In this chapter, we'll explore the most prominent design trends shaping the web in recent times, including their characteristics, applications, and potential impact on user experience.

Section 1: Understanding the Importance of Design Trends

1.1: The Role of Design Trends in Web Development

Discuss the significance of design trends in web development and their impact on user perception, brand identity, and website performance. Explain how following design trends can help websites stay relevant, competitive, and aligned with evolving user expectations.

1.2: Balancing Trends with Timelessness

Emphasize the importance of striking a balance between following design trends and maintaining a timeless aesthetic. Discuss how timeless design principles such as usability, accessibility, and clarity can complement and anchor trend-driven elements to create enduring and effective web experiences.

Section 2: Current Design Trends in Web Development

2.1: Minimalism and Simplified Design

Explore the enduring trend of minimalism in web design, characterized by clean layouts, ample white space, and simplified aesthetics. Discuss the benefits of minimalist design for improving readability, reducing cognitive load, and conveying clarity and sophistication.

2.2: Dark Mode and Light-Mode Switching

Discuss the rising popularity of dark mode interfaces across web and mobile platforms. Explain how dark mode enhances visual comfort in low-light environments, conserves battery life on OLED screens, and provides a sleek and modern alternative to traditional light-mode interfaces.

2.3: Neumorphism and Soft UI

Introduce the emerging design trend of neumorphism, characterized by soft shadows, subtle gradients, and tactile elements that mimic physical objects. Discuss the principles of neumorphic design, its visual appeal, and considerations for implementing soft UI elements effectively.

2.4: Bold Typography and Custom Fonts

Explore the trend of using bold typography and custom fonts to create striking visual statements and enhance brand identity. Discuss techniques for pairing fonts, experimenting with typography hierarchy, and leveraging variable fonts and expressive typefaces to add personality and character to web designs.

2.5: Illustrations and Custom Graphics

Discuss the increasing use of illustrations and custom graphics in web design to add personality, storytelling, and visual interest. Explore different illustration styles, techniques for integrating illustrations into website layouts, and the role of custom graphics in brand storytelling and user engagement.

2.6: Microinteractions and Animated UI Elements

Examine the trend of incorporating microinteractions and animated UI elements to create delightful and engaging user experiences. Discuss the principles of motion design, examples of effective microinteractions, and guidelines for implementing animations that enhance usability without overwhelming users.

Section 3: Application of Design Trends in Web Projects

3.1: Case Studies and Examples

Present real-world case studies and examples of websites that effectively utilize current design trends to achieve their objectives. Analyze the design choices, user experiences, and outcomes of each case study to provide insights and inspiration for incorporating design trends into web projects.

3.2: Practical Implementation Tips

Offer practical tips and best practices for implementing design trends in web projects. Discuss considerations such as user context, brand identity, and technical feasibility, and provide guidance on how to adapt design trends to specific project requirements and constraints.

Section 4: Future Directions and Evolving Trends

4.1: Predictions for Future Design Trends

Speculate on potential future design trends and directions based on current technological advancements, cultural shifts, and emerging design movements. Discuss areas such as augmented reality (AR) interfaces, voice-driven experiences, and sustainable design practices that may shape the future of web design.

4.2: Adapting to Evolving User Needs

Highlight the importance of continuous adaptation and innovation in response to evolving user needs and preferences. Encourage web designers and developers to stay curious, experiment with new technologies and techniques, and embrace change as an opportunity for growth and creativity.

Section 5: Conclusion

Summarize the key insights and takeaways from the chapter, emphasizing the importance of staying informed about current design trends and their potential impact on web projects. Encourage readers to leverage design trends thoughtfully, creatively, and strategically to create compelling, user-centered web experiences that resonate with their target audiences.

Title: Collaborating with Team Members: Strategies and Tools for Effective Teamwork in Web Development

Chapter 1: Introduction to Collaboration in Web Development

1.1 Understanding Collaboration:

- Definition of collaboration in the context of web development.
- Importance of collaboration for successful project outcomes.
- Overview of key benefits of effective collaboration in web development teams.

1.2 Collaboration Challenges:

- Common challenges faced by web development teams in collaborating effectively.
- Discussion on communication breakdowns, misalignment of goals, and role ambiguity.
- Impact of poor collaboration on project timelines, quality, and team morale.

Chapter 2: Building a Collaborative Culture

2.1 Cultivating Collaboration:

- Strategies for fostering a culture of collaboration within web development teams.
- Encouraging open communication, trust, and mutual respect among team members.
- Promoting a collaborative mindset that values diversity of perspectives and contributions.

2.2 Team Dynamics and Roles:

- Defining team roles and responsibilities to clarify expectations and promote accountability.
- Understanding team dynamics and leveraging individual strengths for collective success.
- Techniques for building cohesive and high-performing teams in web development projects.

Chapter 3: Effective Communication Strategies

3.1 Clear Communication Channels:

- Selection and utilization of appropriate communication channels for different types of interactions.
- Balancing synchronous and asynchronous communication to accommodate diverse team needs.
- Establishing guidelines for effective communication practices within web development teams.

3.2 Active Listening and Feedback:

- Importance of active listening in fostering understanding and collaboration among team members.
- Providing constructive feedback to facilitate continuous improvement and growth.
- Techniques for creating a culture of feedback and constructive criticism in web development teams.

Chapter 4: Leveraging Collaboration Tools

4.1 Project Management Platforms:

- Overview of popular project management tools such as Trello, Asana, and Jira.
- Utilizing project management platforms for task allocation, tracking progress, and resource management.
- Integrating project management tools with other collaboration platforms for seamless workflow management.

4.2 Version Control Systems:

- Introduction to version control systems like Git and SVN for managing codebase changes.
- Importance of version control in enabling collaborative development and ensuring code integrity.
- Best practices for branching, merging, and resolving conflicts in version-controlled environments.

4.3 Communication and Collaboration Tools:

- Exploring communication tools like Slack, Microsoft Teams, and Discord for real-time interaction.
- Leveraging collaboration features such as chat, video conferencing, and file sharing to enhance teamwork.
- Integrating communication tools with project management platforms for streamlined collaboration.

Chapter 5: Overcoming Collaboration Challenges

5.1 Addressing Time Zone Differences:

- Strategies for mitigating challenges arising from team members located in different time zones.
- Establishing overlapping work hours, asynchronous communication norms, and flexible scheduling.
- Leveraging time zone management tools and techniques to facilitate global collaboration.

5.2 Resolving Conflict and Misalignment:

- Identifying and addressing conflicts arising from differences in opinions, goals, or priorities.
- Techniques for resolving conflicts constructively through effective communication and negotiation.
- Implementing conflict resolution strategies to promote harmony and productivity within teams.

5.3 Managing Remote Work Challenges:

- Addressing common challenges associated with remote work arrangements, such as isolation and communication barriers.
- Strategies for maintaining team cohesion, motivation, and accountability in remote settings.
- Leveraging remote work technologies and best practices to optimize collaboration and productivity.

Chapter 6: Case Studies and Best Practices

6.1 Real-world Collaboration Examples:

- Case studies showcasing successful collaboration practices in web development projects.
- Analysis of collaboration strategies, tools, and workflows adopted by high-performing teams.
- Extracting key lessons and best practices from real-world examples to inform readers.

6.2 Implementation Tips and Recommendations:

- Practical tips and recommendations for implementing effective collaboration strategies in web development teams.
- Guidance on selecting and integrating collaboration tools, fostering team communication, and addressing common challenges.

- Insights from industry experts and experienced practitioners on optimizing collaboration processes for improved project outcomes.

Chapter 7: Conclusion and Future Outlook

7.1 Summary of Key Insights:

- Recap of key concepts, strategies, and tools discussed in the chapter.
- Emphasis on the importance of collaboration in achieving project success and fostering team cohesion.

7.2 Looking Ahead:

- Reflection on the evolving landscape of collaboration in web development.
- Anticipation of future trends, technologies, and challenges shaping collaboration practices.
- Encouragement for continuous learning and adaptation to stay ahead in the dynamic field of web development collaboration.

Note: Each section will delve into detailed explanations, practical examples, and actionable insights to provide comprehensive guidance on collaborating effectively in web development teams.

Title: Lesson 9: A/B Testing and Optimization in Web Development

Chapter 1: Introduction to A/B Testing and Optimization

1.1 Understanding A/B Testing:

- Definition of A/B testing and its significance in web development.
- Explanation of how A/B testing allows developers to compare two versions of a webpage to determine which one performs better.

1.2 Importance of Optimization:

- Discussion on the importance of optimization in maximizing website performance.
- Overview of optimization strategies and their impact on user experience, conversions, and overall business goals.

Chapter 2: The A/B Testing Process

2.1 Setting Objectives and Hypotheses:

- Establishing clear objectives for A/B testing campaigns.
- Formulating hypotheses to test specific changes or variations on a webpage.

2.2 Designing Test Variations:

- Identifying elements to be tested, such as headlines, calls-to-action, or layout.
- Creating variations of webpages with different design or content elements.

2.3 Implementing A/B Testing Tools:

- Introduction to A/B testing tools and platforms, such as Google Optimize, Optimizely, or VWO.
- Step-by-step guide on implementing A/B tests using selected tools.

2.4 Running A/B Tests:

- Executing A/B tests according to established parameters and timelines.
- Monitoring test performance and collecting relevant data on user interactions.

2.5 Analyzing Results:

- Interpreting A/B test results to determine statistical significance and draw actionable insights.

- Understanding key metrics such as conversion rate, bounce rate, and time on page.

Chapter 3: Optimization Strategies

3.1 Conversion Rate Optimization (CRO):

- Overview of CRO techniques aimed at improving conversion rates.
- Strategies for optimizing conversion funnels, forms, and checkout processes.

3.2 User Experience (UX) Optimization:

- Importance of UX optimization in enhancing user satisfaction and engagement.
- Techniques for improving website navigation, page load times, and mobile responsiveness.

3.3 Content Optimization:

- Strategies for optimizing website content for readability, relevance, and search engine visibility.
- Leveraging keyword research, content audits, and A/B testing to improve content effectiveness.

3.4 Design Optimization:

- Principles of design optimization for aesthetics and usability.
- Techniques for optimizing visual elements, color schemes, and typography to enhance user experience.

Chapter 4: Advanced A/B Testing Techniques

4.1 Multivariate Testing:

- Introduction to multivariate testing and its advantages over traditional A/B testing.
- Strategies for testing multiple variables simultaneously to identify optimal combinations.

4.2 Personalization Testing:

- Overview of personalization testing techniques for delivering customized experiences to users.
- Strategies for segmenting audiences and tailoring content based on user behavior and preferences.

4.3 Split URL Testing:

- Explanation of split URL testing as an alternative method for A/B testing.

- Guidance on setting up and running split URL tests to compare different website versions.

Chapter 5: Best Practices and Considerations

5.1 Sample Size and Duration:

- Importance of determining appropriate sample sizes and test durations for reliable results.
- Guidelines for calculating sample sizes and determining test durations based on statistical significance.

5.2 Test Prioritization:

- Strategies for prioritizing A/B testing initiatives based on potential impact and resource constraints.
- Considerations for balancing short-term wins with long-term optimization goals.

5.3 Data Integrity and Interpretation:

- Best practices for ensuring data integrity and accuracy in A/B testing experiments.
- Techniques for avoiding common pitfalls and biases in data interpretation.

Chapter 6: Case Studies and Examples

6.1 E-commerce A/B Testing:

- Case studies showcasing A/B testing success stories in e-commerce websites.
- Analysis of A/B testing strategies used to improve conversion rates, cart abandonment, and revenue.

6.2 SaaS A/B Testing:

- Case studies demonstrating A/B testing techniques in Software as a Service (SaaS) applications.
- Examples of A/B tests conducted to optimize user onboarding, feature adoption, and subscription upgrades.

Chapter 7: Conclusion and Future Trends

7.1 Summary of Key Insights:

- Recap of key concepts and strategies discussed in the chapter.

- Emphasis on the importance of A/B testing and optimization in driving continuous improvement in web development.

7.2 Future Trends in A/B Testing:

- Discussion on emerging trends and technologies shaping the future of A/B testing.
- Anticipation of advancements in machine learning, automation, and predictive analytics in optimization practices.

Note: Each section will provide in-depth explanations, practical examples, and actionable insights to guide readers in implementing effective A/B testing and optimization strategies in their web development project

Lesson 10: Monitoring Performance and Analytics in Web Development

Chapter 1: Introduction to Performance Monitoring and Analytics

1.1 Understanding Performance Monitoring:

- Definition of performance monitoring in the context of web development.
- Importance of monitoring website performance for user experience, SEO, and business objectives.

1.2 Role of Analytics in Web Development:

- Overview of analytics tools and techniques for tracking user behavior, traffic, and conversions.
- Discussion on how analytics data informs decision-making and optimization strategies.

Chapter 2: Key Performance Metrics

2.1 Website Speed and Load Time:

- Importance of fast website loading times for user satisfaction and search engine rankings.
- Techniques for measuring and optimizing page load times using tools like Google PageSpeed Insights and GTmetrix.

2.2 Page Views and Sessions:

- Explanation of page views and sessions as fundamental metrics for website traffic analysis.
- Strategies for increasing page views and sessions through content optimization and marketing efforts.

2.3 Bounce Rate and Exit Rate:

- Definition of bounce rate and exit rate as indicators of user engagement and website performance.
- Techniques for reducing bounce and exit rates through improved content, navigation, and user experience.

2.4 Conversion Rate and Goal Completion:

- Importance of conversion rate and goal completion metrics for assessing website effectiveness.

- Strategies for optimizing conversion funnels and increasing goal completion rates through A/B testing and UX optimization.

Chapter 3: Web Analytics Tools and Platforms

3.1 Google Analytics:

- Overview of Google Analytics as a comprehensive web analytics platform.
- Introduction to key features such as audience insights, behavior tracking, and conversion tracking.

3.2 Adobe Analytics:

- Introduction to Adobe Analytics as an enterprise-level analytics solution.
- Overview of features for advanced segmentation, attribution modeling, and predictive analytics.

3.3 Hotjar:

- Overview of Hotjar as a user behavior analytics tool.
- Explanation of features such as heatmaps, session recordings, and feedback polls for understanding user interactions.

3.4 Mixpanel:

- Introduction to Mixpanel as a product analytics platform.
- Overview of features for tracking user journeys, analyzing retention, and conducting cohort analysis.

Chapter 4: Setting Up Analytics Tracking

4.1 Installing Tracking Codes:

- Step-by-step guide on installing tracking codes for Google Analytics and other analytics platforms.
- Integration of tracking codes into website HTML or using tag management systems like Google Tag Manager.

4.2 Configuring Goals and Events:

- Definition of goals and events in analytics tracking and their significance for measuring conversions.
- Guidance on setting up goals and events in Google Analytics to track specific user interactions and conversions.

4.3 Customizing Dashboards and Reports:

- Techniques for customizing dashboards and reports in analytics platforms to monitor performance metrics.
- Creating custom reports, segments, and dashboards tailored to specific business objectives and KPIs.

Chapter 5: Analyzing and Interpreting Data

5.1 Data Visualization Techniques:

- Importance of data visualization for simplifying complex analytics data and insights.
- Introduction to visualization techniques such as charts, graphs, and heatmaps for presenting analytics data effectively.

5.2 Identifying Trends and Patterns:

- Strategies for identifying trends and patterns in analytics data to inform decision-making.
- Analysis of historical data to uncover insights into user behavior, traffic sources, and content performance.

5.3 User Segmentation and Audience Analysis:

- Importance of user segmentation for understanding audience demographics, interests, and behaviors.
- Techniques for segmenting users based on demographic data, traffic sources, and behavior metrics.

Chapter 6: Optimization Strategies Based on Analytics Insights

6.1 Content Optimization:

- Leveraging analytics insights to optimize website content for relevance, engagement, and conversions.
- Techniques for identifying high-performing content and optimizing underperforming pages.

6.2 Conversion Rate Optimization (CRO):

- Using analytics data to identify conversion bottlenecks and opportunities for improvement.
- Implementing A/B testing and optimization strategies to increase conversion rates and goal completions.

6.3 Performance Optimization:

- Utilizing analytics insights to identify performance bottlenecks and optimize website speed and responsiveness.
- Techniques for optimizing server response times, reducing page load times, and improving overall website performance.

Chapter 7: Reporting and Actionable Insights

7.1 Generating Regular Reports:

- Importance of regular reporting for monitoring performance trends and tracking progress towards goals.
- Best practices for generating and sharing reports with stakeholders, team members, and clients.

7.2 Extracting Actionable Insights:

- Techniques for extracting actionable insights from analytics data to drive optimization strategies.
- Prioritizing actions based on data-driven insights and aligning them with business objectives and KPIs.

Chapter 8: Case Studies and Examples

8.1 E-commerce Analytics Case Study:

- Case study showcasing how e-commerce businesses use analytics data to optimize conversions and revenue.
- Analysis of strategies implemented and results achieved through analytics-driven optimization.

8.2 Content Analytics Case Study:

- Case study demonstrating how content publishers leverage analytics insights to optimize content strategy and engagement.
- Examples of content optimization techniques and their impact on audience engagement metrics.

Chapter 9: Challenges and Considerations

9.1 Data Privacy and Compliance:

- Discussion on data privacy regulations such as GDPR and CCPA and their implications for analytics tracking.

- Strategies for ensuring compliance with data privacy laws while collecting and analyzing user data.

9.2 Data Integrity and Accuracy:

- Challenges related to data integrity and accuracy in analytics tracking, such as bot traffic and data sampling.
- Techniques for validating and verifying analytics data to ensure reliability and accuracy.

Chapter 10: Future Trends in Web Analytics

10.1 Predictive Analytics and AI:

- Anticipation of advancements in predictive analytics and artificial intelligence in web analytics.
- Exploration of how predictive modeling and AI-driven insights will shape the future of analytics-driven optimization.

10.2 Cross-Platform Analytics:

- Discussion on the importance of cross-platform analytics for tracking user interactions across multiple devices and touchpoints.
- Emerging trends in cross-platform analytics tools and techniques for seamless user tracking and attribution.

Chapter 11: Conclusion and Next Steps

11.1 Summary of Key Insights:

- Recap of key concepts, strategies, and tools discussed in the chapter.
- Emphasis on the importance of monitoring performance and analytics in driving continuous improvement in web development.

11.2 Actionable Takeaways:

- Actionable takeaways for readers to implement in their web development projects, including setting up analytics tracking, analyzing data, and optimizing performance based on insights.

11.3 Future Directions:

- Reflection on future trends and opportunities in web analytics and performance monitoring.
- Encouragement for readers to stay updated on emerging technologies and best practices to stay ahead in the dynamic field of web development.

Note: Each section will provide detailed explanations, practical examples, and actionable insights to guide readers in effectively monitoring website performance and leveraging analytics data to drive optimization strategies in their web development projects.

Chapter 1: Introduction to Adding Pages

1.1 Understanding the Importance of Adding Pages:

- Explanation of why adding pages is a fundamental aspect of website development.
- Importance of having a well-structured and organized website with relevant content.

1.2 Purpose of Adding Pages:

- Discussion on the various purposes served by adding pages to a website, such as providing information, showcasing products or services, and engaging users.

Chapter 2: Planning Your Website Structure

2.1 Defining Website Goals and Objectives:

- Importance of defining clear goals and objectives for the website.
- Techniques for aligning website structure with overarching business or project objectives.

2.2 Understanding User Needs and Expectations:

- Conducting user research to understand the needs, preferences, and expectations of the target audience.
- Techniques for creating user personas and identifying key user journeys.

2.3 Creating a Site Map:

- Explanation of what a site map is and its importance in planning website structure.
- Step-by-step guide on creating a site map to visualize the hierarchy and organization of website pages.

Chapter 3: Choosing the Right Pages

3.1 Core Pages:

- Introduction to core pages that are essential for every website, such as Home, About Us, Contact Us, and Services/Products.
- Explanation of the purpose and content typically found on each core page.

3.2 Additional Pages:

- Discussion on additional pages that may be relevant based on the nature of the website and its goals.
- Examples of additional pages such as Portfolio, Blog, Testimonials, FAQ, and Terms of Service.

Chapter 4: Creating Content for Pages

4.1 Content Strategy:

- Importance of developing a content strategy to ensure consistency and relevance across website pages.
- Techniques for defining the tone, style, and messaging of website content.

4.2 Writing Engaging Copy:

- Tips and best practices for writing engaging and persuasive copy for website pages.
- Techniques for capturing attention, addressing user needs, and guiding users through the content.

4.3 Visual Content:

- Importance of visual content such as images, videos, and infographics in enhancing the appeal and effectiveness of website pages.
- Guidelines for selecting and incorporating visual content to complement written copy.

Chapter 5: Adding Pages in Website Builders

5.1 Using Website Builders:

- Introduction to website builders such as Wix, WordPress, Squarespace, and Shopify.
- Explanation of how website builders simplify the process of adding and managing pages without requiring coding knowledge.

5.2 Step-by-Step Guide to Adding Pages:

- Detailed walkthrough of the process of adding pages in popular website builders.
- Demonstration of how to create new pages, set page titles, URLs, and navigation menus.

Chapter 6: Customizing Page Layouts

6.1 Choosing Templates:

- Importance of selecting the right template or theme for website pages.
- Considerations for choosing templates based on design aesthetic, functionality, and customization options.

6.2 Layout Options:

- Overview of different layout options available for website pages, such as full-width, sidebar, grid, and column layouts.
- Tips for selecting layout options that best showcase the content and achieve the desired user experience.

6.3 Customizing Page Elements:

- Techniques for customizing page elements such as headers, footers, navigation menus, and sidebars.
- Explanation of how to add widgets, buttons, forms, and other interactive elements to enhance page functionality.

Chapter 7: Optimizing Pages for Search Engines

7.1 On-Page SEO Basics:

- Introduction to on-page SEO and its importance in improving search engine visibility.
- Techniques for optimizing page titles, meta descriptions, headings, and content for relevant keywords.

7.2 Image Optimization:

- Importance of optimizing images for search engines and user experience.
- Guidelines for optimizing image filenames, alt text, captions, and sizes to improve page load times and accessibility.

7.3 Mobile Responsiveness:

- Explanation of why mobile responsiveness is crucial for website pages.
- Techniques for ensuring that pages display correctly and function seamlessly across various devices and screen sizes.

Chapter 8: Adding Navigation Menus and Internal Links

8.1 Designing Navigation Menus:

- Importance of well-designed navigation menus for intuitive user navigation.

- Tips for organizing navigation menus to reflect the website's structure and prioritize important pages.

8.2 Creating Internal Links:

- Explanation of the benefits of internal linking for SEO and user experience.
- Techniques for strategically adding internal links between related pages to guide users and improve website crawlability.

Chapter 9: Reviewing and Testing Pages

9.1 Content Review:

- Importance of reviewing website content for accuracy, clarity, and relevance.
- Techniques for conducting content audits and revisions to ensure consistency and quality.

9.2 Cross-Browser and Cross-Device Testing:

- Explanation of why cross-browser and cross-device testing is essential for website pages.
- Techniques for testing pages across different web browsers, devices, and screen resolutions to ensure compatibility and usability.

Chapter 10: Conclusion and Next Steps

10.1 Summary of Key Insights:

- Recap of key concepts and strategies discussed in the chapter.
- Emphasis on the importance of adding well-planned and optimized pages to create a user-friendly and effective website.

10.2 Actionable Takeaways:

- Actionable takeaways for readers to implement in their website development projects, including planning page structure, creating engaging content, and optimizing for search engines.

10.3 Future Directions:

- Reflection on emerging trends and technologies in website development and the importance of staying updated to meet evolving user needs and expectations.

Note: Each section will provide detailed explanations, practical examples, and actionable insights to guide readers in effectively adding pages to their website development projects.

Introduction to Creating New Pages

1.1 Understanding the Importance of New Pages:

- Explanation of why regularly creating new pages is crucial for website growth and user engagement.
- Importance of adding fresh content to attract visitors, improve SEO, and keep the website relevant.

1.2 Goals and Objectives:

- Discussion on setting clear goals and objectives for creating new pages.
- Importance of aligning page creation with overall business objectives, target audience needs, and content strategy.

Chapter 2: Identifying Content Needs

2.1 Audience Analysis:

- Techniques for conducting audience analysis to understand the preferences, interests, and pain points of target users.
- Importance of audience personas in guiding content creation decisions.

2.2 Content Gap Analysis:

- Explanation of content gap analysis and its role in identifying areas where new pages are needed.
- Techniques for analyzing competitors, keyword research, and user feedback to identify content gaps.

2.3 Keyword Research:

- Importance of keyword research in identifying topics and search terms relevant to the target audience.
- Techniques for conducting keyword research using tools like Google Keyword Planner, SEMrush, and Ahrefs.

Chapter 3: Planning New Pages

3.1 Content Strategy:

- Importance of developing a content strategy to guide page creation efforts.
- Techniques for defining content themes, formats, and distribution channels.

3.2 Content Calendar:

- Explanation of the content calendar and its role in organizing and scheduling new page creation.
- Techniques for creating a content calendar to ensure consistent publishing and alignment with marketing initiatives.

3.3 Wireframing and Mockups:

- Introduction to wireframing and mockups as tools for visualizing new page layouts and content structure.
- Techniques for creating wireframes using software tools like Sketch, Adobe XD, or wireframing kits.

Chapter 4: Content Creation

4.1 Writing Engaging Copy:

- Tips and best practices for writing compelling and engaging copy for new pages.
- Techniques for capturing audience attention, addressing pain points, and guiding users through the content.

4.2 Visual Content Creation:

- Importance of incorporating visual content such as images, videos, and infographics into new pages.
- Guidelines for creating and sourcing visual content that enhances the user experience and reinforces key messages.

4.3 Multimedia Integration:

- Techniques for integrating multimedia elements into new pages to increase engagement and convey information effectively.
- Considerations for optimizing multimedia content for fast loading times and accessibility.

Chapter 5: Creating New Pages in Website Builders

5.1 Using Website Builders:

- Introduction to website builders such as Wix, WordPress, Squarespace, and Shopify for creating new pages.
- Explanation of how website builders simplify the process of page creation without requiring coding knowledge.

5.2 Step-by-Step Guide to Creating New Pages:

- Detailed walkthrough of the process of creating new pages in popular website builders.

- Demonstration of how to choose page templates, add content blocks, and customize layouts.

Chapter 6: Page Optimization for SEO

6.1 On-Page SEO Optimization:

- Explanation of on-page SEO techniques for optimizing new pages for search engines.
- Techniques for optimizing page titles, meta descriptions, headings, and content for relevant keywords.

6.2 Image Optimization:

- Importance of image optimization for SEO and user experience.
- Guidelines for optimizing image filenames, alt text, captions, and sizes to improve page rankings and accessibility.

6.3 Mobile Responsiveness:

- Explanation of the importance of mobile responsiveness for new pages.
- Techniques for ensuring that new pages display correctly and function seamlessly across various devices and screen sizes.

Chapter 7: User Experience (UX) Optimization

7.1 Navigation and Layout:

- Importance of intuitive navigation and layout for new pages.
- Techniques for designing clear navigation menus, organizing content logically, and maintaining consistency across pages.

7.2 Call-to-Action (CTA) Optimization:

- Strategies for optimizing call-to-action elements on new pages to encourage user interaction and conversions.
- Techniques for designing persuasive CTAs that stand out and align with page objectives.

7.3 Accessibility Considerations:

- Importance of accessibility considerations for new pages to ensure inclusivity and compliance with web accessibility standards.
- Techniques for designing accessible page layouts, content, and navigation.

Chapter 8: Review and Testing

8.1 Content Review:

- Importance of reviewing new page content for accuracy, clarity, and alignment with objectives.
- Techniques for conducting content audits and revisions to ensure quality and consistency.

8.2 User Testing:

- Explanation of the importance of user testing for new pages to gather feedback and identify usability issues.
- Techniques for conducting user testing sessions and incorporating feedback to improve page design and functionality.

Chapter 9: Launch and Promotion

9.1 Page Launch Plan:

- Importance of planning and coordinating the launch of new pages to maximize visibility and impact.
- Techniques for creating a launch plan, including scheduling social media posts, email announcements, and paid promotions.

9.2 Promotion Strategies:

- Strategies for promoting new pages to increase visibility and drive traffic.
- Techniques for leveraging content marketing, social media, email marketing, and influencer partnerships to promote new pages.

Chapter 10: Monitoring and Optimization

10.1 Performance Monitoring:

- Importance of monitoring the performance of new pages to track user engagement, conversions, and SEO rankings.
- Techniques for using web analytics tools to gather data and insights on page performance.

10.2 Continuous Optimization:

- Explanation of the importance of continuous optimization for new pages to maintain relevance and effectiveness.
- Techniques for analyzing performance data, identifying optimization opportunities, and implementing changes to improve page performance.

Chapter 11: Conclusion and Next Steps

11.1 Summary of Key Insights:

- Recap of key concepts and strategies discussed in the chapter.
- Emphasis on the importance of strategic planning, quality content creation, and ongoing optimization for successful new page creation.

11.2 Actionable Takeaways:

- Actionable takeaways for readers to implement in their website development projects, including audience research, content planning, and optimization strategies.

11.3 Future Directions:

- Reflection on emerging trends and technologies in website development and content creation.
- Encouragement for readers to stay updated on industry developments and continue refining their skills in page creation and optimization.

Introduction to Page Layout Customization

1.1 Understanding Page Layouts:

- Definition of page layouts in website development and their importance for user experience and visual appeal.
- Explanation of how customizable page layouts allow designers and developers to create unique and engaging web pages.

1.2 Importance of Customization:

- Discussion on the significance of customizing page layouts to align with branding, content hierarchy, and user interaction goals.
- Examples of how customized page layouts can enhance usability, accessibility, and overall website performance.

Chapter 2: Choosing Layout Options

2.1 Types of Layouts:

- Overview of common page layout options such as full-width, boxed, grid-based, and multi-column layouts.
- Explanation of the characteristics and suitability of each layout type for different types of content and design aesthetics.

2.2 Responsive Design Considerations:

- Importance of responsive design in choosing and customizing page layouts to ensure optimal viewing experiences across devices.
- Techniques for adapting layout designs for various screen sizes and resolutions through media queries and flexible grids.

2.3 Accessibility and User Experience:

- Discussion on how page layout choices impact accessibility and user experience for all visitors, including those with disabilities.
- Techniques for designing inclusive layouts that prioritize readability, navigation, and interaction for diverse user needs.

Chapter 3: Customizing Layout Elements

3.1 Header Customization:

- Importance of header customization in establishing brand identity and providing navigation cues.

- Techniques for customizing header elements such as logos, menus, navigation bars, and call-to-action buttons.

3.2 Footer Customization:

- Significance of footer customization in providing additional navigation options, contact information, and legal disclosures.
- Techniques for customizing footer elements such as copyright notices, social media links, and site maps.

3.3 Sidebar and Widget Areas:

- Discussion on the role of sidebars and widget areas in adding supplementary content, navigation aids, and interactive features.
- Techniques for customizing sidebar layouts, widget placement, and content modules to support user engagement and content discovery.

Chapter 4: Designing Page Sections

4.1 Hero Sections:

- Importance of hero sections in capturing user attention and conveying key messages or calls to action.
- Techniques for designing impactful hero sections with compelling visuals, concise copy, and clear CTAs.

4.2 Content Sections:

- Discussion on designing content sections to present information in a structured and visually appealing manner.
- Techniques for organizing content sections with clear headings, text hierarchy, and multimedia elements to enhance readability and engagement.

4.3 Call-to-Action (CTA) Sections:

- Significance of CTA sections in encouraging user interaction and driving conversions.
- Techniques for designing effective CTA sections with persuasive copy, contrasting visuals, and prominent placement.

Chapter 5: Customizing Page Templates

5.1 Template Selection:

- Overview of pre-designed page templates available in website builders and content management systems.

- Guidance on selecting templates that align with project requirements, design preferences, and functionality needs.

5.2 Template Customization:

- Techniques for customizing page templates to suit specific branding guidelines, content structures, and user experience objectives.
- Examples of template customization options such as color schemes, typography choices, and layout adjustments.

5.3 Creating Custom Templates:

- Discussion on creating custom page templates from scratch to achieve unique design concepts or functional requirements.
- Techniques for designing and coding custom templates using HTML, CSS, and JavaScript to meet project specifications.

Chapter 6: Testing and Iteration

6.1 Cross-Browser and Cross-Device Testing:

- Importance of testing customized page layouts across different web browsers, devices, and screen sizes.
- Techniques for conducting thorough testing to ensure consistent rendering and usability across various platforms.

6.2 User Feedback and Iterative Design:

- Discussion on the value of soliciting user feedback and iterating on page layouts based on user preferences and behaviors.
- Techniques for gathering user feedback through surveys, usability testing, and analytics insights to inform layout improvements.

6.3 Performance Optimization:

- Considerations for optimizing customized page layouts for performance, including page load times and resource utilization.
- Techniques for optimizing images, scripts, and code structure to enhance page speed and overall user experience.

Chapter 7: Conclusion and Next Steps

7.1 Summary of Key Insights:

- Recap of key concepts and strategies discussed in the chapter.
- Emphasis on the importance of page layout customization in creating engaging and user-friendly web experiences.

7.2 Actionable Takeaways:

- Actionable takeaways for readers to implement in their website development projects, including layout selection, customization techniques, and testing strategies.

7.3 Future Directions:

- Reflection on emerging trends and technologies in page layout customization, such as modular design systems and AI-driven personalization.
- Encouragement for readers to continue exploring new tools and techniques to push the boundaries of creativity and user experience in web design.

Note: Each section will provide detailed explanations, practical examples, and actionable insights to guide readers in effectively customizing page layouts for their website development projects.

Introduction to Adding Content

1.1 Understanding the Importance of Content:

- Definition of content in website development and its crucial role in engaging users, conveying information, and achieving business objectives.
- Explanation of how well-crafted content enhances user experience, improves SEO, and drives conversions.

1.2 Types of Content:

- Overview of various types of content commonly added to web pages, including text, images, videos, infographics, and interactive elements.
- Discussion on the characteristics and benefits of each content type in communicating messages and achieving specific goals.

Chapter 2: Planning Content Strategy

2.1 Audience Analysis:

- Techniques for conducting audience analysis to understand the preferences, needs, and behaviors of target users.
- Importance of creating audience personas and mapping user journeys to tailor content to specific audience segments.

2.2 Content Goals and Objectives:

- Importance of defining clear content goals and objectives aligned with overall business objectives.
- Techniques for setting SMART (Specific, Measurable, Achievable, Relevant, Time-bound) goals to guide content creation efforts.

2.3 Content Calendar:

- Explanation of the content calendar and its role in organizing and scheduling content creation and publication.
- Techniques for creating a content calendar to ensure consistency, relevance, and alignment with marketing initiatives.

Chapter 3: Creating Text Content

3.1 Writing Engaging Copy:

- Tips and best practices for writing compelling and persuasive copy that captures attention and resonates with target audiences.

- Techniques for crafting clear, concise, and user-focused copy that addresses user needs and motivates action.

3.2 Formatting and Typography:

- Importance of formatting and typography in enhancing readability and visual appeal of text content.
- Techniques for selecting appropriate fonts, font sizes, line spacing, and paragraph styles to improve readability and comprehension.

3.3 SEO Optimization:

- Introduction to on-page SEO techniques for optimizing text content to improve search engine visibility and rankings.
- Guidelines for incorporating relevant keywords, optimizing meta tags, headings, and content structure to enhance SEO performance.

Chapter 4: Adding Visual Content

4.1 Image Selection and Optimization:

- Importance of selecting high-quality images that complement and reinforce textual content.
- Techniques for optimizing images for web use, including resizing, compression, and adding descriptive alt text for accessibility and SEO.

4.2 Video Integration:

- Discussion on the benefits of integrating videos into web pages to engage users and convey complex information.
- Techniques for embedding videos from platforms like YouTube or Vimeo, optimizing video playback, and ensuring compatibility across devices.

4.3 Infographics and Interactive Elements:

- Importance of infographics and interactive elements in presenting data and engaging users visually.
- Techniques for creating and integrating infographics, charts, graphs, and interactive features to enhance user experience and understanding.

Chapter 5: Structuring and Organizing Content

5.1 Content Hierarchy:

- Techniques for structuring content hierarchically to prioritize important information and guide user attention.

- Importance of clear headings, subheadings, and bullet points in organizing content for readability and scannability.

5.2 Content Blocks and Sections:

- Discussion on dividing content into logical blocks and sections to improve comprehension and navigation.
- Techniques for using white space, visual cues, and content grouping to create cohesive and digestible content layouts.

5.3 Call-to-Action (CTA) Placement:

- Importance of strategic CTA placement to prompt user action and drive conversions.
- Techniques for placing CTAs strategically throughout content, aligning with user intent and content context.

Chapter 6: Integrating Dynamic Content

6.1 Blog Posts and Articles:

- Techniques for adding blog posts and articles to web pages to provide fresh, relevant content and engage users.
- Importance of consistent publishing schedules, topical relevance, and reader engagement in blog content strategy.

6.2 User-Generated Content:

- Discussion on the benefits of integrating user-generated content such as reviews, testimonials, and comments to build trust and social proof.
- Techniques for soliciting and moderating user-generated content while maintaining brand integrity and relevance.

6.3 Dynamic Widgets and Plugins:

- Introduction to dynamic widgets and plugins for adding interactive elements, social media feeds, and personalized recommendations to web pages.
- Techniques for selecting, configuring, and integrating dynamic content elements to enhance user engagement and functionality.

Chapter 7: Content Optimization and Maintenance

7.1 Content SEO Audit:

- Techniques for conducting content SEO audits to assess keyword relevance, readability, and engagement metrics.

- Importance of updating and optimizing content based on SEO audit findings to improve search engine rankings and user experience.

7.2 Content Performance Monitoring:

- Discussion on the importance of monitoring content performance metrics such as page views, bounce rates, and time on page.
- Techniques for using web analytics tools to track content performance and identify areas for improvement or optimization.

7.3 Content Maintenance and Updates:

- Importance of regular content maintenance and updates to keep information accurate, relevant, and up-to-date.
- Techniques for implementing content management processes, archival strategies, and version control to ensure content freshness and accuracy.

Chapter 8: Conclusion and Next Steps

8.1 Summary of Key Insights:

- Recap of key concepts and strategies discussed in the chapter.
- Emphasis on the importance of strategic content creation, optimization, and maintenance for effective website development.

8.2 Actionable Takeaways:

- Actionable takeaways for readers to implement in their website development projects, including content planning, creation, and optimization strategies.

8.3 Future Directions:

- Reflection on emerging trends and technologies in content creation and integration, such as AI-driven content generation and immersive storytelling formats.
- Encouragement for readers to stay updated on industry developments and continue refining their content creation skills to meet evolving user needs and expectations.

Note: Each section will provide detailed explanations, practical examples, and actionable insights to guide readers in effectively adding content to their web pages for improved user experience and engagement.

Introduction to Dynamic Content

1.1 Understanding Dynamic Content:

- Definition of dynamic content in website development and its role in creating personalized, interactive, and engaging user experiences.
- Explanation of how dynamic content differs from static content and its benefits for improving user engagement and driving conversions.

1.2 Importance of Dynamic Content:

- Discussion on the significance of incorporating dynamic content to cater to user preferences, enhance website usability, and increase user interaction.
- Examples of dynamic content elements such as personalized recommendations, real-time updates, and interactive widgets.

Chapter 2: Types of Dynamic Content

2.1 Personalized Recommendations:

- Explanation of personalized recommendation systems that analyze user behavior and preferences to suggest relevant content or products.
- Techniques for implementing recommendation algorithms and displaying personalized content based on user interactions and preferences.

2.2 Real-Time Updates:

- Discussion on real-time updates such as live feeds, notifications, and dynamic data displays that provide users with timely and relevant information.
- Techniques for integrating real-time data sources, APIs, and event-driven updates to deliver dynamic content that reflects current events and user actions.

2.3 Interactive Widgets and Elements:

- Importance of interactive widgets and elements such as sliders, carousels, accordions, and interactive maps in enhancing user engagement and interactivity.
- Techniques for designing and implementing interactive elements using HTML, CSS, and JavaScript to create dynamic user experiences.

Chapter 3: Implementing Dynamic Content

3.1 Content Management Systems (CMS):

- Overview of content management systems such as WordPress, Drupal, and Joomla that support dynamic content creation and management.
- Explanation of how CMS platforms enable content editors to update, schedule, and publish dynamic content without requiring technical expertise.

3.2 Database Integration:

- Discussion on integrating databases such as MySQL, MongoDB, or Firebase with web applications to store and retrieve dynamic content.
- Techniques for creating database-driven applications and querying dynamic content based on user inputs or predefined criteria.

3.3 API Integration:

- Importance of integrating application programming interfaces (APIs) to access external data sources and services for dynamic content generation.
- Techniques for consuming APIs, handling data responses, and dynamically updating content based on API interactions.

Chapter 4: Personalization and User Engagement

4.1 User Profiling and Segmentation:

- Techniques for creating user profiles and segments based on demographic, behavioral, or contextual data to deliver personalized dynamic content.
- Importance of segmentation in tailoring content recommendations, offers, and messages to specific user groups for maximum relevance and impact.

4.2 Adaptive Content Delivery:

- Discussion on adaptive content delivery techniques that dynamically adjust content presentation based on user preferences, device characteristics, or environmental factors.
- Techniques for implementing adaptive layouts, responsive designs, and content prioritization strategies to optimize user experience across devices and contexts.

4.3 Interactive Experiences:

- Importance of creating interactive experiences through quizzes, surveys, polls, and user-generated content to foster user engagement and participation.
- Techniques for designing and implementing interactive content elements that encourage user interaction, feedback, and contribution.

Chapter 5: Dynamic Content Optimization

5.1 Performance Optimization:

- Techniques for optimizing dynamic content delivery to ensure fast page loading times and responsive user experiences.
- Importance of caching, lazy loading, and content delivery network (CDN) integration to minimize latency and improve performance for dynamic content.

5.2 A/B Testing and Optimization:

- Discussion on using A/B testing and experimentation to optimize dynamic content elements such as headlines, images, or call-to-action buttons.
- Techniques for designing and implementing A/B tests, analyzing results, and iterating on dynamic content variations to improve engagement and conversions.

5.3 Data Analytics and Insights:

- Importance of leveraging data analytics and insights to monitor user interactions, track engagement metrics, and derive actionable insights for dynamic content optimization.
- Techniques for using web analytics tools, heatmaps, and user behavior tracking to understand user preferences and behavior patterns for continuous improvement.

Chapter 6: Compliance and Security

6.1 Data Privacy and GDPR Compliance:

- Techniques for ensuring compliance with data privacy regulations such as the General Data Protection Regulation (GDPR) when collecting and processing user data for dynamic content personalization.
- Importance of obtaining user consent, implementing data protection measures, and maintaining transparency in data handling practices.

6.2 Security Best Practices:

- Discussion on security best practices for protecting dynamic content systems from common vulnerabilities such as SQL injection, cross-site scripting (XSS), and data breaches.
- Techniques for implementing security controls, encryption, and access management to safeguard sensitive user data and content assets.

6.3 Accessibility Considerations:

- Importance of accessibility considerations in designing and implementing dynamic content experiences that are usable and accessible to users with disabilities.

- Techniques for following web accessibility guidelines, providing alternative text for multimedia content, and ensuring keyboard navigation and screen reader compatibility.

Chapter 7: Conclusion and Next Steps

7.1 Summary of Key Insights:

- Recap of key concepts and strategies discussed in the chapter.
- Emphasis on the importance of incorporating dynamic content to enhance user engagement, personalization, and interactivity.

7.2 Actionable Takeaways:

- Actionable takeaways for readers to implement in their website development projects, including dynamic content strategies, implementation techniques, and optimization strategies.

7.3 Future Directions:

- Reflection on emerging trends and technologies in dynamic content creation and personalization, such as AI-driven content generation and machine learning-based recommendation systems.
- Encouragement for readers to explore advanced dynamic content solutions and stay updated on industry developments to deliver cutting-edge user experiences.

Note: Each section will provide detailed explanations, practical examples, and actionable insights to guide readers in effectively incorporating dynamic content into their website development projects for enhanced user engagement and interactivity.

Introduction to Navigation Menus

1.1 Understanding the Role of Navigation Menus:

- Definition of navigation menus and their importance in guiding users through a website's content and features.
- Explanation of how navigation menus contribute to user experience, website usability, and information architecture.

1.2 Types of Navigation Menus:

- Overview of different types of navigation menus, including traditional top navigation bars, sidebars, footer menus, and hamburger menus.
- Discussion on the characteristics and suitability of each menu type based on website goals, content structure, and design preferences.

Chapter 2: Designing Navigation Structures

2.1 Information Architecture:

- Techniques for designing effective information architecture to organize website content into logical categories and hierarchies.
- Importance of user-centric navigation structures that align with user needs, tasks, and browsing behaviors.

2.2 Navigation Labels and Categories:

- Strategies for creating clear and descriptive navigation labels that accurately represent the content and functionality of each section.
- Techniques for categorizing and grouping navigation items to facilitate intuitive navigation and content discovery.

2.3 Visual Hierarchy and Layout:

- Importance of visual hierarchy and layout in designing navigation menus that prioritize important sections and guide user attention.
- Techniques for using typography, color, spacing, and visual cues to create a clear and visually appealing navigation layout.

Chapter 3: Implementing Navigation Menus

3.1 HTML and CSS Basics:

- Overview of HTML and CSS fundamentals for creating and styling navigation menus.

- Explanation of HTML markup for structuring navigation lists and CSS styles for customizing menu appearance, layout, and responsiveness.

3.2 Static Navigation Menus:

- Techniques for creating static navigation menus using HTML and CSS, including basic list-based menus and styled navigation bars.
- Discussion on responsive design principles for adapting static menus to different screen sizes and devices.

3.3 Dynamic Navigation Menus:

- Introduction to dynamic navigation menus generated from content management systems (CMS) or JavaScript frameworks.
- Techniques for integrating dynamic menus that automatically update based on website structure, content changes, or user interactions.

Chapter 4: Advanced Navigation Features

4.1 Mega Menus:

- Explanation of mega menus as large, multi-column dropdown menus that display additional navigation options and content.
- Techniques for designing and implementing mega menus to accommodate complex website structures and extensive content hierarchies.

4.2 Sticky and Fixed Menus:

- Discussion on sticky and fixed navigation menus that remain visible as users scroll down the page.
- Techniques for implementing sticky headers and fixed menus using CSS positioning or JavaScript to improve navigation accessibility and convenience.

4.3 Mobile Navigation Solutions:

- Importance of mobile-friendly navigation solutions for providing seamless user experiences on smartphones and tablets.
- Techniques for designing mobile navigation patterns such as off-canvas menus, accordion menus, and bottom navigation bars for optimal mobile usability.

Chapter 5: Accessibility and Usability Considerations

5.1 Keyboard Navigation:

- Techniques for ensuring keyboard accessibility in navigation menus to accommodate users who rely on keyboard navigation or screen readers.

- Importance of keyboard focus styles, tab order, and aria attributes for improving navigation accessibility and usability.

5.2 Semantic Markup and ARIA Roles:

- Discussion on using semantic HTML markup and Accessible Rich Internet Applications (ARIA) roles to enhance navigation menu accessibility for assistive technologies.
- Techniques for applying ARIA roles such as menu, menuitem, and navigation to improve screen reader support and navigation semantics.

5.3 Color Contrast and Visual Feedback:

- Importance of color contrast and visual feedback in navigation menus for users with visual impairments or color blindness.
- Techniques for ensuring sufficient color contrast ratios and providing alternative visual cues such as hover effects or focus states for improved usability.

Chapter 6: Testing and Optimization

6.1 Usability Testing:

- Importance of usability testing to evaluate navigation menu effectiveness, usability, and user satisfaction.
- Techniques for conducting usability tests, gathering feedback from users, and identifying navigation usability issues for optimization.

6.2 A/B Testing:

- Discussion on using A/B testing to compare different navigation menu designs, layouts, or features to determine optimal configurations.
- Techniques for designing A/B tests, measuring performance metrics, and iterating on navigation menu variations based on test results.

6.3 Performance Optimization:

- Importance of optimizing navigation menu performance for fast loading times and responsive user experiences.
- Techniques for optimizing menu code, minimizing HTTP requests, and leveraging caching and content delivery networks (CDNs) for improved performance.

Chapter 7: Conclusion and Next Steps

7.1 Summary of Key Insights:

- Recap of key concepts and strategies discussed in the chapter.
- Emphasis on the importance of well-designed navigation menus for improving website usability, accessibility, and user experience.

7.2 Actionable Takeaways:

- Actionable takeaways for readers to implement in their website development projects, including navigation menu design principles, implementation techniques, and optimization strategies.

7.3 Future Directions:

- Reflection on emerging trends and technologies in navigation menu design, such as voice-based navigation and AI-driven personalization.
- Encouragement for readers to stay updated on industry developments and continue refining their navigation menu design skills to meet evolving user needs and expectations.

Note: Each section will provide detailed explanations, practical examples, and actionable insights to guide readers in effectively creating navigation menus for their website development projects.

Introduction to Navigation Structure Design

1.1 Understanding the Importance of Navigation Structure:

- Definition of navigation structure and its crucial role in organizing website content and facilitating user navigation.
- Explanation of how a well-designed navigation structure contributes to user experience, website usability, and content discoverability.

1.2 Goals of Navigation Structure Design:

- Discussion on the goals and objectives of navigation structure design, including intuitive navigation, efficient content access, and logical information architecture.
- Explanation of how navigation structure design aligns with user needs, business goals, and website objectives.

Chapter 2: User-Centered Navigation Design Principles

2.1 User Research and Analysis:

- Techniques for conducting user research and analysis to understand user needs, preferences, and behavior patterns.
- Importance of user personas, user journeys, and usability testing in informing navigation structure design decisions.

2.2 Clarity and Simplicity:

- Strategies for ensuring clarity and simplicity in navigation structure design to minimize cognitive load and facilitate intuitive navigation.
- Techniques for using clear labels, logical groupings, and hierarchical organization to simplify navigation options.

2.3 Consistency and Familiarity:

- Importance of consistency and familiarity in navigation structure design to enhance usability and reduce user confusion.
- Techniques for maintaining consistent navigation patterns, terminology, and visual cues across different sections of the website.

Chapter 3: Organizing Content Hierarchies

3.1 Information Architecture Principles:

- Overview of information architecture principles for organizing website content into logical categories, hierarchies, and navigation paths.
- Techniques for creating a clear and intuitive information architecture that reflects user mental models and content relationships.

3.2 Hierarchical Navigation Structures:

- Explanation of hierarchical navigation structures such as top-level navigation, submenus, and breadcrumb trails for organizing content hierarchies.
- Techniques for designing hierarchical navigation structures that accommodate diverse content types and user browsing preferences.

3.3 Faceted Navigation and Filters:

- Introduction to faceted navigation and filtering systems for allowing users to refine content based on specific criteria or attributes.
- Techniques for implementing faceted navigation interfaces with filter options, sorting controls, and dynamic search functionality.

Chapter 4: Designing Accessible and Inclusive Navigation

4.1 Accessibility Guidelines:

- Overview of web accessibility guidelines and best practices for designing navigation structures that are accessible to users with disabilities.
- Techniques for adhering to WCAG (Web Content Accessibility Guidelines) standards, providing alternative text for images, and ensuring keyboard navigation support.

4.2 Inclusive Design Principles:

- Discussion on inclusive design principles for designing navigation structures that accommodate diverse user needs, preferences, and abilities.
- Techniques for considering accessibility, language preferences, cultural differences, and cognitive abilities in navigation structure design.

4.3 Mobile-Friendly Navigation:

- Importance of designing mobile-friendly navigation structures for optimal user experience on smartphones and tablets.
- Techniques for implementing responsive design principles, touch-friendly navigation elements, and mobile-specific navigation patterns.

Chapter 5: Navigation Design Patterns and Trends

5.1 Mega Menus and Dropdowns:

- Explanation of mega menus and dropdown menus as popular navigation design patterns for accommodating large amounts of content.
- Techniques for designing visually appealing and user-friendly mega menus with clear categorization and hover interactions.

5.2 Hamburger Menus and Off-Canvas Navigation:

- Introduction to hamburger menus and off-canvas navigation as space-saving solutions for mobile and minimalist website designs.
- Techniques for implementing off-canvas navigation panels with smooth animations and intuitive gestures for mobile users.

5.3 Card-Based Navigation:

- Discussion on card-based navigation as a versatile design pattern for organizing content into visually appealing and digestible chunks.
- Techniques for designing card-based navigation interfaces with interactive elements, swipe gestures, and dynamic content previews.

Chapter 6: Navigation Usability Testing and Optimization

6.1 Usability Testing Methods:

- Techniques for conducting usability testing to evaluate navigation structure effectiveness, user satisfaction, and task completion rates.
- Importance of usability testing methods such as card sorting, tree testing, and clickstream analysis in identifying navigation usability issues.

6.2 Iterative Design and Optimization:

- Discussion on iterative design and optimization processes for refining navigation structures based on user feedback and usability test results.
- Techniques for implementing iterative design cycles, gathering stakeholder feedback, and prioritizing navigation structure improvements.

6.3 Performance Monitoring and Analytics:

- Importance of monitoring navigation structure performance metrics such as bounce rates, exit rates, and navigation paths.
- Techniques for using web analytics tools, heatmaps, and user behavior tracking to identify navigation structure optimization opportunities.

Chapter 7: Conclusion and Next Steps

7.1 Summary of Key Insights:

- Recap of key concepts and principles discussed in the chapter.

- Emphasis on the importance of user-centered navigation structure design for enhancing website usability and user experience.

7.2 Actionable Takeaways:

- Actionable takeaways for readers to implement in their website development projects, including navigation structure design principles, usability testing techniques, and optimization strategies.

7.3 Future Directions:

- Reflection on emerging trends and technologies in navigation structure design, such as voice-based navigation and AI-driven personalization.
- Encouragement for readers to stay updated on industry developments and continue refining their navigation structure design skills to meet evolving user needs and expectations.

Note: Each section will provide detailed explanations, practical examples, and actionable insights to guide readers in effectively designing user-friendly navigation structures for their website development projects.

Introduction to Navigation Enhancements

1.1 Understanding Navigation Enhancement:

- Definition of navigation enhancements and their role in improving user experience, engagement, and usability.
- Explanation of how navigation enhancements go beyond basic navigation structures to provide additional functionality and interactivity.

1.2 Importance of Navigation Enhancements:

- Discussion on the significance of implementing navigation enhancements to streamline navigation, increase content discoverability, and drive user engagement.
- Examples of navigation enhancements such as search functionality, breadcrumbs, and contextual navigation.

Chapter 2: Search Functionality

2.1 Introduction to Search:

- Overview of search functionality as a navigation enhancement that allows users to find specific content quickly and efficiently.
- Importance of implementing search features in websites with large amounts of content or complex navigation structures.

2.2 Search Design Best Practices:

- Techniques for designing effective search interfaces with intuitive search bars, autocomplete suggestions, and advanced filtering options.
- Importance of relevance ranking, typo tolerance, and semantic search algorithms for delivering accurate and relevant search results.

2.3 Integrating Search into Navigation:

- Strategies for integrating search functionality into navigation menus, headers, or sidebars for easy access and visibility.
- Techniques for designing seamless transitions between navigation browsing and search interactions to support diverse user navigation preferences.

Chapter 3: Breadcrumbs Navigation

3.1 Understanding Breadcrumbs:

- Explanation of breadcrumbs navigation as a hierarchical trail that shows the user's current location within the website's navigation hierarchy.
- Importance of breadcrumbs for providing context, orientation, and easy navigation back to higher-level pages.

3.2 Types of Breadcrumbs:

- Overview of different types of breadcrumbs, including location-based, path-based, and attribute-based breadcrumbs.
- Discussion on the characteristics and suitability of each breadcrumb type based on website structure and user navigation needs.

3.3 Implementing Breadcrumbs:

- Techniques for implementing breadcrumbs navigation using HTML markup and CSS styling, or through content management systems (CMS) and website platforms.
- Importance of dynamic breadcrumb generation based on user navigation paths and website hierarchy changes.

Chapter 4: Contextual Navigation

4.1 Definition of Contextual Navigation:

- Introduction to contextual navigation as dynamic navigation options that change based on the user's current context or content selection.
- Explanation of how contextual navigation enhances user experience by providing relevant options and shortcuts.

4.2 Techniques for Contextual Navigation:

- Strategies for implementing contextual navigation features such as related links, next/previous navigation, and content-based navigation menus.
- Importance of contextual navigation in guiding users to related content, encouraging exploration, and reducing bounce rates.

4.3 Dynamic Navigation Components:

- Discussion on dynamic navigation components such as related articles, recommended products, or related categories that adapt based on user interactions or content attributes.
- Techniques for integrating dynamic navigation components into website templates, content pages, and product listings for personalized user experiences.

Chapter 5: Interactive Navigation Elements

5.1 Definition of Interactive Navigation Elements:

- Overview of interactive navigation elements such as accordions, tabs, and expandable menus that allow users to interactively explore content.
- Importance of interactive navigation elements in conserving screen space, organizing content hierarchies, and providing engaging user experiences.

5.2 Design and Implementation Techniques:

- Techniques for designing and implementing interactive navigation elements using HTML, CSS, and JavaScript frameworks.
- Importance of accessibility considerations, touch-friendly design, and responsive layouts for optimal user interaction across devices and screen sizes.

5.3 Examples of Interactive Navigation:

- Examples of websites and applications that effectively utilize interactive navigation elements to enhance user engagement and navigation experience.
- Analysis of design patterns, usability principles, and best practices employed in interactive navigation implementations.

Chapter 6: Performance Optimization

6.1 Performance Considerations for Navigation Enhancements:

- Importance of performance optimization for navigation enhancements to ensure fast loading times and responsive user interactions.
- Techniques for optimizing search functionality, breadcrumb rendering, and dynamic navigation components to minimize latency and improve user experience.

6.2 Lazy Loading and Content Preloading:

- Discussion on lazy loading and content preloading techniques to optimize navigation enhancements by prioritizing critical resources and deferring non-essential content.
- Techniques for lazy loading search results, breadcrumb trails, and dynamically loaded navigation components to improve page load performance.

6.3 Caching and Content Delivery:

- Importance of caching strategies and content delivery networks (CDNs) in optimizing navigation enhancement components for global accessibility and scalability.
- Techniques for leveraging browser caching, server-side caching, and CDN caching to deliver navigation enhancements efficiently to users worldwide.

Chapter 7: Testing and Optimization Strategies

7.1 Usability Testing for Navigation Enhancements:

- Techniques for conducting usability testing to evaluate the effectiveness, usability, and user satisfaction of navigation enhancements.
- Importance of usability testing methods such as task-based testing, navigation scenario testing, and user feedback collection in identifying usability issues and optimization opportunities.

7.2 A/B Testing and Iterative Optimization:

- Discussion on using A/B testing and iterative optimization techniques to refine navigation enhancements based on user feedback and performance data.
- Techniques for designing A/B tests, defining test objectives, measuring key performance indicators (KPIs), and iterating on navigation enhancement variations to improve user engagement and conversion rates.

7.3 Analytics and Performance Monitoring:

- Importance of analytics and performance monitoring in tracking user interactions, navigation behavior, and navigation enhancement performance metrics.
- Techniques for using web analytics tools, heatmaps, and performance monitoring dashboards to gather insights and make data-driven decisions for navigation enhancement optimization.

Chapter 8: Conclusion and Next Steps

8.1 Summary of Key Insights:

- Recap of key concepts and strategies discussed in the chapter.
- Emphasis on the importance of implementing navigation enhancements to improve user experience, engagement, and usability in website development projects.

8.2 Actionable Takeaways:

- Actionable takeaways for readers to implement in their website development projects, including techniques for implementing search functionality, breadcrumbs navigation, contextual navigation, and interactive navigation elements.

8.3 Future Directions:

- Reflection on emerging trends and technologies in navigation enhancement design, such as AI-driven personalization, voice-based navigation, and augmented reality (AR) interfaces.
- Encouragement for readers to explore innovative navigation enhancement strategies and continue refining their navigation design skills to meet evolving user needs and expectations.

Note: Each section will provide detailed explanations, practical examples, and actionable insights to guide readers in effectively implementing navigation enhancements in their website development projects.

Introduction to Navigation Testing and Optimization

1.1 Understanding Navigation Testing and Optimization:

- Definition of navigation testing and optimization and their significance in improving user experience, engagement, and conversion rates.
- Explanation of how navigation testing involves evaluating the effectiveness and usability of navigation elements, while optimization focuses on refining navigation based on insights and data.

1.2 Importance of Navigation Testing and Optimization:

- Discussion on the importance of navigation testing and optimization in identifying usability issues, improving user satisfaction, and maximizing website performance.
- Examples of how well-tested and optimized navigation can lead to increased user engagement, higher conversion rates, and improved search engine rankings.

Chapter 2: Usability Testing Methods

2.1 Task-Based Testing:

- Explanation of task-based testing methodologies for evaluating navigation effectiveness by observing users as they complete specific tasks or scenarios.
- Techniques for designing test scenarios, recruiting participants, and analyzing task completion rates, errors, and user satisfaction.

2.2 Navigation Scenario Testing:

- Introduction to navigation scenario testing, which involves presenting users with hypothetical navigation challenges and observing their navigation strategies and decision-making processes.
- Techniques for creating realistic navigation scenarios, measuring user responses, and identifying navigation usability issues and pain points.

2.3 User Feedback Collection:

- Importance of gathering user feedback through surveys, interviews, and usability sessions to understand user perceptions, preferences, and navigation challenges.
- Techniques for structuring feedback collection methods, asking targeted questions, and synthesizing qualitative data to inform navigation optimization efforts.

Chapter 3: A/B Testing and Iterative Optimization

3.1 Introduction to A/B Testing:

- Overview of A/B testing as a method for comparing two or more variations of navigation elements to determine which performs better in terms of user engagement, conversion rates, or other key metrics.
- Explanation of the A/B testing process, including hypothesis formulation, test design, implementation, and results analysis.

3.2 Designing A/B Tests for Navigation:

- Strategies for designing A/B tests specifically focused on navigation elements, such as menu layouts, navigation labels, button placements, and call-to-action (CTA) designs.
- Techniques for defining test objectives, selecting test variations, setting up tracking metrics, and ensuring statistical validity in navigation A/B tests.

3.3 Iterative Optimization:

- Discussion on the iterative optimization process, which involves continuously refining navigation elements based on A/B test results, user feedback, and performance metrics.
- Importance of iteration cycles, data-driven decision-making, and incremental improvements in achieving optimal navigation design and user experience.

Chapter 4: Analytics and Performance Monitoring

4.1 Key Performance Indicators (KPIs) for Navigation:

- Overview of key performance indicators (KPIs) used to measure navigation effectiveness, including bounce rates, exit rates, time on page, page views, and conversion rates.
- Explanation of how each KPI provides insights into different aspects of navigation usability, engagement, and conversion effectiveness.

4.2 Web Analytics Tools:

- Introduction to web analytics tools such as Google Analytics, Adobe Analytics, and Mixpanel for tracking navigation-related metrics and user behavior patterns.
- Techniques for setting up custom event tracking, goal tracking, and conversion funnels to monitor user interactions with navigation elements.

4.3 Heatmaps and User Behavior Tracking:

- Importance of heatmaps and user behavior tracking tools for visualizing user interactions with navigation elements, such as clicks, hovers, scrolls, and attention patterns.
- Techniques for interpreting heatmap data, identifying navigation usability issues, and making informed optimization decisions based on user behavior insights.

Chapter 5: Performance Optimization Techniques

5.1 Page Load Speed Optimization:

- Strategies for optimizing navigation performance by reducing page load times through techniques such as image optimization, minification of CSS and JavaScript files, and leveraging browser caching.
- Importance of fast navigation load times in improving user satisfaction, reducing bounce rates, and enhancing overall website performance.

5.2 Mobile-Friendly Navigation Optimization:

- Discussion on optimizing navigation for mobile devices by implementing responsive design principles, touch-friendly navigation elements, and mobile-specific navigation patterns.
- Techniques for ensuring seamless navigation experiences across various screen sizes, resolutions, and device types to cater to mobile users effectively.

5.3 Accessibility and Inclusivity Optimization:

- Importance of optimizing navigation for accessibility and inclusivity by adhering to web accessibility standards such as WCAG (Web Content Accessibility Guidelines) and implementing keyboard navigation support, alternative text for images, and semantic HTML markup.
- Techniques for conducting accessibility audits, addressing accessibility issues, and ensuring navigation elements are usable by all users, including those with disabilities.

Chapter 6: Continuous Improvement Strategies

6.1 Feedback Loop Integration:

- Importance of establishing a feedback loop between navigation testing, optimization efforts, and user feedback collection to facilitate continuous improvement.
- Techniques for incorporating user feedback into navigation optimization decisions, prioritizing optimization efforts, and addressing navigation usability issues iteratively.

6.2 Cross-Functional Collaboration:

- Discussion on the importance of cross-functional collaboration between design, development, and marketing teams in implementing navigation enhancements and optimization strategies.
- Techniques for fostering collaboration, communication, and knowledge sharing across teams to ensure alignment with business goals and user needs in navigation optimization efforts.

6.3 Stay Updated on Industry Trends:

- Importance of staying updated on industry trends, best practices, and emerging technologies in navigation testing and optimization to remain competitive and deliver exceptional user experiences.
- Techniques for staying informed through industry publications, conferences, webinars, and networking with peers in the web development community.

Chapter 7: Conclusion and Next Steps

7.1 Summary of Key Insights:

- Recap of key concepts and strategies discussed in the chapter.
- Emphasis on the importance of navigation testing and optimization in improving user experience, engagement, and conversion rates on websites.

7.2 Actionable Takeaways:

- Actionable takeaways for readers to implement in their website development projects, including techniques for conducting usability testing, A/B testing, analytics tracking, and performance optimization.

7.3 Future Directions:

- Reflection on emerging trends and technologies in navigation testing and optimization, such as AI-driven personalization, voice-based navigation, and augmented reality (AR) interfaces.
- Encouragement for readers to explore innovative testing and optimization strategies and continue refining their navigation optimization skills to meet evolving user needs and expectations.

Note: Each section will provide detailed explanations, practical examples, and actionable insights to guide readers in effectively testing and optimizing navigation elements in their website development projects.

Introduction to Consistency Across Pages

1.1 Understanding Consistency:

- Definition of consistency in the context of website development and its importance in providing a seamless user experience.
- Explanation of how consistency across pages enhances usability, brand identity, and navigational clarity for website visitors.

1.2 Importance of Consistency:

- Discussion on the significance of maintaining consistency across pages to build user trust, reduce cognitive load, and improve overall website usability.
- Examples of how consistent design elements, navigation structures, and content presentation contribute to a cohesive user experience.

Chapter 2: Elements of Consistency

2.1 Visual Consistency:

- Explanation of visual consistency principles such as color schemes, typography, layout grids, and design elements that maintain a cohesive visual identity across pages.
- Techniques for establishing visual consistency through style guides, design templates, and standardized design elements.

2.2 Navigational Consistency:

- Discussion on navigational consistency, including consistent placement, labeling, and behavior of navigation elements such as menus, buttons, and links.
- Techniques for ensuring consistent navigation patterns across pages to facilitate intuitive browsing and reduce user confusion.

2.3 Content Consistency:

- Importance of content consistency in maintaining a unified tone, voice, and messaging across pages to reinforce brand identity and communicate effectively with users.
- Techniques for creating content guidelines, editorial standards, and content templates to ensure consistency in writing style, formatting, and messaging.

Chapter 3: Designing Consistent Layouts

3.1 Grid-Based Layouts:

- Overview of grid-based layout systems for designing consistent page layouts with balanced proportions, alignment, and visual hierarchy.
- Techniques for using grid frameworks such as Bootstrap, Foundation, or CSS Grid to create responsive and consistent layouts across pages.

3.2 Component-Based Design:

- Introduction to component-based design methodologies for building reusable design elements and UI components that ensure consistency across pages.
- Techniques for designing modular UI components such as headers, footers, cards, and forms for consistent integration across website pages.

3.3 Responsive Design Principles:

- Discussion on responsive design principles for ensuring consistency in layout and visual presentation across different devices and screen sizes.
- Techniques for using fluid layouts, flexible images, and media queries to create consistent user experiences on desktops, tablets, and smartphones.

Chapter 4: Maintaining Consistent Navigation

4.1 Centralized Navigation Systems:

- Explanation of centralized navigation systems that maintain consistent navigation elements across all pages, such as global navigation menus or site-wide footers.
- Techniques for designing and implementing centralized navigation systems using HTML, CSS, and JavaScript for seamless navigation across pages.

4.2 Breadth and Depth of Navigation:

- Importance of maintaining consistent breadth and depth of navigation across pages to ensure users can easily access all sections of the website.
- Techniques for balancing the breadth (number of navigation options) and depth (level of nesting) of navigation menus to provide comprehensive yet streamlined navigation experiences.

4.3 Contextual Navigation Elements:

- Discussion on the role of contextual navigation elements such as breadcrumbs, related links, and call-to-action buttons in providing supplementary navigation options that remain consistent across pages.
- Techniques for integrating contextual navigation elements into page layouts and designs for enhanced user guidance and exploration.

Chapter 5: Ensuring Content Consistency

5.1 Style Guides and Brand Standards:

- Importance of style guides and brand standards in maintaining consistent content presentation, including writing style, tone of voice, visual imagery, and brand messaging.
- Techniques for creating and enforcing style guides that define content standards and guidelines for consistency across all pages.

5.2 Content Templates and Modules:

- Explanation of content templates and modular content design approaches for ensuring consistent content layouts and structures across pages.
- Techniques for designing reusable content modules such as article cards, product listings, or service descriptions that maintain consistency in presentation and formatting.

5.3 Editorial Workflows and Quality Assurance:

- Discussion on establishing editorial workflows and quality assurance processes to ensure consistency in content creation, editing, and publishing.
- Techniques for implementing content review cycles, proofreading checks, and version control systems to maintain high-quality, consistent content across pages.

Chapter 6: Continuous Monitoring and Improvement

6.1 Regular Audits and Reviews:

- Importance of conducting regular audits and reviews to identify inconsistencies, errors, or deviations from established design and content standards across pages.
- Techniques for performing visual inspections, content audits, and user testing sessions to detect and address inconsistencies proactively.

6.2 User Feedback and Iterative Refinement:

- Discussion on the value of gathering user feedback and incorporating iterative refinement cycles to continuously improve consistency across pages.
- Techniques for collecting user feedback through surveys, usability tests, and feedback forms, and using insights to refine design and content elements for enhanced consistency.

6.3 Performance Monitoring and Analytics:

- Importance of monitoring performance metrics and analytics data to assess the impact of consistency efforts on user engagement, conversion rates, and overall website performance.

- Techniques for tracking key performance indicators (KPIs) such as bounce rates, time on page, and conversion funnels to measure the effectiveness of consistency initiatives.

Chapter 7: Conclusion and Next Steps

7.1 Summary of Key Insights:

- Recap of key concepts and strategies discussed in the chapter.
- Emphasis on the importance of maintaining consistency across pages to enhance user experience and achieve business objectives in website development projects.

7.2 Actionable Takeaways:

- Actionable takeaways for readers to implement in their website development projects, including techniques for designing consistent layouts, maintaining navigation consistency, and ensuring content coherence.

7.3 Future Directions:

- Reflection on emerging trends and technologies in maintaining consistency across pages, such as design systems, AI-driven automation, and voice user interfaces.
- Encouragement for readers to stay updated on industry best practices and continue refining their consistency maintenance strategies to meet evolving user needs and expectations.

Note: Each section will provide detailed explanations, practical examples, and actionable insights to guide readers in effectively maintaining consistency across pages in their website development projects.

Introduction to Advanced Elements

1.1 Understanding Advanced Elements:

- Definition of advanced elements in website development and their role in enhancing functionality, interactivity, and user experience.
- Explanation of how advanced elements go beyond basic HTML elements to include dynamic components, interactive widgets, and multimedia integration.

1.2 Importance of Advanced Elements:

- Discussion on the significance of incorporating advanced elements to create engaging, dynamic, and feature-rich websites that meet modern user expectations.
- Examples of advanced elements such as sliders, carousels, accordions, interactive forms, and multimedia players that elevate website functionality and user engagement.

Chapter 2: Advanced Form Elements

2.1 Dynamic Form Fields:

- Explanation of dynamic form fields that adjust or change based on user input or predefined conditions, such as dropdown menus, date pickers, and conditional fields.
- Techniques for implementing dynamic form fields using JavaScript, jQuery, or front-end frameworks like React or Vue.js to enhance form usability and user experience.

2.2 Multi-Step Forms:

- Introduction to multi-step forms that break lengthy or complex input processes into sequential steps or stages, improving user comprehension and completion rates.
- Techniques for designing and implementing multi-step forms using progressive disclosure patterns, validation feedback, and clear navigation indicators.

2.3 Form Validation and Feedback:

- Importance of form validation and feedback mechanisms to guide users in submitting accurate and error-free data, reducing form abandonment and submission errors.
- Techniques for implementing client-side and server-side form validation, providing real-time feedback, and displaying error messages to users effectively.

Chapter 3: Interactive UI Components

3.1 Modal Windows and Dialogs:

- Overview of modal windows and dialogs as overlay elements that temporarily interrupt the main content flow to display critical information, alerts, or interactive content.
- Techniques for creating modal windows using HTML, CSS, and JavaScript libraries like Bootstrap or jQuery UI for presenting notifications, messages, or interactive forms.

3.2 Tooltips and Popovers:

- Explanation of tooltips and popovers as small, contextual UI elements that provide supplementary information or actions when users hover or click on specific elements.
- Techniques for implementing tooltips and popovers using CSS and JavaScript libraries like Popper.js or Tippy.js to enhance user guidance and interaction.

3.3 Drag-and-Drop Interfaces:

- Importance of drag-and-drop interfaces for intuitive content manipulation and interaction, such as reordering items, uploading files, or organizing elements.
- Techniques for implementing drag-and-drop functionality using HTML5 Drag and Drop API or JavaScript libraries like interact.js or Sortable.js for seamless user interactions.

Chapter 4: Multimedia Integration

4.1 Video Players and Galleries:

- Overview of video players and galleries for showcasing multimedia content, such as videos, slideshows, or image carousels, with customizable playback controls and navigation options.
- Techniques for embedding video players using HTML5 video tags, integrating video galleries with JavaScript plugins like Plyr or Fancybox, and optimizing multimedia content for performance.

4.2 Audio Players and Soundtracks:

- Explanation of audio players and soundtracks for embedding audio content, such as music tracks, podcasts, or sound effects, with playback controls and playlist management features.

- Techniques for integrating audio players using HTML5 audio tags, customizing audio playback behavior, and enhancing soundtracks with JavaScript libraries like Howler.js or Wavesurfer.js.

4.3 Interactive Maps and Geolocation:

- Importance of interactive maps and geolocation features for displaying geographic information, locations, or routes, and enabling user interaction such as zooming, panning, or searching.
- Techniques for embedding interactive maps using Google Maps API, Mapbox, or Leaflet.js, and implementing geolocation functionality to customize user experiences based on location data.

Chapter 5: Advanced Animation and Effects

5.1 CSS Animations and Transitions:

- Overview of CSS animations and transitions for adding motion, visual effects, and interactivity to website elements, such as fading, sliding, or rotating effects.
- Techniques for creating CSS animations and transitions using keyframes, transitions properties, and animation libraries like Animate.css for dynamic visual experiences.

5.2 JavaScript Animation Libraries:

- Explanation of JavaScript animation libraries for creating complex animations, interactive effects, and immersive storytelling experiences, such as scrolling animations, parallax effects, or particle systems.
- Techniques for integrating JavaScript animation libraries like GreenSock (GSAP), ScrollMagic, or Three.js to unleash creative possibilities and enhance user engagement with dynamic animations.

5.3 Scroll-Based Interactions:

- Importance of scroll-based interactions for designing engaging and interactive experiences that respond to user scrolling behavior, such as revealing content, triggering animations, or navigating between sections.
- Techniques for implementing scroll-based interactions using JavaScript libraries like ScrollMagic or AOS (Animate On Scroll), and designing scroll-driven effects with CSS scroll-snap properties or Intersection Observer API.

Chapter 6: Accessibility and Usability Considerations

6.1 Accessibility Best Practices:

- Importance of accessibility considerations in designing and implementing advanced elements to ensure inclusive user experiences for all users, including those with disabilities.
- Techniques for implementing accessibility features such as keyboard navigation, focus management, and screen reader compatibility, and conducting accessibility audits to identify and address usability barriers.

6.2 Performance Optimization:

- Discussion on performance optimization techniques for advanced elements to ensure fast loading times, smooth interactions, and optimal user experiences across devices and network conditions.
- Techniques for optimizing code, assets, and media files, implementing lazy loading, and leveraging browser caching and compression techniques to improve website performance without compromising functionality.

6.3 User Testing and Iterative Design:

- Importance of user testing and iterative design in refining advanced elements to meet user needs, preferences, and usability expectations.
- Techniques for conducting usability testing sessions, gathering user feedback, and iterating on design iterations based on insights and observations to enhance user satisfaction and engagement.

Chapter 7: Conclusion and Next Steps

7.1 Summary of Key Insights:

- Recap of key concepts and techniques discussed in the chapter.
- Emphasis on the role of advanced elements in elevating website functionality, interactivity, and user experience to meet the demands of modern web users.

7.2 Actionable Takeaways:

- Actionable takeaways for readers to implement in their website development projects, including techniques for incorporating advanced form elements, interactive UI components, multimedia integration, animation effects, and accessibility considerations.

7.3 Future Directions:

- Reflection on emerging trends and technologies in advanced web development, such as progressive web apps (PWAs), web components, and immersive experiences, and encouragement for readers to explore and experiment with innovative approaches to advanced elements in their projects.

Note: Each section will provide detailed explanations, practical examples, and actionable insights to guide readers in exploring and implementing advanced elements effectively in their website development projects.

: Introduction to Custom Forms

1.1 Understanding Custom Forms:

- Definition of custom forms in website development and their significance in collecting user input, gathering data, and facilitating user interactions.
- Explanation of how custom forms go beyond standard HTML form elements to offer personalized styling, advanced functionality, and seamless integration with website design.

1.2 Importance of Custom Forms:

- Discussion on the importance of custom forms in enhancing user experience, improving form completion rates, and capturing accurate data for various purposes such as lead generation, feedback collection, and e-commerce transactions.
- Examples of industries and use cases where custom forms play a critical role in engaging users and achieving business objectives.

Chapter 2: Designing Custom Form Layouts

2.1 Layout Considerations:

- Exploration of layout considerations for custom forms, including alignment, spacing, grouping, and visual hierarchy, to optimize usability and readability.
- Techniques for designing intuitive and user-friendly form layouts that guide users through the input process and minimize errors.

2.2 Responsive Design:

- Importance of responsive design principles in designing custom forms that adapt seamlessly to various screen sizes and devices.
- Techniques for creating responsive form layouts using fluid grids, flexible inputs, and media queries to ensure accessibility and usability across desktops, tablets, and smartphones.

2.3 Branding and Visual Consistency:

- Discussion on branding and visual consistency in custom form design to reinforce brand identity and maintain a cohesive user experience.
- Techniques for incorporating brand colors, typography, logos, and visual elements into custom form designs while ensuring consistency with the overall website aesthetic.

Chapter 3: Advanced Form Fields and Validation

3.1 Custom Input Fields:

- Overview of custom input fields beyond basic text inputs, including checkboxes, radio buttons, dropdowns, sliders, date pickers, and file uploads.
- Techniques for customizing input fields using HTML, CSS, and JavaScript to match specific design requirements and improve user interaction.

3.2 Form Validation:

- Explanation of form validation techniques to ensure data accuracy, completeness, and integrity before submission.
- Techniques for implementing client-side and server-side form validation using HTML5 attributes, JavaScript validation functions, and backend validation scripts to provide real-time feedback and error prevention.

3.3 Conditional Logic and Dynamic Fields:

- Importance of conditional logic and dynamic fields in custom forms to display or hide certain fields based on user input or predefined conditions.
- Techniques for implementing conditional logic using JavaScript or form builder plugins to create dynamic and adaptive form experiences that streamline user interactions.

Chapter 4: Custom Styling and Visual Enhancements

4.1 CSS Styling Techniques:

- Overview of CSS styling techniques for customizing form elements, including borders, backgrounds, fonts, colors, and transitions.
- Techniques for applying CSS styles selectively to form elements using class names, pseudo-classes, and CSS preprocessors to achieve desired visual effects and brand consistency.

4.2 Custom Icons and Graphics:

- Discussion on the role of custom icons and graphics in enhancing the visual appeal and usability of custom forms.
- Techniques for incorporating custom icons, illustrations, and graphics into form designs using icon fonts, SVG graphics, or raster images to provide visual cues and improve user engagement.

4.3 Animation and Microinteractions:

- Importance of animation and microinteractions in custom form design to provide feedback, guidance, and delight to users during the input process.

- Techniques for adding subtle animations, transitions, hover effects, and microinteractions to form elements using CSS animations, JavaScript libraries, or animation frameworks to enhance user experience.

Chapter 5: Accessibility and Usability Considerations

5.1 Accessibility Best Practices:

- Importance of accessibility considerations in custom form design to ensure inclusivity and usability for users with disabilities.
- Techniques for implementing accessibility features such as keyboard navigation, focus management, ARIA attributes, and semantic markup to improve form accessibility and compliance with accessibility standards.

5.2 Usability Testing and Feedback:

- Discussion on the importance of usability testing and feedback collection in refining custom form designs based on user preferences, behaviors, and pain points.
- Techniques for conducting usability testing sessions, gathering user feedback through surveys or interviews, and iterating on form designs to address usability issues and improve user satisfaction.

5.3 Performance Optimization:

- Importance of performance optimization in custom form development to ensure fast loading times and smooth user interactions.
- Techniques for optimizing form performance by minimizing HTTP requests, optimizing code and assets, implementing lazy loading, and leveraging browser caching to improve overall form responsiveness and user experience.

Chapter 6: Integrating with Backend Systems

6.1 Form Submission and Data Handling:

- Overview of form submission processes and data handling techniques to securely collect, process, and store user input.
- Techniques for integrating custom forms with backend systems using server-side scripting languages like PHP, Node.js, or Python to handle form submissions, validate input, and store data in databases.

6.2 Email Notifications and Alerts:

- Importance of email notifications and alerts in custom form workflows to notify users, administrators, or stakeholders about form submissions and important events.

- Techniques for setting up email notifications using server-side scripting, third-party email services, or form builder integrations to send automated emails based on form submissions or user actions.

6.3 Form Analytics and Tracking:

- Discussion on the role of form analytics and tracking in monitoring form performance, user behavior, and conversion rates.
- Techniques for implementing form analytics using tools like Google Analytics, Hotjar, or form builder analytics features to track form interactions, submission rates, abandonment rates, and conversion funnels for optimization purposes.

Chapter 7: Conclusion and Next Steps

7.1 Summary of Key Insights:

- Recap of key concepts and techniques discussed in the chapter.
- Emphasis on the importance of custom forms in website development and the role they play in enhancing user experience and achieving business goals.

7.2 Actionable Takeaways:

- Actionable takeaways for readers to implement in their website development projects, including techniques for designing custom form layouts, implementing advanced form fields and validation, custom styling and visual enhancements, accessibility and usability considerations, integration with backend systems, and performance optimization.

7.3 Future Directions:

- Reflection on emerging trends and technologies in custom form development, such as conversational forms, progressive web forms, and AI-powered form assistants, and encouragement for readers to explore and experiment with innovative approaches to custom forms in their projects.

Understanding Database Integration:

- Definition of database integration in website development and its role in storing, retrieving, and managing dynamic data.
- Explanation of how database integration enables websites to interact with structured data, such as user profiles, product listings, and transaction records, to provide personalized and dynamic content.

1.2 Importance of Database Integration:

- Discussion on the importance of database integration in enhancing website functionality, scalability, and data management capabilities.
- Examples of industries and use cases where database integration is crucial, such as e-commerce websites, content management systems (CMS), customer relationship management (CRM) systems, and online booking platforms.

Chapter 2: Types of Databases

2.1 Relational Databases:

- Overview of relational databases and their structured data model based on tables, rows, and columns.
- Discussion on popular relational database management systems (RDBMS) such as MySQL, PostgreSQL, Microsoft SQL Server, and Oracle Database, and their suitability for various web development projects.

2.2 NoSQL Databases:

- Introduction to NoSQL databases and their non-relational data models, including document-oriented, key-value, columnar, and graph databases.
- Explanation of NoSQL database systems like MongoDB, Cassandra, Redis, and Neo4j, and their advantages in handling unstructured or semi-structured data and scaling horizontally.

2.3 NewSQL Databases:

- Explanation of NewSQL databases as a hybrid approach combining the scalability of NoSQL databases with the ACID compliance of traditional relational databases.
- Overview of NewSQL database systems like Google Spanner, CockroachDB, and NuoDB, and their capabilities in supporting distributed transactions and high availability.

Chapter 3: Integrating Databases with Web Applications

3.1 Backend Frameworks and ORMs:

- Discussion on backend frameworks and object-relational mapping (ORM) libraries that facilitate database integration in web applications.
- Overview of popular backend frameworks like Express.js (Node.js), Django (Python), Ruby on Rails (Ruby), and Laravel (PHP), and their ORM counterparts such as Sequelize, Django ORM, ActiveRecord, and Eloquent.

3.2 RESTful APIs and Web Services:

- Explanation of RESTful APIs and web services as mechanisms for exposing database functionality to client-side applications.
- Techniques for building RESTful APIs using frameworks like Express.js, Flask, Ruby on Rails, or Laravel, and integrating them with frontend technologies like React, Angular, or Vue.js for data retrieval and manipulation.

3.3 GraphQL and Data Querying:

- Introduction to GraphQL as a query language and runtime for APIs, enabling clients to request and receive precisely the data they need.
- Techniques for implementing GraphQL APIs using libraries like Apollo Server, GraphQL.js, or Prisma, and leveraging GraphQL's flexibility and efficiency in querying databases to optimize data fetching in web applications.

Chapter 4: Database Design and Modeling

4.1 Entity-Relationship Modeling:

- Overview of entity-relationship (ER) modeling as a technique for designing relational database schemas based on entities, attributes, and relationships.
- Techniques for creating ER diagrams using tools like Lucidchart, draw.io, or Microsoft Visio, and translating ER models into database tables with normalized or denormalized structures.

4.2 Data Modeling Best Practices:

- Discussion on data modeling best practices for designing efficient, scalable, and maintainable database schemas.
- Techniques for defining primary keys, foreign keys, indexes, constraints, and data types, and optimizing database schema design for performance, data integrity, and flexibility.

4.3 Database Normalization:

- Explanation of database normalization as a process for organizing data into logical and efficient structures to minimize redundancy and dependency.

- Techniques for applying normalization rules (e.g., First Normal Form, Second Normal Form, Third Normal Form) to decompose database tables and ensure data consistency and integrity.

Chapter 5: Database Administration and Security

5.1 Database Administration Tasks:

- Overview of database administration tasks such as installation, configuration, backup and recovery, performance tuning, and monitoring.
- Techniques for performing routine database maintenance tasks using management tools like phpMyAdmin, pgAdmin, SQL Server Management Studio, or MongoDB Compass.

5.2 Data Security Measures:

- Discussion on data security measures to protect sensitive information stored in databases from unauthorized access, breaches, and cyber attacks.
- Techniques for implementing data encryption, access control, authentication, authorization, and auditing mechanisms to enforce data security policies and compliance with regulatory requirements.

5.3 Disaster Recovery and Backup Strategies:

- Explanation of disaster recovery and backup strategies to ensure data availability and integrity in case of system failures, data corruption, or natural disasters.
- Techniques for implementing regular backups, redundant storage, failover mechanisms, and disaster recovery plans to minimize data loss and downtime in database systems.

Chapter 6: Advanced Database Concepts

6.1 Data Warehousing and Analytics:

- Overview of data warehousing and analytics solutions for aggregating, analyzing, and visualizing large volumes of data stored in databases.
- Techniques for building data warehouses, data marts, and OLAP cubes, and using business intelligence (BI) tools like Tableau, Power BI, or Google Data Studio for data analysis and reporting.

6.2 Distributed Databases and Scalability:

- Discussion on distributed databases and their role in distributing data across multiple nodes or clusters to achieve horizontal scalability and fault tolerance.

- Techniques for implementing distributed database systems like sharding, replication, partitioning, and distributed consensus algorithms to handle large-scale data processing and high availability requirements.

6.3 Real-Time Data Processing:

- Explanation of real-time data processing techniques for processing and analyzing streaming data in near real-time, such as event-driven architectures, message queues, and stream processing frameworks.
- Techniques for building real-time data pipelines using technologies like Apache Kafka, Apache Flink, Amazon Kinesis, or Google Cloud Dataflow, and integrating them with databases for real-time analytics and decision-making.

Chapter 7: Conclusion and Next Steps

7.1 Summary of Key Insights:

- Recap of key concepts and techniques discussed in the chapter.
- Emphasis on the importance of database integration in website development and its implications for data-driven decision-making and business success.

7.2 Actionable Takeaways:

- Actionable takeaways for readers to implement in their website development projects, including techniques for choosing appropriate database systems, integrating databases with web applications, designing efficient database schemas, implementing data security measures, and exploring advanced database concepts.

7.3 Future Directions:

- Reflection on emerging trends and technologies in database integration, such as serverless databases, blockchain-based databases, and AI-driven analytics, and encouragement for readers to stay updated on evolving database technologies and practices to drive innovation in their projects.

Note: Each section will provide detailed explanations, practical examples, and actionable insights to guide readers in understanding and implementing database integration effectively in their website development projects.

Understanding Member Areas:

- Definition of member areas in website development and their role in providing personalized and exclusive content, features, and interactions to registered users.
- Explanation of how member areas enhance user engagement, loyalty, and retention by offering value-added services, community access, and membership benefits.

1.2 Importance of Member Areas:

- Discussion on the importance of member areas in fostering user relationships, driving conversions, and monetizing website traffic.
- Examples of industries and use cases where member areas add value, such as subscription-based content platforms, online communities, e-learning portals, and membership-based e-commerce sites.

Chapter 2: Planning and Designing Member Areas

2.1 User Registration and Authentication:

- Overview of user registration and authentication processes for member areas, including sign-up forms, login pages, and password management.
- Techniques for designing user-friendly registration forms, implementing secure authentication methods (e.g., email/password, social login, two-factor authentication), and handling user sessions and authentication tokens.

2.2 Profile Management:

- Discussion on profile management features in member areas, such as user profiles, account settings, and preferences.
- Techniques for allowing users to update their profile information, manage notification settings, customize preferences, and view their activity history within the member area.

2.3 Access Control and Permissions:

- Explanation of access control and permissions in member areas to regulate user access to content, features, and functionality based on roles and privileges.
- Techniques for implementing role-based access control (RBAC), permission levels, and content visibility rules to restrict or grant access to specific sections of the member area.

Chapter 3: Content Management and Personalization

3.1 Content Delivery:

- Overview of content management features in member areas for delivering personalized and targeted content to users.
- Techniques for organizing content into categories, tags, or collections, and leveraging user preferences, behavior data, and membership levels to recommend relevant content and experiences.

3.2 User-generated Content:

- Discussion on user-generated content (UGC) features in member areas, such as forums, comments, reviews, and user-generated submissions.
- Techniques for facilitating user contributions, moderating user-generated content, and fostering community engagement and collaboration within the member area.

3.3 Personalization and Recommendations:

- Explanation of personalization and recommendation engines in member areas to tailor content, products, and recommendations to individual user preferences and behaviors.
- Techniques for implementing personalization algorithms, collaborative filtering, content-based filtering, and machine learning models to deliver personalized experiences and drive user engagement.

Chapter 4: Community Building and Engagement

4.1 Discussion Forums and Social Networking:

- Overview of community-building features in member areas, including discussion forums, social networking tools, and interactive features.
- Techniques for creating online communities, fostering user interactions, facilitating discussions, and promoting user-generated content within the member area.

4.2 Member Events and Activities:

- Discussion on member events and activities features to engage users and encourage participation within the member area.
- Techniques for organizing virtual events, live webinars, workshops, challenges, and contests, and integrating event calendars, RSVPs, and reminders into the member area.

4.3 Gamification and Rewards:

- Explanation of gamification and rewards systems in member areas to incentivize user engagement and loyalty.

- Techniques for implementing gamified features such as points, badges, leaderboards, achievements, and loyalty programs to motivate users, drive desired behaviors, and enhance the overall member experience.

Chapter 5: Monetization Strategies

5.1 Subscription Models:

- Overview of subscription-based monetization models for member areas, including freemium, tiered pricing, and subscription bundles.
- Techniques for designing subscription plans, offering trial periods, managing subscription billing cycles, and integrating payment gateways to monetize access to premium content and features.

5.2 Premium Content and Digital Products:

- Discussion on premium content and digital product offerings in member areas, such as exclusive articles, courses, eBooks, and downloadable resources.
- Techniques for creating, pricing, and selling digital products, implementing digital rights management (DRM), and delivering purchased content securely to members.

5.3 Advertising and Sponsorships:

- Explanation of advertising and sponsorship opportunities in member areas to generate revenue through display ads, sponsored content, affiliate marketing, and partnerships.
- Techniques for implementing ad placements, tracking ad performance, managing ad campaigns, and attracting advertisers or sponsors to the member area.

Chapter 6: Analytics and Optimization

6.1 User Engagement Metrics:

- Overview of user engagement metrics and KPIs for measuring the effectiveness of member areas in driving user interactions, retention, and satisfaction.
- Techniques for tracking metrics such as active users, session duration, page views, content consumption, community participation, and conversion rates using web analytics tools and dashboard reports.

6.2 A/B Testing and Optimization:

- Discussion on A/B testing and optimization techniques to improve the performance and user experience of member areas.

- Techniques for conducting A/B tests on user interfaces, content layouts, calls-to-action, and engagement features, and using data-driven insights to iterate and optimize member area design and functionality.

6.3 Feedback Collection and User Surveys:

- Explanation of feedback collection and user survey strategies to gather insights, preferences, and suggestions from members.
- Techniques for implementing feedback forms, user satisfaction surveys, and NPS (Net Promoter Score) surveys, and analyzing feedback data to identify areas for improvement and prioritize feature enhancements.

Chapter 7: Conclusion and Next Steps

7.1 Summary of Key Insights:

- Recap of key concepts and techniques discussed in the chapter.
- Emphasis on the importance of member areas in website development and their role in driving user engagement, loyalty, and revenue generation.

7.2 Actionable Takeaways:

- Actionable takeaways for readers to implement in their website development projects, including techniques for planning and designing member areas, optimizing content management and personalization, building online communities, monetizing member areas, and analyzing user engagement metrics.

7.3 Future Directions:

- Reflection on emerging trends and technologies in member areas, such as AI-driven personalization, blockchain-based memberships, and virtual communities, and encouragement for readers to explore innovative approaches to member area development in their projects.

Note: Each section will provide detailed explanations, practical examples, and actionable insights to guide readers in understanding and implementing member areas effectively in their website development projects.

Introduction to Bookings and Appointments

1.1 Understanding Bookings and Appointments:

- Definition of bookings and appointments in website development and their significance in facilitating scheduling, reservations, and time management for businesses and service providers.
- Explanation of how bookings and appointments streamline the booking process, improve customer experience, and optimize resource utilization for businesses across various industries.

1.2 Importance of Bookings and Appointments:

- Discussion on the importance of bookings and appointments functionality in enhancing operational efficiency, increasing revenue opportunities, and reducing no-shows and scheduling conflicts.
- Examples of businesses and service providers that benefit from bookings and appointments solutions, such as healthcare facilities, salons, spas, restaurants, fitness centers, and tour operators.

Chapter 2: Types of Booking Systems

2.1 Appointment Scheduling Systems:

- Overview of appointment scheduling systems for booking individual appointments, consultations, and meetings with clients or customers.
- Discussion on features such as calendar views, availability checking, time slot selection, appointment reminders, and rescheduling capabilities offered by appointment scheduling software.

2.2 Reservation Management Systems:

- Introduction to reservation management systems for booking tables, seats, rooms, or resources at specific times or dates.
- Explanation of features such as table layouts, capacity management, reservation confirmation, waitlist management, and table turn tracking provided by reservation management platforms.

2.3 Event Booking Platforms:

- Overview of event booking platforms for scheduling and managing events, workshops, classes, or group activities.
- Discussion on features such as event registration, ticketing, attendee management, session scheduling, and event promotion offered by event booking software.

Chapter 3: Implementing Booking and Appointment Systems

3.1 Backend Infrastructure:

- Explanation of backend infrastructure requirements for implementing booking and appointment systems, including database design, server-side scripting, and API integrations.
- Techniques for designing database schemas, building server-side logic for handling booking requests, and integrating with external APIs for calendar synchronization, payment processing, or notification services.

3.2 Frontend User Interface:

- Discussion on frontend user interface design considerations for booking and appointment systems, including intuitive booking forms, interactive calendars, and responsive layouts.
- Techniques for creating user-friendly booking interfaces, providing real-time availability updates, and optimizing the user experience for seamless booking and scheduling interactions.

3.3 Integration with Business Processes:

- Overview of integration considerations for aligning booking and appointment systems with existing business processes and workflows.
- Techniques for integrating booking systems with CRM software, point-of-sale (POS) systems, inventory management tools, or customer communication platforms to streamline operations and enhance customer service.

Chapter 4: Customizing Booking and Appointment Solutions

4.1 Branding and Customization:

- Explanation of branding and customization options for tailoring booking and appointment solutions to match the visual identity and branding guidelines of businesses.
- Techniques for customizing colors, fonts, logos, and themes, and adding custom fields or branding elements to booking forms and confirmation emails.

4.2 Flexible Booking Rules and Policies:

- Discussion on flexible booking rules and policies to accommodate various business requirements, scheduling constraints, and service offerings.
- Techniques for configuring booking rules such as minimum notice periods, maximum booking durations, buffer times between appointments, and cancellation policies to optimize resource utilization and minimize disruptions.

4.3 Multi-channel Booking Options:

- Overview of multi-channel booking options for enabling customers to book appointments or reservations through different channels, including websites, mobile apps, social media platforms, or third-party booking aggregators.
- Techniques for implementing omnichannel booking integrations, providing consistent booking experiences across channels, and syncing booking data across multiple touchpoints for centralized management.

Chapter 5: Managing Bookings and Appointments

5.1 Calendar Management:

- Explanation of calendar management features for organizing and visualizing bookings, appointments, and availability schedules.
- Techniques for managing calendars, viewing and editing bookings, blocking off time slots, and handling scheduling conflicts or overlapping appointments effectively.

5.2 Automated Reminders and Notifications:

- Discussion on automated reminders and notifications to keep customers informed about upcoming appointments, reservations, or events.
- Techniques for sending email reminders, SMS notifications, or push notifications to confirm bookings, provide appointment details, and send follow-up messages or satisfaction surveys.

5.3 Resource Allocation and Optimization:

- Overview of resource allocation and optimization strategies for maximizing resource utilization and capacity management in booking and appointment systems.
- Techniques for monitoring resource availability, analyzing booking patterns, optimizing scheduling algorithms, and adjusting capacity based on demand fluctuations to minimize idle time and maximize revenue potential.

Chapter 6: Integration with Payment Systems

6.1 Online Payment Processing:

- Explanation of online payment processing capabilities for accepting payments and deposits at the time of booking.
- Discussion on payment gateway integrations, secure payment processing protocols (e.g., SSL encryption), and PCI compliance requirements for handling online transactions securely.

6.2 Billing and Invoicing:

- Overview of billing and invoicing features for generating invoices, receipts, or payment reminders for booked services or reservations.
- Techniques for automating billing cycles, calculating service fees or taxes, generating invoices, and sending invoices to customers via email or integrated billing platforms.

6.3 Refund and Cancellation Handling:

- Discussion on refund and cancellation policies and procedures for handling customer requests to cancel or reschedule bookings.
- Techniques for processing refunds, applying cancellation fees or penalties, managing refund requests, and updating booking statuses and availability in real-time to accommodate changes.

Chapter 7: Analytics and Reporting

7.1 Performance Metrics and KPIs:

- Explanation of performance metrics and key performance indicators (KPIs) for evaluating the effectiveness and efficiency of booking and appointment systems.
- Discussion on metrics such as booking conversion rates, booking lead times, appointment attendance rates, customer satisfaction scores, and revenue generated per booking.

7.2 Data Analysis and Insights:

- Overview of data analysis and insights derived from booking and appointment data to identify trends, patterns, and opportunities for optimization.
- Techniques for analyzing booking trends, customer demographics, service popularity, peak booking times, and revenue generation patterns using business intelligence tools or built-in reporting features.

7.3 Continuous Improvement and Optimization:

- Discussion on the importance of continuous improvement and optimization based on analytics and insights gathered from booking and appointment data.
- Techniques for implementing iterative improvements, A/B testing new features or booking workflows, and incorporating customer feedback to enhance the user experience and drive business growth.

Chapter 8: Conclusion and Next Steps

8.1 Summary of Key Insights:

- Recap of key concepts and techniques discussed in the chapter.
- Emphasis on the importance of bookings and appointments functionality in website development and its impact on customer experience, operational efficiency, and revenue generation.

8.2 Actionable Takeaways:

- Actionable takeaways for readers to implement in their website development projects, including techniques for planning and designing booking and appointment systems, customizing solutions to meet business needs, managing bookings effectively, integrating with payment systems, and analyzing performance metrics.

8.3 Future Directions:

- Reflection on emerging trends and technologies in bookings and appointments solutions, such as AI-driven scheduling algorithms, voice-enabled booking assistants, and blockchain-based reservation systems, and encouragement for readers to explore innovative approaches to booking and appointment management in their projects.

Note: Each section will provide detailed explanations, practical examples, and actionable insights to guide readers in understanding and implementing bookings and appointments functionality effectively in their website development projects.

Introduction to Online Stores

1.1 Understanding Online Stores:

- Definition of online stores in website development and their role in facilitating e-commerce transactions, product sales, and digital storefronts.
- Explanation of how online stores enable businesses to reach global audiences, operate 24/7, and leverage digital marketing channels to drive sales and revenue.

1.2 Importance of Online Stores:

- Discussion on the importance of online stores in modern commerce, including their ability to expand market reach, reduce operational costs, and provide convenient shopping experiences for customers.
- Examples of successful online stores across various industries, highlighting their impact on sales growth, brand visibility, and customer engagement.

Chapter 2: Planning and Designing Online Stores

2.1 Market Research and Target Audience:

- Overview of market research and target audience analysis for planning online stores, including identifying niche markets, analyzing customer demographics, and understanding consumer behavior.
- Techniques for conducting market research, creating buyer personas, and defining target audience segments to tailor product offerings and marketing strategies.

2.2 E-commerce Platform Selection:

- Discussion on e-commerce platform options for building online stores, including hosted platforms (e.g., Shopify, BigCommerce), self-hosted platforms (e.g., WooCommerce, Magento), and open-source solutions.
- Comparison of platform features, pricing structures, scalability, customization options, and integrations to help businesses choose the right e-commerce platform for their needs.

2.3 User Experience Design:

- Explanation of user experience (UX) design principles for creating intuitive and engaging online store interfaces that drive conversions and customer satisfaction.
- Techniques for designing user-friendly navigation, clear product listings, seamless checkout processes, responsive layouts, and visually appealing product displays to enhance the shopping experience.

Chapter 3: Setting Up Online Stores

3.1 Product Catalog Management:

- Overview of product catalog management features for organizing and displaying products in online stores, including product categories, attributes, variations, and pricing.
- Techniques for adding and editing product listings, uploading product images and descriptions, managing inventory levels, and configuring product options such as size, color, and quantity.

3.2 Payment Gateway Integration:

- Discussion on payment gateway integration for processing online transactions securely and accepting payments from customers.
- Explanation of payment gateway options, payment processing fees, PCI compliance requirements, and techniques for integrating payment gateways into e-commerce platforms to enable seamless checkout experiences.

3.3 Shipping and Order Fulfillment:

- Explanation of shipping and order fulfillment processes for delivering products to customers efficiently and accurately.
- Techniques for configuring shipping options, calculating shipping rates, managing order fulfillment workflows, generating shipping labels, and tracking order shipments to ensure timely delivery and customer satisfaction.

Chapter 4: Marketing and Promotion Strategies

4.1 Search Engine Optimization (SEO):

- Overview of SEO strategies for improving the visibility and ranking of online stores in search engine results pages (SERPs).
- Techniques for optimizing product pages, meta tags, URLs, and site structure, conducting keyword research, generating high-quality backlinks, and implementing local SEO tactics to attract organic traffic and increase sales.

4.2 Content Marketing:

- Discussion on content marketing strategies for engaging and informing customers through valuable content such as blog posts, product guides, tutorials, and videos.
- Techniques for creating compelling content, optimizing content for search engines, promoting content through social media channels, and leveraging content marketing to drive traffic, leads, and conversions.

4.3 Social Media Marketing:

- Explanation of social media marketing strategies for promoting online stores and engaging with customers on popular social media platforms such as Facebook, Instagram, Twitter, and Pinterest.
- Techniques for creating engaging social media posts, running targeted advertising campaigns, building communities and followers, and leveraging user-generated content to showcase products and drive sales.

Chapter 5: Customer Relationship Management (CRM)

5.1 Customer Data Management:

- Overview of customer data management features for capturing, storing, and analyzing customer information in online stores.
- Techniques for collecting customer data through registration forms, purchase histories, and interaction tracking, and leveraging customer relationship management (CRM) tools to segment customers, personalize communications, and nurture relationships.

5.2 Customer Support and Engagement:

- Discussion on customer support and engagement strategies for providing exceptional service and building trust with online store customers.
- Techniques for offering multiple support channels (e.g., live chat, email, phone), responding promptly to inquiries and complaints, resolving issues effectively, and proactively engaging customers through personalized interactions and follow-ups.

5.3 Loyalty Programs and Retention:

- Explanation of loyalty programs and retention strategies for rewarding loyal customers and encouraging repeat purchases in online stores.
- Techniques for implementing loyalty rewards, referral programs, VIP tiers, and special offers to incentivize customer loyalty, increase customer lifetime value (CLV), and reduce churn.

Chapter 6: Analytics and Performance Tracking

6.1 Sales and Conversion Tracking:

- Overview of sales and conversion tracking metrics for monitoring the performance of online stores and optimizing sales funnels.

- Techniques for tracking key metrics such as conversion rates, average order value (AOV), cart abandonment rates, and sales attribution using e-commerce analytics tools and dashboards.

6.2 Website Traffic Analysis:

- Discussion on website traffic analysis techniques for understanding user behavior, traffic sources, and engagement patterns in online stores.
- Techniques for analyzing website traffic data, identifying top-performing pages, measuring user engagement metrics (e.g., bounce rate, session duration), and optimizing website content and navigation based on insights gathered.

6.3 A/B Testing and Optimization:

- Explanation of A/B testing and optimization strategies for experimenting with different website elements, layouts, and marketing tactics to improve online store performance.
- Techniques for conducting A/B tests on product pages, checkout processes, pricing strategies, and promotional offers, and using data-driven insights to iterate and optimize online store design and functionality.

Chapter 7: Security and Compliance

7.1 Payment Security:

- Overview of payment security measures for protecting customer payment data and preventing fraud in online transactions.
- Explanation of PCI DSS compliance requirements, SSL encryption protocols, tokenization techniques, and fraud detection tools to ensure secure payment processing in online stores.

7.2 Data Privacy and GDPR Compliance:

- Discussion on data privacy and GDPR compliance considerations for handling customer data and personal information in online stores.
- Techniques for implementing privacy policies, obtaining user consent for data processing, providing transparency and control over data usage, and ensuring compliance with GDPR regulations to protect customer privacy rights.

7.3 Website Security:

- Explanation of website security best practices for safeguarding online stores against cyber threats, malware attacks, and data breaches.
- Techniques for implementing security measures such as web application firewalls (WAFs), regular security audits, software patches and updates, secure hosting environments, and backup and recovery procedures to maintain the integrity and availability of online store data.

Chapter 8: Conclusion and Next Steps

8.1 Summary of Key Insights:

- Recap of key concepts and techniques discussed in the chapter.
- Emphasis on the importance of online stores in website development and their role in driving e-commerce success for businesses of all sizes and industries.

8.2 Actionable Takeaways:

- Actionable takeaways for readers to implement in their online store development projects, including strategies for planning and designing online stores, setting up e-commerce platforms, marketing and promoting products, managing customer relationships, analyzing performance metrics, and ensuring security and compliance.

8.3 Future Directions:

- Reflection on emerging trends and technologies in e-commerce, such as mobile commerce, voice commerce, augmented reality (AR) shopping experiences, and blockchain-based payment solutions, and encouragement for readers to explore innovative approaches to online store development in their projects.

Note: Each section will provide detailed explanations, practical examples, and actionable insights to guide readers in understanding and implementing online store functionality effectively in their website development projects.

Introduction to Advanced Media Elements

1.1 Understanding Advanced Media Elements:

- Definition of advanced media elements in website development, including interactive multimedia content such as videos, animations, audio clips, and interactive graphics.
- Explanation of how advanced media elements enhance user engagement, convey information effectively, and create immersive user experiences on websites.

1.2 Importance of Advanced Media Elements:

- Discussion on the importance of incorporating advanced media elements into websites to capture audience attention, communicate brand messages, and differentiate from competitors.
- Examples of websites and applications that leverage advanced media elements to showcase products, tell stories, educate users, and entertain audiences effectively.

Chapter 2: Video Integration and Customization

2.1 Video Integration Techniques:

- Overview of video integration techniques for embedding videos from external sources (e.g., YouTube, Vimeo) or hosting videos directly on web servers.
- Techniques for embedding videos using HTML5 video tags, iframe embed codes, or video hosting platforms' embed APIs, and configuring video playback options such as autoplay, loop, and controls.

2.2 Video Customization Options:

- Discussion on video customization options for enhancing video playback experiences and optimizing video performance on websites.
- Techniques for customizing video player controls, aspect ratios, resolutions, and quality settings, as well as implementing video overlays, annotations, and interactive elements to engage viewers.

Chapter 3: Animation and Motion Graphics

3.1 Animation Techniques:

- Overview of animation techniques for adding motion and visual interest to web pages through CSS animations, JavaScript libraries, and animation frameworks.

- Techniques for creating animated transitions, effects, and sequences using CSS keyframes, JavaScript animation libraries (e.g., GSAP, Anime.js), and SVG animations to enhance user interactions and storytelling.

3.2 Motion Graphics Design:

- Discussion on motion graphics design principles for creating visually appealing and dynamic animations for web interfaces.
- Techniques for designing motion graphics using vector graphics software (e.g., Adobe After Effects, Animate CC), incorporating motion design principles such as timing, easing, and anticipation, and optimizing motion graphics for web delivery and performance.

Chapter 4: Audio Integration and Enhancement

4.1 Audio Integration Techniques:

- Overview of audio integration techniques for embedding audio files into web pages and controlling audio playback using HTML5 audio elements or JavaScript audio APIs.
- Techniques for embedding audio files in various formats (e.g., MP3, OGG, WAV), configuring audio player controls, and implementing audio playlists or background music loops to enhance user experiences.

4.2 Audio Enhancement Options:

- Discussion on audio enhancement options for improving audio quality, accessibility, and user interactions on websites.
- Techniques for optimizing audio files for web delivery, adding audio effects (e.g., equalization, reverb, compression), implementing audio visualizations, and synchronizing audio with visual content to create immersive multimedia experiences.

Chapter 5: Interactive Graphics and Visual Effects

5.1 Interactive Graphics Techniques:

- Overview of interactive graphics techniques for creating dynamic and interactive visual elements using HTML5 canvas, WebGL, and JavaScript libraries.
- Techniques for drawing and animating graphics on the web canvas, implementing interactivity (e.g., mouse interactions, touch events), and integrating interactive graphics with other web content to create engaging user experiences.

5.2 Visual Effects Design:

- Discussion on visual effects design principles for adding visual enhancements and effects to web interfaces, such as parallax scrolling, particle effects, and shaders.
- Techniques for designing and implementing visual effects using CSS animations, JavaScript libraries (e.g., Three.js, PixiJS), and WebGL shaders to create immersive and visually stunning web experiences.

Chapter 6: Optimization and Performance

6.1 Media Optimization Strategies:

- Overview of media optimization strategies for improving website performance and user experience by optimizing media assets for faster loading times and reduced bandwidth usage.
- Techniques for optimizing image files (e.g., JPEG compression, SVG optimization), video files (e.g., video compression, streaming optimization), audio files (e.g., audio compression, format selection), and animation assets (e.g., sprite sheets, CSS animations) to minimize file sizes and enhance performance.

6.2 Performance Best Practices:

- Discussion on performance best practices for managing advanced media elements effectively and optimizing their delivery for different devices and network conditions.
- Techniques for lazy loading media assets, implementing responsive design principles, leveraging content delivery networks (CDNs), and using performance monitoring tools to identify and address performance bottlenecks related to advanced media elements.

Chapter 7: Accessibility and Compatibility

7.1 Accessibility Considerations:

- Overview of accessibility considerations for ensuring that advanced media elements are accessible to users with disabilities and compatible with assistive technologies.
- Techniques for providing alternative text descriptions for media elements, implementing keyboard and screen reader navigation support, and adhering to accessibility standards (e.g., WCAG) to improve inclusivity and compliance.

7.2 Cross-Browser and Device Compatibility:

- Discussion on cross-browser and device compatibility challenges associated with advanced media elements and techniques for ensuring consistent rendering and functionality across different web browsers and devices.
- Techniques for testing and debugging media element compatibility issues, using progressive enhancement and graceful degradation strategies, and adopting modern web standards and APIs to maximize compatibility and interoperability.

Chapter 8: Security and Privacy

8.1 Media Security Measures:

- Overview of media security measures for protecting against security threats such as content theft, hotlinking, and unauthorized access to media assets.
- Techniques for implementing access controls, digital rights management (DRM) solutions, and encryption protocols to secure media files and prevent unauthorized distribution or usage.

8.2 Privacy Considerations:

- Discussion on privacy considerations related to advanced media elements and techniques for safeguarding user privacy and data confidentiality.
- Techniques for implementing privacy controls, obtaining user consent for media usage and tracking, and complying with data protection regulations (e.g., GDPR) to ensure privacy compliance and build user trust.

Chapter 9: Future Trends and Innovations

9.1 Emerging Technologies:

- Exploration of emerging technologies and trends shaping the future of advanced media elements in website development, such as virtual reality (VR), augmented reality (AR), 360-degree video, and spatial audio.
- Discussion on how these technologies are revolutionizing multimedia experiences on the web and opening up new opportunities for creative expression and interactive storytelling.

9.2 Innovative Applications:

- Showcase of innovative applications and use cases of advanced media elements in website development across industries, including e-learning platforms, virtual tours, interactive storytelling, and immersive brand experiences.
- Examples of websites pushing the boundaries of multimedia innovation and leveraging advanced media elements to engage audiences and deliver memorable user experiences.

Chapter 10: Conclusion and Next Steps

10.1 Summary of Key Insights:

- Recap of key concepts and techniques discussed in the chapter.
- Emphasis on the importance of incorporating advanced media elements effectively in website development to enhance user engagement, communication, and storytelling.

10.2 Actionable Takeaways:

- Actionable takeaways for readers to implement in their website development projects, including strategies for integrating and customizing advanced media elements, optimizing performance and accessibility, ensuring security and privacy, and exploring future trends and innovations.

10.3 Future Directions:

- Reflection on the evolving landscape of advanced media elements in website development and encouragement for readers to stay updated on emerging technologies, experiment with innovative techniques, and push the boundaries of multimedia creativity in their projects.

Introduction to Custom Code Integration

1.1 Understanding Custom Code Integration:

- Definition of custom code integration in website development and its significance in extending the functionality and customization capabilities of websites.
- Explanation of how custom code integration allows developers to implement unique features, integrate third-party services, and tailor website behavior to specific requirements.

1.2 Importance of Custom Code Integration:

- Discussion on the importance of custom code integration for addressing unique business needs, implementing specialized functionalities, and enhancing user experiences on websites.
- Examples of scenarios where custom code integration can add value, such as integrating custom analytics tracking, implementing complex UI components, or integrating with external APIs for data exchange.

Chapter 2: Types of Custom Code Integration

2.1 Frontend Customization:

- Overview of frontend customization techniques involving custom HTML, CSS, and JavaScript code to modify the appearance and behavior of web pages.
- Techniques for implementing custom UI components, animations, interactive elements, and responsive design layouts using frontend frameworks (e.g., React, Vue.js) and libraries (e.g., jQuery).

2.2 Backend Integration:

- Discussion on backend integration techniques for implementing custom server-side logic, data processing, and database interactions.
- Techniques for integrating server-side scripting languages (e.g., PHP, Node.js), databases (e.g., MySQL, MongoDB), and serverless computing platforms (e.g., AWS Lambda, Google Cloud Functions) to handle dynamic content generation and data management.

2.3 Third-Party API Integration:

- Explanation of third-party API integration for connecting websites with external services, platforms, and data sources to leverage additional functionalities.
- Techniques for integrating popular APIs such as payment gateways, social media platforms, mapping services, and e-commerce platforms to enable

features like online payments, social login, mapping, and product synchronization.

Chapter 3: Custom Code Implementation

3.1 Planning and Architecture:

- Overview of the planning and architecture phase for custom code implementation, including requirements gathering, system design, and architecture planning.
- Techniques for defining project goals, identifying technical requirements, creating wireframes, and designing system architecture to guide the custom code development process.

3.2 Development and Implementation:

- Discussion on the development and implementation phase for writing and deploying custom code solutions.
- Techniques for writing clean, maintainable code, following coding best practices and standards, implementing version control, and deploying custom code changes to production environments safely.

3.3 Testing and Quality Assurance:

- Explanation of the testing and quality assurance phase for ensuring the functionality, performance, and security of custom code solutions.
- Techniques for conducting unit tests, integration tests, and end-to-end tests, performing code reviews, debugging issues, and addressing security vulnerabilities to deliver high-quality custom code solutions.

Chapter 4: Common Use Cases of Custom Code Integration

4.1 E-commerce Customizations:

- Overview of custom code integration use cases in e-commerce websites, such as custom product catalogs, shopping cart modifications, checkout process enhancements, and integration with third-party payment gateways.
- Techniques for implementing custom product attributes, pricing rules, discount codes, shipping calculations, and order management workflows to meet specific business requirements.

4.2 Content Management System (CMS) Customizations:

- Discussion on custom code integration use cases in content management systems (CMS) for extending functionality, customizing templates, and integrating with external services.

- Techniques for implementing custom post types, taxonomies, templates, and plugins/extensions to add new features, improve content management workflows, and enhance website performance.

4.3 User Authentication and Authorization:

- Explanation of custom code integration use cases for implementing user authentication and authorization mechanisms, including custom login/signup forms, role-based access control (RBAC), and single sign-on (SSO) solutions.
- Techniques for integrating authentication providers (e.g., OAuth, LDAP), implementing password hashing, session management, and access control lists (ACLs), and securing user data and authentication tokens.

Chapter 5: Performance Optimization and Security Considerations

5.1 Performance Optimization:

- Overview of performance optimization techniques for custom code integration to improve website speed, responsiveness, and user experience.
- Techniques for optimizing code efficiency, minimizing HTTP requests, caching resources, lazy loading content, and leveraging content delivery networks (CDNs) to enhance website performance.

5.2 Security Considerations:

- Discussion on security considerations for custom code integration to protect websites against common security threats such as SQL injection, cross-site scripting (XSS), and cross-site request forgery (CSRF).
- Techniques for implementing secure coding practices, input validation, output encoding, parameterized queries, and implementing security headers and HTTPS encryption to mitigate security risks.

Chapter 6: Documentation and Maintenance

6.1 Documentation Practices:

- Overview of documentation practices for documenting custom code solutions, APIs, and system architecture to facilitate knowledge transfer and collaboration among developers.
- Techniques for writing clear, comprehensive documentation, including code comments, API documentation, developer guides, and troubleshooting instructions to aid in future maintenance and support.

6.2 Maintenance and Support:

- Discussion on maintenance and support practices for managing custom code solutions over their lifecycle, including bug fixes, feature enhancements, and software updates.
- Techniques for implementing version control, bug tracking, release management, and providing ongoing support and maintenance services to ensure the long-term stability and performance of custom code solutions.

Chapter 7: Future Trends and Innovations

7.1 Serverless Computing:

- Exploration of serverless computing trends and their impact on custom code integration, including serverless architectures, function as a service (FaaS) platforms, and microservices.
- Discussion on how serverless computing enables scalable, cost-effective, and event-driven custom code solutions and simplifies infrastructure management for developers.

7.2 Machine Learning and AI Integration:

- Discussion on the integration of machine learning (ML) and artificial intelligence (AI) technologies into custom code solutions to enable advanced functionalities such as natural language processing (NLP), image recognition, and predictive analytics.
- Exploration of how ML/AI integration can enhance user experiences, automate business processes, and enable personalized recommendations and content delivery on websites.

Chapter 8: Conclusion and Next Steps

8.1 Summary of Key Insights:

- Recap of key concepts and techniques discussed in the chapter.
- Emphasis on the importance of custom code integration in website development and its role in extending functionality, meeting specific business requirements, and delivering tailored user experiences.

8.2 Actionable Takeaways:

- Actionable takeaways for readers to implement in their website development projects, including strategies for planning and architecture, development and implementation, testing and quality assurance, performance optimization, security considerations, documentation and maintenance, and exploring future trends and innovations.

8.3 Future Directions:

- Reflection on the evolving landscape of custom code integration in website development and encouragement for readers to stay updated on emerging technologies, experiment with innovative techniques, and leverage custom code solutions to drive business growth and innovation.

Understanding Performance Optimization

1.1 Importance of Performance Optimization:

- Discuss the significance of performance optimization in website development for improving user experience, increasing engagement, and achieving business goals.
- Explore how website performance impacts key metrics such as page load times, bounce rates, conversion rates, and search engine rankings.

1.2 Goals of Performance Optimization:

- Define the goals of performance optimization, including reducing page load times, improving responsiveness, minimizing resource usage, and enhancing overall user satisfaction.
- Discuss how performance optimization aligns with broader objectives such as enhancing accessibility, usability, and scalability.

Chapter 2: Website Performance Metrics

2.1 Key Performance Indicators (KPIs):

- Identify and explain key performance indicators (KPIs) for measuring website performance, including page load time, time to first byte (TTFB), render time, and total page size.
- Discuss how KPIs vary across different devices, browsers, and network conditions, and their impact on user perception and behavior.

2.2 Tools for Performance Monitoring:

- Introduce tools and techniques for monitoring website performance, including web analytics platforms, performance testing tools (e.g., Google PageSpeed Insights, GTmetrix), and browser developer tools.
- Discuss how to interpret performance metrics, diagnose performance bottlenecks, and prioritize optimization efforts based on data insights.

Chapter 3: Frontend Optimization Techniques

3.1 Minification and Compression:

- Explain the concepts of minification and compression for reducing the size of HTML, CSS, and JavaScript files.

- Discuss techniques for removing whitespace, comments, and unnecessary characters, as well as using gzip compression to reduce file sizes and improve download speeds.

3.2 Image Optimization:

- Explore image optimization techniques for reducing image file sizes without sacrificing quality.
- Discuss image formats (e.g., JPEG, PNG, WebP), compression algorithms, resolution optimization, lazy loading, and responsive image techniques to minimize image loading times.

3.3 Browser Caching:

- Discuss browser caching mechanisms for storing static resources locally to reduce server requests and improve page load times.
- Explain how to leverage HTTP caching headers (e.g., Cache-Control, Expires) and cache-control directives to control caching behavior and cache busting techniques to invalidate cache when necessary.

Chapter 4: Backend Optimization Strategies

4.1 Server-Side Performance Optimization:

- Explore server-side performance optimization strategies for improving server response times and reducing database queries.
- Discuss techniques such as server-side caching (e.g., Redis, Memcached), database indexing, query optimization, and asynchronous processing to streamline backend operations.

4.2 Content Delivery Networks (CDNs):

- Explain the concept of content delivery networks (CDNs) and their role in optimizing content delivery and reducing latency.
- Discuss how CDNs distribute website content across geographically distributed servers, cache static assets, and accelerate content delivery to users worldwide.

4.3 Load Balancing and Scalability:

- Discuss load balancing techniques for distributing incoming traffic across multiple servers to improve reliability, performance, and scalability.
- Explore horizontal and vertical scaling strategies, auto-scaling mechanisms, and cloud computing services (e.g., AWS Elastic Load Balancing, Google Cloud Load Balancing) to handle fluctuating traffic loads efficiently.

Chapter 5: Responsive Design and Mobile Optimization

5.1 Responsive Web Design (RWD):

- Explain the principles of responsive web design (RWD) and its impact on performance optimization.
- Discuss techniques for designing flexible layouts, using fluid grids, media queries, and responsive images to ensure a consistent user experience across devices.

5.2 Mobile Optimization:

- Explore mobile optimization strategies for improving performance on mobile devices, including optimizing viewport meta tags, prioritizing above-the-fold content, and reducing mobile-specific issues such as touch delays and viewport scaling.

5.3 Accelerated Mobile Pages (AMP):

- Introduce the concept of Accelerated Mobile Pages (AMP) and their role in optimizing performance for mobile web pages.
- Discuss how AMP HTML, AMP JS, and AMP Cache enable faster rendering and better user experiences on mobile devices, and how to implement AMP in website development projects.

Chapter 6: Best Practices for Performance Optimization

6.1 Prioritizing Critical Rendering Path:

- Discuss the critical rendering path and its role in optimizing page rendering and user perception.
- Explore techniques for prioritizing critical resources, optimizing CSS and JavaScript delivery, and deferring non-essential tasks to improve time to first render and perceived performance.

6.2 Asynchronous Loading:

- Explain asynchronous loading techniques for loading resources such as JavaScript and CSS files asynchronously to prevent render-blocking and improve page load times.
- Discuss methods for deferring JavaScript execution, loading scripts asynchronously, and optimizing CSS delivery to enhance website performance.

6.3 Continuous Monitoring and Optimization:

- Emphasize the importance of continuous monitoring and optimization as an iterative process in website performance optimization.

- Discuss techniques for setting up performance monitoring tools, conducting regular performance audits, and implementing feedback loops to identify performance issues and make ongoing improvements.

Chapter 7: Performance Testing and Benchmarking

7.1 Performance Testing Techniques:

- Introduce performance testing techniques for evaluating website performance under various conditions and scenarios.
- Discuss methodologies such as load testing, stress testing, and soak testing, as well as tools and frameworks for automating performance testing processes.

7.2 Benchmarking and Comparison:

- Discuss benchmarking techniques for comparing website performance against industry standards, competitors, and previous versions.
- Explore tools and services for benchmarking performance metrics, analyzing comparative data, and identifying areas for improvement based on benchmarking results.

Chapter 8: Security Considerations for Performance Optimization

8.1 Security Implications of Performance Optimization:

- Discuss the security implications of performance optimization techniques and the potential risks associated with aggressive optimization strategies.
- Explore how performance optimization measures such as caching, CDN usage, and third-party integrations can impact security posture and introduce vulnerabilities if not implemented properly.

8.2 Mitigating Security Risks:

- Provide guidance on mitigating security risks while optimizing website performance, including implementing security best practices, securing communication channels, and conducting security assessments and audits.

Chapter 9: Future Trends in Performance Optimization

9.1 Emerging Technologies:

- Explore emerging technologies and trends in performance optimization, such as HTTP/3, WebAssembly, and browser-level optimizations.

- Discuss how these technologies are shaping the future of web performance and opening up new possibilities for optimizing website performance.

9.2 Progressive Web Apps (PWAs):

- Discuss the role of Progressive Web Apps (PWAs) in performance optimization and their potential to deliver fast, reliable, and engaging user experiences.
- Explore how PWAs leverage technologies such as service workers, app shells, and push notifications to improve performance, offline capabilities, and user engagement.

Chapter 10: Conclusion and Next Steps

10.1 Summary of Key Insights:

- Recap key concepts and techniques discussed in the chapter.
- Emphasize the importance of performance optimization in website development and its impact on user experience, engagement, and business success.

10.2 Actionable Takeaways:

- Provide actionable takeaways for readers to implement in their website development projects, including frontend and backend optimization techniques, responsive design strategies, performance testing methodologies, and security considerations.

10.3 Future Directions:

- Reflect on the future of performance optimization in website development and encourage readers to stay updated on emerging technologies, experiment with innovative techniques, and continuously optimize their websites to meet evolving user expectations and business needs.

Understanding the Importance:

- Discuss the significance of testing and troubleshooting in website development to ensure quality, reliability, and performance.
- Explain how thorough testing and effective troubleshooting can help identify and resolve issues before they impact users and business objectives.

1.2 Goals of Testing and Troubleshooting:

- Define the goals of testing and troubleshooting, including identifying bugs and errors, validating functionality, ensuring compatibility, and optimizing performance.
- Discuss how these goals align with broader objectives such as delivering a seamless user experience, meeting project requirements, and achieving business success.

Chapter 2: Types of Testing in Website Development

2.1 Functional Testing:

- Discuss functional testing techniques for verifying that individual components and features of a website perform as expected.
- Explore methods such as unit testing, integration testing, and end-to-end testing to validate functionality across different levels of the application stack.

2.2 Compatibility Testing:

- Explain compatibility testing strategies for ensuring that websites render and function correctly across different browsers, devices, and operating systems.
- Discuss techniques such as cross-browser testing, device testing, and responsive design testing to identify and address compatibility issues.

2.3 Performance Testing:

- Explore performance testing methodologies for evaluating the speed, responsiveness, and scalability of websites under various conditions.
- Discuss techniques such as load testing, stress testing, and capacity testing to assess website performance and identify bottlenecks.

2.4 Security Testing:

- Discuss security testing techniques for identifying vulnerabilities and weaknesses in website security measures.
- Explore methods such as penetration testing, vulnerability scanning, and code analysis to assess the security posture of websites and mitigate potential risks.

Chapter 3: Testing Strategies and Best Practices

3.1 Test Planning and Preparation:

- Discuss the importance of test planning and preparation in ensuring comprehensive test coverage and effective resource utilization.
- Explore techniques for defining test objectives, creating test plans, identifying test scenarios, and preparing test environments.

3.2 Test Execution and Reporting:

- Explain the process of test execution and reporting, including running test cases, recording test results, and documenting issues.
- Discuss strategies for prioritizing tests, executing test suites, and generating test reports to communicate findings to stakeholders.

3.3 Test Automation:

- Discuss the benefits of test automation for improving testing efficiency, repeatability, and coverage.
- Explore popular test automation tools and frameworks for frontend testing (e.g., Selenium, Cypress) and backend testing (e.g., Postman, SoapUI).

Chapter 4: Troubleshooting Techniques

4.1 Issue Identification and Analysis:

- Discuss techniques for identifying and analyzing issues in website development, including error logging, monitoring tools, and user feedback.
- Explore strategies for categorizing and prioritizing issues based on severity, impact, and urgency.

4.2 Root Cause Analysis:

- Explain the concept of root cause analysis (RCA) and its importance in identifying the underlying causes of issues.
- Discuss methodologies such as the 5 Whys technique, fishbone diagrams, and Pareto analysis for conducting root cause analysis and addressing systemic issues.

4.3 Debugging and Problem Solving:

- Explore debugging techniques for troubleshooting issues in website code and configurations.
- Discuss strategies for isolating problems, reproducing issues, and using debugging tools (e.g., browser developer tools, IDE debuggers) to identify and fix errors.

Chapter 5: Testing and Troubleshooting Tools

5.1 Browser Developer Tools:

- Discuss the features and capabilities of browser developer tools for debugging and testing websites.
- Explore functionalities such as inspecting HTML/CSS, debugging JavaScript, monitoring network activity, and emulating device characteristics.

5.2 Testing Platforms and Services:

- Introduce testing platforms and services for automating and scaling testing efforts.
- Discuss cloud-based testing services (e.g., BrowserStack, Sauce Labs), test management tools (e.g., TestRail, Zephyr), and continuous integration (CI) platforms (e.g., Jenkins, Travis CI) for streamlining testing workflows.

5.3 Performance Monitoring Tools:

- Explore performance monitoring tools for tracking website performance metrics and identifying performance bottlenecks.
- Discuss tools such as Google PageSpeed Insights, GTmetrix, and New Relic for monitoring page load times, server response times, and resource utilization.

Chapter 6: Continuous Testing and Improvement

6.1 Continuous Integration/Continuous Deployment (CI/CD):

- Discuss the role of continuous integration/continuous deployment (CI/CD) pipelines in automating testing and deployment processes.
- Explore how CI/CD pipelines enable continuous testing, integration, and delivery of code changes to production environments, reducing cycle times and enhancing development agility.

6.2 Agile Testing Practices:

- Explore agile testing practices for incorporating testing activities into agile development workflows.
- Discuss techniques such as test-driven development (TDD), behavior-driven development (BDD), and acceptance test-driven development (ATDD) for integrating testing into iterative development cycles.

Chapter 7: Collaboration and Communication

7.1 Collaborative Problem-Solving:

- Discuss the importance of collaboration and communication in effective testing and troubleshooting.
- Explore strategies for fostering collaboration among development teams, QA teams, and stakeholders to share knowledge, coordinate efforts, and resolve issues efficiently.

7.2 Reporting and Documentation:

- Discuss best practices for reporting testing findings and documenting troubleshooting efforts.
- Explore techniques for writing clear, concise bug reports, documenting resolutions, and maintaining knowledge bases to facilitate knowledge transfer and future troubleshooting.

Chapter 8: Future Trends and Innovations

8.1 AI-Powered Testing:

- Explore the emerging trend of AI-powered testing and its potential to revolutionize testing processes.
- Discuss how AI and machine learning technologies can automate test case generation, predict failure points, and optimize testing strategies based on historical data.

8.2 Shift-Left Testing:

- Discuss the concept of shift-left testing and its role in shifting testing activities earlier in the development lifecycle.
- Explore how shift-left testing practices such as code reviews, pair programming, and early test automation can improve code quality, reduce defects, and accelerate time to market.

Chapter 9: Conclusion and Next Steps

9.1 Summary of Key Insights:

- Recap key concepts and techniques discussed in the chapter.
- Emphasize the importance of testing and troubleshooting in website development and its impact on product quality, user satisfaction, and business success.

9.2 Actionable Takeaways:

- Provide actionable takeaways for readers to implement in their testing and troubleshooting processes, including test planning and execution strategies, debugging techniques, and collaboration practices.

9.3 Future Directions:

- Reflect on the future of testing and troubleshooting in website development and encourage readers to stay updated on emerging technologies, adopt innovative practices, and continuously improve their testing and troubleshooting capabilities to meet evolving challenges and opportunities.

Introduction to Mobile-Friendly Websites

1.1 Understanding Mobile Responsiveness:

- Define the concept of mobile-friendliness in website design and development.
- Discuss the importance of mobile responsiveness in catering to the growing number of users accessing the internet through mobile devices.

1.2 Impact of Mobile-Friendliness:

- Explore the significance of having a mobile-friendly website in enhancing user experience, improving search engine rankings, and driving business growth.
- Discuss how mobile-friendliness impacts factors such as bounce rates, conversion rates, and user engagement.

Chapter 2: Responsive Web Design Principles

2.1 Flexible Layouts:

- Explain the principle of flexible layouts in responsive web design.
- Discuss techniques such as fluid grids, flexible images, and CSS media queries for creating layouts that adapt to different screen sizes and resolutions.

2.2 Fluid Typography:

- Explore the concept of fluid typography and its role in responsive design.
- Discuss techniques for scaling typography proportionally based on viewport size and maintaining readability across devices.

2.3 Scalable Images:

- Discuss strategies for optimizing images for mobile devices without compromising quality.
- Explore techniques such as responsive images, CSS image resizing, and image compression for delivering high-quality images across various screen sizes and resolutions.

Chapter 3: Mobile-Friendly Navigation

3.1 Simplified Navigation Menus:

- Discuss the importance of simplified navigation menus for mobile users.
- Explore techniques for creating collapsible menus, hamburger menus, and navigation bars that prioritize essential content and streamline navigation on small screens.

3.2 Thumb-Friendly Design:

- Explain the concept of thumb-friendly design and its significance in mobile navigation.
- Discuss techniques for placing interactive elements within easy reach of the user's thumb, optimizing touch targets, and reducing the need for pinch-zoom gestures.

3.3 Touch Gestures and Interactions:

- Explore touch gestures and interactions that enhance the mobile user experience.
- Discuss techniques for implementing swipe gestures, touch sliders, and interactive animations to engage users and provide intuitive navigation on touchscreen devices.

Chapter 4: Mobile-Friendly Content

4.1 Prioritizing Content:

- Discuss strategies for prioritizing content and presenting key information prominently on mobile devices.
- Explore techniques such as content hierarchy, concise messaging, and strategic placement of call-to-action buttons to guide users through the mobile experience.

4.2 Optimizing Forms and Inputs:

- Explore best practices for optimizing forms and input fields for mobile users.
- Discuss techniques such as using native form elements, minimizing input requirements, and implementing input masks and validation to streamline the form submission process on mobile devices.

4.3 Adaptive Content Layouts:

- Discuss the concept of adaptive content layouts and its role in delivering personalized experiences across devices.
- Explore techniques for adapting content layouts based on device characteristics, user preferences, and contextual factors to optimize content consumption on mobile devices.

Chapter 5: Performance Optimization for Mobile

5.1 Minimizing Page Load Times:

- Discuss the importance of minimizing page load times for mobile users.

- Explore techniques for optimizing images, leveraging browser caching, and minimizing HTTP requests to improve website performance on mobile devices.

5.2 Mobile-Friendly Optimization Tools:

- Introduce tools and resources for testing and optimizing websites for mobile devices.
- Discuss mobile-friendly testing tools such as Google's Mobile-Friendly Test, PageSpeed Insights, and Lighthouse, as well as performance optimization techniques recommended by these tools.

5.3 Progressive Web Apps (PWAs):

- Introduce the concept of Progressive Web Apps (PWAs) and their role in providing native-like experiences on mobile devices.
- Discuss how PWAs leverage service workers, app shells, and web app manifests to enhance performance, offline capabilities, and user engagement on mobile devices.

Chapter 6: Mobile SEO and Accessibility

6.1 Mobile SEO Best Practices:

- Discuss mobile SEO best practices for optimizing websites for search engines.
- Explore techniques such as mobile-friendly design, responsive web design, and optimizing page speed and performance to improve mobile search rankings and visibility.

6.2 Accessibility Considerations:

- Explore accessibility considerations for mobile-friendly websites.
- Discuss techniques for ensuring accessibility compliance, including semantic HTML markup, proper alt text for images, and keyboard navigation support for mobile users with disabilities.

6.3 Voice Search Optimization:

- Discuss the growing importance of voice search optimization for mobile users.
- Explore techniques for optimizing content for voice search queries, including natural language optimization, featured snippets, and structured data markup to improve visibility in voice search results.

Chapter 7: Testing and Iteration

7.1 Cross-Browser and Cross-Device Testing:

- Discuss the importance of cross-browser and cross-device testing for ensuring mobile compatibility.
- Explore techniques for testing websites across different browsers, devices, and operating systems to identify and resolve compatibility issues.

7.2 User Testing and Feedback:

- Discuss the value of user testing and feedback in refining the mobile user experience.
- Explore techniques for conducting usability tests, collecting user feedback, and iteratively improving the mobile experience based on user insights and observations.

Chapter 8: Conclusion and Next Steps

8.1 Summary of Key Insights:

- Recap key concepts and techniques discussed in the chapter.
- Emphasize the importance of making websites mobile-friendly and provide actionable insights for implementing mobile-friendly design principles.

8.2 Implementation Strategies:

- Provide implementation strategies for optimizing existing websites for mobile devices and designing new websites with mobile-friendliness in mind.
- Discuss steps for conducting mobile audits, prioritizing mobile optimization efforts, and collaborating with designers, developers, and stakeholders to create exceptional mobile experiences.

8.3 Future Directions:

- Reflect on the future of mobile web design and encourage readers to stay updated on emerging trends, technologies, and user behaviors to continuously evolve and improve their mobile-friendly websites.

Understanding Search Engine Optimization (SEO):

- Define SEO and its significance in digital marketing and online visibility.
- Discuss the role of SEO in improving website rankings, increasing organic traffic, and enhancing user experience.

1.2 Importance of SEO for Websites:

- Explore the importance of SEO for websites in attracting targeted traffic, generating leads, and achieving business objectives.
- Discuss how SEO impacts brand visibility, credibility, and competitiveness in search engine results pages (SERPs).

Chapter 2: On-Page SEO Optimization

2.1 Keyword Research and Analysis:

- Discuss the importance of keyword research in on-page SEO optimization.
- Explore techniques for identifying relevant keywords, analyzing search volume and competition, and selecting strategic keywords for optimization.

2.2 Content Optimization:

- Explore content optimization techniques for improving search engine rankings.
- Discuss strategies for optimizing title tags, meta descriptions, headings, and body content to align with targeted keywords and user intent.

2.3 Technical SEO Optimization:

- Discuss technical SEO optimization techniques for improving website performance and crawlability.
- Explore strategies for optimizing URL structure, internal linking, site speed, mobile-friendliness, and schema markup to enhance search engine visibility.

Chapter 3 Off-Page SEO Optimization

3.1 Link Building Strategies:

- Discuss link building strategies for improving off-page SEO.
- Explore techniques for acquiring high-quality backlinks from authoritative websites, including guest blogging, influencer outreach, and content promotion.

3.2 Social Media Engagement:

- Explore the role of social media engagement in off-page SEO optimization.

- Discuss strategies for leveraging social media platforms to amplify content reach, build brand authority, and attract natural backlinks.

3.3 Online Reputation Management:

- Discuss the importance of online reputation management in off-page SEO.
- Explore strategies for monitoring and managing online reviews, mentions, and brand sentiment to maintain a positive online presence and enhance search engine rankings.

Chapter 4: Local SEO Optimization

4.1 Local Search Ranking Factors:

- Discuss local search ranking factors and their impact on local SEO.
- Explore techniques for optimizing Google My Business listings, local citations, and location-based keywords to improve visibility in local search results.

4.2 Local Content Optimization:

- Discuss strategies for optimizing local content for search engines.
- Explore techniques for creating location-specific landing pages, optimizing business directories, and generating localized content to attract local customers and improve local search rankings.

4.3 Online Reviews and Reputation Management:

- Explore the role of online reviews and reputation management in local SEO.
- Discuss strategies for soliciting and managing online reviews, responding to customer feedback, and building trust and credibility with local audiences.

Chapter 5: Mobile SEO Optimization

5.1 Mobile-Friendly Design:

- Discuss the importance of mobile-friendly design for mobile SEO optimization.
- Explore techniques for optimizing website layout, navigation, and usability for mobile users to enhance search engine rankings and user experience.

5.2 Accelerated Mobile Pages (AMP):

- Discuss the role of Accelerated Mobile Pages (AMP) in mobile SEO optimization.
- Explore techniques for implementing AMP to improve website speed, reduce bounce rates, and boost search engine rankings on mobile devices.

5.3 Voice Search Optimization:

- Explore the growing importance of voice search optimization for mobile SEO.

- Discuss strategies for optimizing content for voice search queries, including natural language optimization, featured snippets, and schema markup to improve visibility in voice search results.

Chapter 6: SEO Performance Tracking and Analysis

6.1 SEO Metrics and KPIs:

- Discuss key SEO metrics and KPIs for tracking and measuring SEO performance.
- Explore metrics such as organic traffic, keyword rankings, backlink profile, and conversion rates to evaluate the effectiveness of SEO efforts.

6.2 SEO Tools and Analytics:

- Introduce SEO tools and analytics platforms for tracking and analyzing SEO performance.
- Discuss tools such as Google Analytics, Google Search Console, and third-party SEO tools for monitoring website traffic, keyword performance, and search engine visibility.

6.3 SEO Audits and Reporting:

- Discuss the importance of SEO audits and reporting in assessing website performance and identifying optimization opportunities.
- Explore techniques for conducting comprehensive SEO audits, generating actionable insights, and presenting findings to stakeholders through detailed SEO reports.

Chapter 7: Advanced SEO Strategies

7.1 Semantic SEO and Natural Language Processing (NLP):

- Explore advanced SEO strategies such as semantic SEO and natural language processing (NLP).
- Discuss how search engines use NLP to understand user queries and content context, and explore techniques for optimizing content for semantic search.

7.2 Structured Data Markup:

- Discuss the importance of structured data markup in advanced SEO optimization.
- Explore techniques for implementing schema.org markup to enhance search engine visibility, rich snippet display, and click-through rates in search engine results.

7.3 Machine Learning and AI in SEO:

- Explore the role of machine learning and artificial intelligence (AI) in advanced SEO strategies.
- Discuss how machine learning algorithms analyze user behavior, search patterns, and content relevance to improve search engine rankings and provide more personalized search results.

Chapter 8: SEO Trends and Future Directions

8.1 Voice Search and Conversational SEO:

- Explore emerging trends such as voice search and conversational SEO.
- Discuss how advancements in natural language processing and voice recognition technology are shaping the future of search engine optimization.

8.2 Video and Visual Search Optimization:

- Discuss the growing importance of video and visual search optimization in SEO.
- Explore strategies for optimizing video content, image metadata, and visual search experiences to improve visibility in search engine results.

8.3 Localized and Personalized Search:

- Explore the trend towards localized and personalized search experiences.
- Discuss how search engines are incorporating location-based data, user preferences, and behavioral signals to deliver more relevant and personalized search results to users.

Chapter 9: Conclusion and Next Steps

9.1 Summary of Key Insights:

- Recap key concepts and techniques discussed in the chapter.
- Emphasize the importance of SEO optimization for improving website visibility, attracting targeted traffic, and achieving business objectives.

9.2 Implementation Strategies:

- Provide implementation strategies for optimizing websites for search engines.
- Discuss steps for conducting keyword research, optimizing content, building backlinks, and tracking SEO performance to improve search engine rankings and drive organic traffic.

9.3 Future Directions:

- Reflect on the future of SEO optimization and encourage readers to stay updated on emerging trends, technologies, and algorithm updates to adapt and evolve their SEO strategies accordingly.

Introduction to Website Testing and Previewing

1.1 Understanding the Importance of Testing:

- Define the concept of website testing and its significance in ensuring quality, functionality, and user experience.
- Discuss the role of testing in identifying and fixing errors, bugs, and usability issues before launching a website.

1.2 Previewing for Design and Functionality:

- Explore the importance of previewing websites for design and functionality.
- Discuss how previewing allows designers and developers to assess layout, navigation, responsiveness, and interactivity across different devices and browsers.

Chapter 2: Types of Website Testing

2.1 Functional Testing:

- Discuss functional testing techniques for assessing website functionality and performance.
- Explore methods such as unit testing, integration testing, and end-to-end testing to verify that website features and functionalities work as intended.

2.2 Usability Testing:

- Explore usability testing techniques for evaluating website usability and user experience.
- Discuss methods such as user testing, heuristic evaluation, and A/B testing to assess website navigation, content clarity, and task completion.

2.3 Compatibility Testing:

- Discuss compatibility testing techniques for ensuring website compatibility across different devices, browsers, and operating systems.
- Explore methods such as cross-browser testing, responsive design testing, and device testing to identify and fix compatibility issues.

2.4 Performance Testing:

- Discuss performance testing techniques for evaluating website performance and speed.
- Explore methods such as load testing, stress testing, and speed testing to assess website response times, page load times, and server performance.

Chapter 3: Testing Tools and Platforms

3.1 Automated Testing Tools:

- Introduce automated testing tools for streamlining the website testing process.
- Discuss popular automated testing tools such as Selenium, TestComplete, and Puppeteer, and explore their features and capabilities.

3.2 Browser Developer Tools:

- Explore browser developer tools for debugging and testing websites.
- Discuss features such as inspect element, console logs, network monitoring, and device emulation available in browser developer tools for troubleshooting and optimization.

3.3 Online Testing Platforms:

- Introduce online testing platforms for comprehensive website testing.
- Discuss platforms such as BrowserStack, Sauce Labs, and LambdaTest, and explore their features for cross-browser testing, responsive design testing, and device testing.

Chapter 4: Pre-launch Checklist and Best Practices

4.1 Content Review and Proofreading:

- Discuss the importance of content review and proofreading in website testing.
- Explore techniques for reviewing website content, checking for spelling and grammatical errors, and ensuring accuracy and consistency.

4.2 Functional Testing Checklist:

- Provide a functional testing checklist for assessing website functionality.
- Discuss key areas such as navigation, forms, links, multimedia content, and interactive elements to test for functionality and performance.

4.3 Usability Testing Guidelines:

- Provide usability testing guidelines for evaluating website usability and user experience.
- Discuss tasks to assign to users, criteria for evaluating usability, and methods for collecting feedback and insights from usability tests.

Chapter 5: Testing and Previewing Process

5.1 Test Planning and Preparation:

- Discuss the importance of test planning and preparation in the testing process.
- Explore techniques for defining test objectives, creating test cases, and preparing test environments for efficient and effective testing.

5.2 Test Execution and Documentation:

- Discuss the process of test execution and documentation.
- Explore techniques for executing test cases, recording test results, and documenting issues and defects for further analysis and resolution.

5.3 Iterative Testing and Continuous Improvement:

- Discuss the importance of iterative testing and continuous improvement in the website development process.
- Explore techniques for incorporating feedback from testing, making necessary adjustments and improvements, and retesting to ensure ongoing website quality and performance.

Chapter 6: Previewing Your Website

6.1 Cross-Browser Preview:

- Discuss the importance of cross-browser previewing for ensuring website compatibility.
- Explore techniques for previewing websites across different browsers and versions to identify and fix rendering issues and inconsistencies.

6.2 Responsive Design Preview:

- Explore the importance of responsive design previewing for optimizing website layout and usability across devices.
- Discuss techniques for previewing websites on various screen sizes, resolutions, and orientations to ensure responsiveness and user-friendliness.

6.3 User Testing and Feedback:

- Discuss the value of user testing and feedback in previewing websites.
- Explore techniques for soliciting feedback from real users, observing their interactions with the website, and gathering insights to inform further optimization.

Chapter 7: Post-launch Monitoring and Maintenance

7.1 Performance Monitoring:

- Discuss the importance of post-launch performance monitoring for maintaining website quality and performance.

- Explore techniques for monitoring website traffic, performance metrics, and user feedback to identify issues and opportunities for improvement.

7.2 Bug Tracking and Resolution:

- Discuss techniques for tracking and resolving bugs and issues post-launch.
- Explore methods such as bug tracking systems, issue tracking tools, and version control systems for efficiently managing and resolving website issues.

7.3 Continuous Optimization:

- Discuss the importance of continuous optimization for ongoing website success.
- Explore techniques for analyzing website data, implementing performance improvements, and staying proactive in addressing user needs and preferences.

Chapter 8: Conclusion and Next Steps

8.1 Summary of Key Insights:

- Recap key concepts and techniques discussed in the chapter.
- Emphasize the importance of thorough testing and previewing in ensuring website quality, functionality, and user experience.

8.2 Implementation Strategies:

- Provide implementation strategies for incorporating testing and previewing into the website development process.
- Discuss steps for creating a comprehensive testing plan, leveraging testing tools and platforms, and establishing a culture of continuous improvement.

8.3 Future Directions:

- Reflect on the future of website testing and previewing and encourage readers to stay updated on emerging trends, technologies, and best practices to adapt and evolve their testing strategies accordingly.

Introduction to Website Publishing

1.1 Understanding the Importance of Website Publishing:

- Define website publishing and its significance in making a website accessible to the public.
- Discuss the role of website publishing in launching online presence, reaching target audience, and achieving business goals.

1.2 Key Considerations Before Publishing:

- Explore important considerations before publishing a website.
- Discuss factors such as domain registration, hosting selection, content readiness, legal compliance, and security measures to ensure a successful website launch.

Chapter 2: Choosing a Hosting Provider

2.1 Types of Hosting Services:

- Discuss different types of hosting services available for website publishing.
- Explore shared hosting, VPS hosting, dedicated hosting, and cloud hosting options, and discuss their features, benefits, and limitations.

2.2 Selecting a Hosting Provider:

- Provide guidelines for selecting a hosting provider for website publishing.
- Discuss factors such as reliability, performance, scalability, security, customer support, and pricing to consider when choosing a hosting provider.

2.3 Setting Up Hosting Account:

- Guide users through the process of setting up a hosting account with a chosen provider.
- Provide step-by-step instructions for registering a domain, selecting a hosting plan, and configuring account settings to prepare for website deployment.

Chapter 3: Uploading Website Files

3.1 File Transfer Methods:

- Discuss different methods for uploading website files to a hosting server.
- Explore techniques such as FTP (File Transfer Protocol), SFTP (SSH File Transfer Protocol), and web-based file managers for transferring files securely.

3.2 File Structure and Organization:

- Discuss best practices for organizing website files before uploading.
- Provide guidelines for structuring folders, organizing assets, and optimizing file sizes to ensure efficient website management and performance.

3.3 Uploading Website Files:

- Provide step-by-step instructions for uploading website files to the hosting server.
- Discuss techniques for using FTP clients, file managers, and command-line interfaces to transfer files and directories to the correct locations on the server.

Chapter 4: Configuring Domain Settings

4.1 Domain Registration and DNS Configuration:

- Discuss the process of domain registration and DNS (Domain Name System) configuration.
- Explore techniques for registering a domain, updating DNS records, and pointing the domain to the hosting server for website accessibility.

4.2 Domain Redirects and Aliases:

- Discuss domain redirects and aliases for managing multiple domains and subdomains.
- Provide instructions for configuring 301 redirects, domain aliases, and canonical URLs to improve website SEO and user experience.

4.3 SSL Certificate Installation:

- Discuss the importance of SSL (Secure Sockets Layer) certificates for website security.
- Provide guidelines for installing an SSL certificate on the hosting server to enable HTTPS encryption and secure data transmission.

Chapter 5: Testing and Quality Assurance

5.1 Pre-Launch Testing:

- Discuss the importance of pre-launch testing for ensuring website functionality and performance.
- Explore techniques for conducting functional testing, usability testing, cross-browser testing, and performance testing to identify and fix issues before publishing.

5.2 User Acceptance Testing (UAT):

- Discuss the role of user acceptance testing (UAT) in validating website readiness for launch.
- Provide guidelines for involving stakeholders and end users in UAT, collecting feedback, and making necessary adjustments to meet expectations.

5.3 Final Quality Assurance Checks:

- Provide a checklist for final quality assurance checks before website publishing.
- Discuss tasks such as reviewing content accuracy, checking for broken links, validating forms, and ensuring mobile responsiveness to ensure a flawless website launch.

Chapter 6: Publishing Your Website

6.1 Deployment Process:

- Provide an overview of the website deployment process.
- Discuss steps such as syncing files, configuring server settings, updating DNS records, and testing website functionality to ensure a smooth deployment.

6.2 Launch Announcement and Promotion:

- Discuss strategies for announcing and promoting the website launch.
- Explore techniques such as email announcements, social media posts, press releases, and SEO optimization to drive traffic and engagement after publishing.

6.3 Monitoring and Maintenance:

- Discuss the importance of monitoring and maintenance after website publishing.
- Provide guidelines for monitoring website performance, security vulnerabilities, and user feedback, and establishing a maintenance schedule for ongoing updates and improvements.

Chapter 7: Post-Publishing Optimization

7.1 Performance Optimization:

- Discuss strategies for optimizing website performance post-publishing.
- Explore techniques such as caching, image optimization, content delivery network (CDN) integration, and code minification to enhance website speed and responsiveness.

7.2 SEO Optimization:

- Discuss post-publishing SEO optimization strategies for improving search engine visibility.

- Explore techniques such as meta tag optimization, content updates, backlink building, and ongoing keyword research to boost organic traffic and rankings.

7.3 User Engagement and Conversion Optimization:

- Discuss strategies for optimizing user engagement and conversion post-publishing.
- Explore techniques such as user behavior analysis, A/B testing, call-to-action optimization, and content personalization to increase user interaction and drive conversions.

Chapter 8: Conclusion and Next Steps

8.1 Summary of Key Insights:

- Recap key concepts and steps discussed in the chapter.
- Emphasize the importance of thorough preparation, testing, and optimization for successful website publishing.

8.2 Implementation Strategies:

- Provide implementation strategies for readers to apply the knowledge gained from the chapter.
- Discuss steps for following the publishing process, monitoring website performance, and continuously optimizing for better results.

8.3 Future Directions:

- Reflect on the future of website publishing and encourage readers to stay updated on emerging technologies, trends, and best practices to adapt and evolve their publishing strategies accordingly.

Introduction to Website Performance Monitoring

1.1 Understanding Website Performance:

- Define website performance and its significance in user experience and business success.
- Discuss key performance metrics such as page load time, response time, and server uptime, and their impact on user satisfaction and conversion rates.

1.2 Importance of Performance Monitoring:

- Explore the importance of monitoring website performance on an ongoing basis.
- Discuss how performance monitoring helps identify issues, optimize resources, and improve overall website reliability and user experience.

Chapter 2: Key Performance Metrics and Indicators

2.1 Page Load Time:

- Define page load time and its importance in website performance.
- Discuss factors affecting page load time, such as server response time, file size, and network latency, and techniques for optimizing load times.

2.2 Server Response Time:

- Define server response time and its impact on website performance.
- Discuss strategies for reducing server response time, such as server optimization, caching, and content delivery network (CDN) integration.

2.3 Website Uptime:

- Define website uptime and its significance in ensuring accessibility and reliability.
- Discuss methods for monitoring website uptime, detecting downtime incidents, and implementing strategies to minimize downtime and service interruptions.

2.4 User Experience Metrics:

- Explore user experience metrics such as bounce rate, session duration, and conversion rate.
- Discuss how these metrics reflect website performance and user engagement, and strategies for optimizing user experience to improve performance.

Chapter 3: Tools and Techniques for Performance Monitoring

3.1 Website Monitoring Tools:

- Introduce website monitoring tools for tracking performance metrics.
- Discuss popular tools such as Google Analytics, Pingdom, GTmetrix, and New Relic, and their features for monitoring website performance in real-time.

3.2 Synthetic Monitoring:

- Discuss synthetic monitoring techniques for simulating user interactions and testing website performance under controlled conditions.
- Explore tools and services for synthetic monitoring, and how they help identify performance bottlenecks and optimize website performance.

3.3 Real User Monitoring (RUM):

- Discuss real user monitoring (RUM) techniques for capturing performance data from actual user interactions.
- Explore tools and services for RUM, and how they provide insights into user behavior, performance issues, and opportunities for improvement.

3.4 A/B Testing and Experimentation:

- Introduce A/B testing and experimentation techniques for optimizing website performance.
- Discuss how A/B testing helps identify performance improvements, validate changes, and refine user experience based on data-driven insights.

Chapter 4: Performance Optimization Strategies

4.1 Website Speed Optimization:

- Discuss strategies for optimizing website speed to improve performance.
- Explore techniques such as image optimization, code minification, browser caching, and lazy loading to reduce page load times and enhance user experience.

4.2 Server and Hosting Optimization:

- Discuss strategies for optimizing server and hosting infrastructure for better performance.
- Explore techniques such as server scaling, load balancing, server-side caching, and choosing the right hosting provider to improve server response times and uptime.

4.3 Content Delivery Network (CDN) Integration:

- Discuss the role of content delivery networks (CDNs) in improving website performance.

- Explore how CDNs optimize content delivery by caching resources closer to users, reducing latency, and enhancing website scalability and reliability.

4.4 Mobile Optimization:

- Discuss strategies for optimizing website performance on mobile devices.
- Explore techniques such as responsive design, AMP (Accelerated Mobile Pages), and mobile-first development to ensure fast and efficient mobile user experiences.

Chapter 5: Continuous Monitoring and Improvement

5.1 Establishing Baselines and Targets:

- Discuss the importance of establishing performance baselines and targets.
- Explore techniques for setting benchmarks, defining acceptable performance thresholds, and establishing goals for continuous improvement.

5.2 Ongoing Monitoring and Alerting:

- Discuss the importance of ongoing monitoring and alerting for proactive performance management.
- Explore techniques for setting up monitoring alerts, identifying performance anomalies, and responding promptly to performance issues and incidents.

5.3 Performance Analysis and Optimization:

- Discuss the process of performance analysis and optimization.
- Explore techniques for analyzing performance data, identifying optimization opportunities, and implementing changes to improve website performance over time.

Chapter 6: Case Studies and Best Practices

6.1 Case Studies:

- Present case studies of websites that have successfully optimized performance.
- Discuss the challenges faced, strategies implemented, and outcomes achieved in improving website performance and user experience.

6.2 Best Practices:

- Provide best practices for effective website performance monitoring and optimization.
- Discuss tips for prioritizing performance improvements, collaborating across teams, and leveraging automation and data-driven insights for continuous optimization.

Chapter 7: Conclusion and Next Steps

7.1 Summary of Key Insights:

- Recap key concepts and strategies discussed in the chapter.
- Emphasize the importance of ongoing performance monitoring and optimization for ensuring website reliability, user satisfaction, and business success.

7.2 Implementation Strategies:

- Provide implementation strategies for readers to apply the knowledge gained from the chapter.
- Discuss steps for implementing performance monitoring tools, establishing monitoring processes, and prioritizing optimization efforts based on business goals and user needs.

7.3 Future Directions:

- Reflect on the future of website performance monitoring and optimization.
- Discuss emerging trends, technologies, and challenges in website performance management, and encourage readers to stay informed and adaptive in their approach to performance optimization.

Introduction to Ongoing Website Updates and Improvements

1.1 Understanding the Importance of Ongoing Updates:

- Define ongoing updates and improvements for websites.
- Discuss the importance of continually updating and improving websites to meet changing user needs, technological advancements, and business objectives.

1.2 Benefits of Ongoing Updates:

- Explore the benefits of making ongoing updates and improvements to websites.
- Discuss how regular updates enhance user experience, improve security, boost SEO rankings, and drive business growth and innovation.

Chapter 2: Identifying Areas for Improvement

2.1 User Feedback and Analytics:

- Discuss the importance of user feedback and analytics in identifying areas for improvement.
- Explore techniques for collecting and analyzing user feedback, website analytics, and performance metrics to pinpoint areas of weakness and opportunities for enhancement.

2.2 Industry Trends and Best Practices:

- Discuss the role of industry trends and best practices in guiding website updates and improvements.
- Explore resources such as industry reports, case studies, and expert blogs to stay informed about emerging trends, technologies, and design principles.

2.3 Competitor Analysis:

- Discuss the value of competitor analysis in identifying areas for improvement.
- Explore techniques for conducting competitive analysis, benchmarking against competitors, and identifying gaps and opportunities for differentiation and innovation.

Chapter 3: Planning and Prioritizing Updates

3.1 Establishing Update Priorities:

- Discuss the importance of prioritizing updates based on business goals and user needs.

- Explore techniques for categorizing updates into categories such as critical fixes, feature enhancements, and long-term strategic initiatives.

3.2 Creating a Roadmap:

- Discuss the importance of creating a roadmap for ongoing updates and improvements.
- Explore techniques for developing a roadmap that outlines update priorities, timelines, resource allocation, and key milestones to guide implementation and execution.

3.3 Agile Development and Iterative Updates:

- Discuss the benefits of adopting agile development methodologies for ongoing updates.
- Explore agile principles such as iterative development, continuous feedback, and adaptive planning for delivering updates in small, incremental cycles to maximize efficiency and flexibility.

Chapter 4: Implementing Updates and Improvements

4.1 Content Updates:

- Discuss strategies for making ongoing content updates and improvements.
- Explore techniques for updating website copy, images, videos, and other multimedia content to keep information fresh, relevant, and engaging for users.

4.2 Design and User Experience Enhancements:

- Discuss strategies for enhancing website design and user experience through ongoing updates.
- Explore techniques for improving navigation, layout, typography, color scheme, and interactive elements to create a more intuitive, visually appealing, and user-friendly website.

4.3 Functionality Enhancements:

- Discuss strategies for enhancing website functionality through ongoing updates.
- Explore techniques for adding new features, optimizing existing features, and integrating third-party tools and plugins to enhance website performance, usability, and interactivity.

Chapter 5: Testing and Quality Assurance

5.1 Pre-Release Testing:

- Discuss the importance of pre-release testing for ensuring updates are error-free.
- Explore techniques for conducting functional testing, compatibility testing, and user acceptance testing to identify and resolve issues before updates are deployed to production.

5.2 User Acceptance Testing (UAT):

- Discuss the role of user acceptance testing (UAT) in validating updates and improvements.
- Explore techniques for involving stakeholders and end users in UAT, gathering feedback, and making necessary adjustments to ensure updates meet expectations and requirements.

5.3 Continuous Monitoring and Feedback:

- Discuss the importance of continuous monitoring and feedback after updates are deployed.
- Explore techniques for monitoring website performance, user feedback, and analytics data to evaluate the impact of updates and identify opportunities for further refinement and optimization.

Chapter 6: Iterative Optimization and Continuous Improvement

6.1 Data-Driven Optimization:

- Discuss the importance of data-driven optimization for ongoing updates and improvements.
- Explore techniques for analyzing website performance metrics, user behavior data, and A/B testing results to inform decision-making and prioritize optimization efforts.

6.2 Iterative Development Process:

- Discuss the benefits of adopting an iterative development process for continuous improvement.
- Explore techniques for iterating on updates based on feedback, insights, and evolving business objectives to incrementally enhance website performance, usability, and value over time.

6.3 Feedback Loops and Collaboration:

- Discuss the importance of feedback loops and collaboration in driving continuous improvement.
- Explore techniques for fostering communication and collaboration across teams, gathering input from stakeholders and users, and integrating feedback

into the update process to ensure ongoing alignment with goals and expectations.

Chapter 7: Conclusion and Next Steps

7.1 Summary of Key Insights:

- Recap key concepts and strategies discussed in the chapter.
- Emphasize the importance of making ongoing updates and improvements to websites for maintaining relevance, competitiveness, and effectiveness in the digital landscape.

7.2 Implementation Strategies:

- Provide implementation strategies for readers to apply the knowledge gained from the chapter.
- Discuss steps for establishing a culture of continuous improvement, implementing update processes and workflows, and leveraging feedback and data for informed decision-making.

7.3 Future Directions:

- Reflect on the future of ongoing updates and improvements for websites.
- Discuss emerging trends, technologies, and challenges in website development and optimization, and encourage readers to stay informed and adaptive in their approach to driving continuous improvement and innovation.

Introduction to Website Publishing

1.1 Understanding Website Publishing:

- Define website publishing and its significance in making a website accessible to the public.
- Discuss the process of transitioning from website development to publishing, including preparing content, configuring settings, and deploying the website online.

1.2 Importance of Proper Website Publishing:

- Explore the importance of proper website publishing in establishing an online presence.
- Discuss how effective publishing practices contribute to user engagement, search engine visibility, and overall success of the website.

Chapter 2: Preparing Your Website for Publishing

2.1 Finalizing Content and Design:

- Discuss the importance of finalizing website content and design before publishing.
- Explore techniques for reviewing and editing content, optimizing images and multimedia elements, and ensuring consistency and coherence in design.

2.2 Testing and Quality Assurance:

- Discuss the importance of testing and quality assurance before publishing.
- Explore techniques for conducting cross-browser testing, mobile responsiveness testing, and functional testing to identify and resolve issues before making the website live.

2.3 Optimizing for Performance:

- Discuss the importance of optimizing website performance before publishing.
- Explore techniques for optimizing page load times, server response times, and overall website speed to provide a seamless user experience.

Chapter 3: Choosing a Hosting Provider

3.1 Understanding Hosting Options:

- Introduce different hosting options available for publishing a website, such as shared hosting, VPS hosting, and cloud hosting.

- Discuss the pros and cons of each hosting option and how to choose the most suitable one based on website requirements and budget.

3.2 Selecting a Hosting Provider:

- Provide guidelines for selecting a reliable hosting provider.
- Discuss factors to consider, such as uptime guarantees, performance, security features, scalability, and customer support, when choosing a hosting provider.

3.3 Setting Up Hosting Account:

- Walk through the process of setting up a hosting account with a chosen hosting provider.
- Discuss steps such as domain registration, account setup, DNS configuration, and installing necessary software or platforms for website deployment.

Chapter 4: Deploying Your Website

4.1 Uploading Files:

- Discuss different methods for uploading website files to the hosting server.
- Explore techniques such as FTP (File Transfer Protocol), SFTP (Secure File Transfer Protocol), and using hosting control panels for file uploads.

4.2 Configuring Server Settings:

- Discuss the importance of configuring server settings for optimal website performance and security.
- Explore techniques for configuring server settings such as PHP version, file permissions, security certificates, and server-side caching.

4.3 Configuring Domain and DNS:

- Walk through the process of configuring domain settings and DNS (Domain Name System) records for the website.
- Discuss steps such as updating nameservers, setting up DNS records (A, CNAME, MX), and configuring domain redirects if necessary.

Chapter 5: Testing Your Published Website

5.1 Functional Testing:

- Discuss the importance of functional testing after website deployment.
- Explore techniques for testing website functionality, navigation, forms, links, and interactive elements to ensure they work as intended.

5.2 Cross-Browser and Cross-Device Testing:

- Discuss the importance of cross-browser and cross-device testing for ensuring compatibility and responsiveness.
- Explore techniques for testing website performance and appearance across different web browsers, devices, and screen sizes.

5.3 Performance Testing:

- Discuss the importance of performance testing after website deployment.
- Explore techniques for measuring website performance metrics such as page load time, server response time, and overall speed using performance testing tools and services.

Chapter 6: Optimizing for Search Engines

6.1 On-Page SEO Optimization:

- Discuss the importance of on-page SEO optimization for improving search engine visibility.
- Explore techniques for optimizing website content, meta tags, headings, URLs, and images for relevant keywords and user intent.

6.2 Submitting Sitemap to Search Engines:

- Walk through the process of creating and submitting a sitemap to search engines.
- Discuss the importance of sitemaps in helping search engines crawl and index website content effectively.

6.3 Monitoring and Analyzing SEO Performance:

- Discuss the importance of monitoring and analyzing SEO performance after website publishing.
- Explore techniques for using SEO analytics tools such as Google Analytics, Google Search Console, and third-party SEO software to track website traffic, rankings, and user behavior.

Chapter 7: Maintaining and Updating Your Website

7.1 Regular Maintenance Tasks:

- Discuss the importance of regular website maintenance after publishing.
- Explore techniques for performing tasks such as updating plugins, security patches, content refreshes, and backups to ensure website reliability and security.

7.2 Monitoring Website Performance:

- Discuss the importance of monitoring website performance after publishing.
- Explore techniques for using website monitoring tools to track performance metrics, uptime, and user experience, and taking proactive measures to address issues and optimize performance.

7.3 Implementing Ongoing Updates and Improvements:

- Discuss the importance of implementing ongoing updates and improvements to keep the website fresh and relevant.
- Explore techniques for identifying areas for improvement, planning and prioritizing updates, and iterating on website design, content, and functionality based on user feedback and analytics insights.

Chapter 8: Conclusion and Next Steps

8.1 Summary of Key Insights:

- Recap key concepts and strategies discussed in the chapter.
- Emphasize the importance of proper website publishing practices in ensuring website accessibility, performance, and search engine visibility.

8.2 Implementation Strategies:

- Provide implementation strategies for readers to apply the knowledge gained from the chapter.
- Discuss steps for effectively publishing a website, choosing a hosting provider, deploying website files, testing and optimizing for search engines, and maintaining and updating the website for long-term success.

8.3 Future Directions:

- Reflect on the future of website publishing and management.
- Discuss emerging trends, technologies, and challenges in website publishing, and encourage readers to stay informed and adaptive in their approach to website development and maintenance.

Introduction to Domain Configuration

1.1 Understanding Domain Settings:

- Define domain settings and their importance in managing website domains.
- Discuss the role of domain settings in controlling domain registration, DNS configuration, email forwarding, and other domain-related functionalities.

1.2 Significance of Proper Domain Configuration:

- Explore the significance of proper domain configuration for website accessibility, email communication, branding, and online presence.
- Discuss how misconfigured domain settings can lead to issues such as website downtime, email deliverability problems, and security vulnerabilities.

Chapter 2: Domain Registration and Ownership

2.1 Domain Registration Process:

- Walk through the process of registering a domain name with a domain registrar.
- Discuss steps such as searching for available domain names, selecting a registrar, completing registration forms, and providing required contact information.

2.2 Domain Ownership and Registrant Information:

- Discuss the concept of domain ownership and the importance of accurate registrant information.
- Explore techniques for verifying domain ownership, updating registrant contact details, and protecting domain ownership through privacy protection services.

2.3 Domain Registration Privacy:

- Discuss the importance of domain registration privacy and the risks associated with exposing registrant contact information.
- Explore techniques for enabling domain privacy protection services offered by domain registrars to keep registrant information private and shielded from public WHOIS databases.

Chapter 3: Domain Name System (DNS) Configuration

3.1 Understanding DNS Configuration:

- Define the Domain Name System (DNS) and its role in translating domain names into IP addresses.

- Discuss the components of DNS configuration, including DNS records, nameservers, DNS zones, and DNS propagation.

3.2 Nameserver Configuration:

- Walk through the process of configuring nameservers for a domain name.
- Discuss steps such as accessing domain management interfaces, entering custom nameserver information, and verifying nameserver settings with the domain registrar.

3.3 DNS Records Management:

- Explore the management of DNS records for configuring domain settings such as website hosting, email routing, and subdomain delegation.
- Discuss common types of DNS records such as A records, CNAME records, MX records, TXT records, and SPF records, and their respective purposes.

Chapter 4: Email Configuration and Forwarding

4.1 Email Hosting Options:

- Discuss different options for hosting email accounts associated with a domain name.
- Explore techniques for choosing between self-hosted email servers, third-party email hosting providers, and email forwarding services based on business needs and budget.

4.2 Email Forwarding Setup:

- Walk through the process of setting up email forwarding for a domain name.
- Discuss steps such as configuring email forwarding rules, specifying forwarding addresses, and testing email forwarding functionality to ensure proper routing of incoming messages.

4.3 SPF and DKIM Configuration:

- Discuss the importance of SPF (Sender Policy Framework) and DKIM (DomainKeys Identified Mail) authentication for email deliverability and security.
- Explore techniques for configuring SPF and DKIM records in DNS settings to authenticate outgoing emails and prevent spoofing and phishing attacks.

Chapter 5: SSL/TLS Certificate Configuration

5.1 Importance of SSL/TLS Certificates:

- Define SSL/TLS certificates and their importance in securing website connections and data transmission.
- Discuss the role of SSL/TLS certificates in encrypting sensitive information, building trust with visitors, and improving search engine rankings.

5.2 SSL/TLS Certificate Installation:

- Walk through the process of installing an SSL/TLS certificate for a domain name.
- Discuss steps such as generating a certificate signing request (CSR), purchasing or obtaining a certificate from a certificate authority (CA), and installing the certificate on the web server.

5.3 HTTPS Configuration:

- Explore techniques for configuring HTTPS (Hypertext Transfer Protocol Secure) for a domain name to enable secure connections between web servers and client browsers.
- Discuss the benefits of HTTPS for website security, SEO, and user trust, and provide guidance on enforcing HTTPS redirection and resolving mixed content issues.

Chapter 6: Domain Redirects and Alias Configuration

6.1 URL Redirects:

- Discuss the concept of URL redirects and their use cases in directing traffic from one URL to another.
- Explore techniques for configuring URL redirects such as 301 redirects (permanent redirects), 302 redirects (temporary redirects), and wildcard redirects using domain management interfaces or .htaccess files.

6.2 Subdomain Configuration:

- Walk through the process of configuring subdomains for a domain name.
- Discuss steps such as creating subdomain DNS records, setting up subdomain folders or directories on the web server, and configuring subdomain-specific settings such as SSL/TLS certificates and email accounts.

6.3 Domain Alias Setup:

- Discuss the concept of domain aliasing and its benefits in managing multiple domain names pointing to the same website.
- Explore techniques for configuring domain aliases through domain management interfaces or server configurations to ensure consistent branding and accessibility across multiple domain names.

Chapter 7: DNS Security and Protection

7.1 DNS Security Best Practices:

- Discuss best practices for securing DNS settings and preventing DNS-related attacks such as DNS hijacking, DNS cache poisoning, and DDoS (Distributed Denial of Service) attacks.
- Explore techniques for implementing DNSSEC (Domain Name System Security Extensions), DNS filtering, and DNS firewalling to enhance DNS security and resilience.

7.2 Domain Reputation Management:

- Discuss the importance of maintaining a positive domain reputation and the impact of domain reputation on email deliverability and website credibility.
- Explore techniques for monitoring domain reputation, identifying and resolving issues such as blacklisting and phishing reports, and implementing measures to protect domain integrity and trustworthiness.

7.3 DNS Monitoring and Analytics:

- Explore the role of DNS monitoring and analytics in tracking DNS performance, resolving DNS-related issues, and optimizing DNS configuration for better website performance and reliability.
- Discuss techniques for using DNS monitoring tools and services to monitor DNS resolution times, identify bottlenecks, and troubleshoot DNS-related problems proactively.

Chapter 8: Conclusion and Next Steps

8.1 Summary of Key Insights:

- Recap key concepts and strategies discussed in the chapter.
- Emphasize the importance of proper domain configuration in ensuring website accessibility, email functionality, security, and online presence.

8.2 Implementation Strategies:

- Provide implementation strategies for readers to apply the knowledge gained from the chapter.
- Discuss steps for effectively configuring domain settings, managing DNS records, securing email communication, and optimizing SSL/TLS certificates to enhance website performance, security, and usability.

8.3 Future Directions:

- Reflect on the future of domain configuration and management.
- Discuss emerging trends, technologies, and challenges in domain management, and encourage readers to stay informed and adaptive in their approach to domain configuration and security practices.

Introduction to Social Media Promotion

1.1 Understanding Social Media Marketing:

- Define social media marketing and its role in promoting websites and businesses.
- Discuss the importance of social media promotion in increasing brand visibility, driving website traffic, and engaging with target audiences.

1.2 Significance of Social Media Platforms:

- Explore the significance of various social media platforms in reaching different demographics and target markets.
- Discuss the strengths and features of major social media platforms such as Facebook, Instagram, Twitter, LinkedIn, Pinterest, and YouTube, and their suitability for different types of content and marketing objectives.

Chapter 2: Creating a Social Media Strategy

2.1 Setting Clear Objectives:

- Discuss the importance of setting clear objectives and goals for social media promotion.
- Explore techniques for defining SMART (Specific, Measurable, Achievable, Relevant, Time-bound) objectives that align with overall business goals and website promotion objectives.

2.2 Identifying Target Audience:

- Explore techniques for identifying and understanding target audiences on social media platforms.
- Discuss methods such as audience segmentation, persona development, and social listening to gain insights into audience demographics, interests, and behaviors.

2.3 Content Strategy and Planning:

- Discuss the importance of developing a content strategy for social media promotion.
- Explore techniques for planning and creating engaging content, including text posts, images, videos, infographics, and interactive media, that resonate with target audiences and align with brand messaging and objectives.

Chapter 3: Leveraging Social Media Platforms

3.1 Facebook Marketing:

- Discuss strategies for leveraging Facebook as a marketing platform for website promotion.
- Explore techniques for creating Facebook Pages, posting engaging content, running targeted advertising campaigns, and engaging with followers through comments, messages, and live video.

3.2 Instagram Marketing:

- Discuss strategies for leveraging Instagram as a visual marketing platform for website promotion.
- Explore techniques for creating an Instagram Business Profile, posting visually appealing content, using Instagram Stories, IGTV, and Reels, and collaborating with influencers to reach new audiences.

3.3 Twitter Marketing:

- Discuss strategies for leveraging Twitter as a real-time marketing platform for website promotion.
- Explore techniques for tweeting engaging content, using hashtags to increase visibility, participating in Twitter chats and trending topics, and running Twitter ad campaigns to reach target audiences.

3.4 LinkedIn Marketing:

- Discuss strategies for leveraging LinkedIn as a professional networking platform for website promotion.
- Explore techniques for optimizing LinkedIn Company Pages, sharing industry insights and thought leadership content, participating in LinkedIn Groups and discussions, and using LinkedIn Ads for B2B marketing and lead generation.

3.5 Pinterest Marketing:

- Discuss strategies for leveraging Pinterest as a visual discovery platform for website promotion.
- Explore techniques for creating Pinterest Boards, pinning visually appealing images and infographics, optimizing pin descriptions and keywords, and driving traffic to the website through Pinterest Ads and Rich Pins.

3.6 YouTube Marketing:

- Discuss strategies for leveraging YouTube as a video marketing platform for website promotion.
- Explore techniques for creating compelling video content, optimizing video titles, descriptions, and tags for search, engaging with the YouTube community through comments and collaborations, and using YouTube Ads to reach target audiences.

Chapter 4: Engaging with the Audience

4.1 Building Community Engagement:

- Discuss the importance of building community engagement on social media platforms.
- Explore techniques for fostering conversations, responding to comments and messages, running polls and surveys, and hosting contests and giveaways to engage with the audience and build brand loyalty.

4.2 Influencer Marketing:

- Discuss the role of influencer marketing in social media promotion.
- Explore techniques for identifying and partnering with influencers in the niche or industry to amplify brand reach, drive website traffic, and build credibility with their followers.

Chapter 5: Measuring and Analyzing Social Media Performance

5.1 Key Performance Indicators (KPIs):

- Discuss key performance indicators (KPIs) for measuring social media performance.
- Explore metrics such as reach, engagement, clicks, conversions, and return on investment (ROI) to evaluate the effectiveness of social media promotion efforts.

5.2 Social Media Analytics Tools:

- Explore popular social media analytics tools for tracking and analyzing performance metrics.
- Discuss features and functionalities of tools such as Facebook Insights, Instagram Insights, Twitter Analytics, LinkedIn Analytics, Pinterest Analytics, and third-party social media management platforms for monitoring performance and gaining actionable insights.

Chapter 6: Optimization and Iteration

6.1 Optimization Strategies:

- Discuss strategies for optimizing social media promotion efforts based on performance data and insights.

- Explore techniques for refining content strategy, adjusting targeting parameters, experimenting with ad formats, and optimizing posting schedules to maximize engagement and results.

6.2 Iterative Approach:

- Discuss the importance of taking an iterative approach to social media promotion.
- Explore techniques for continuously testing and refining strategies, analyzing results, and adapting tactics based on changing audience preferences, platform algorithms, and industry trends.

Chapter 7: Conclusion and Next Steps

7.1 Summary of Key Insights:

- Recap key concepts and strategies discussed in the chapter.
- Emphasize the importance of strategic planning, audience engagement, and data-driven optimization in effective social media promotion for website success.

7.2 Implementation Strategies:

- Provide implementation strategies for readers to apply the knowledge gained from the chapter.
- Discuss steps for developing a comprehensive social media promotion strategy, selecting appropriate platforms, creating engaging content, measuring performance, and optimizing results for long-term success.

7.3 Future Directions:

- Reflect on the future of social media marketing and website promotion.
- Discuss emerging trends, technologies, and best practices in social media promotion, and encourage readers to stay informed and adaptive in their approach to leveraging social media for website success.

Introduction to Email Marketing

1.1 Understanding Email Marketing:

- Define email marketing and its significance in digital marketing strategies.
- Discuss the role of email marketing in building customer relationships, driving conversions, and generating revenue for businesses.

1.2 Benefits of Email Marketing:

- Explore the benefits of email marketing compared to other marketing channels.
- Discuss advantages such as cost-effectiveness, high ROI (Return on Investment), targeted messaging, and scalability in reaching and engaging with audiences.

Chapter 2: Building an Email Marketing Strategy

2.1 Setting Objectives and Goals:

- Discuss the importance of setting clear objectives and goals for email marketing campaigns.
- Explore techniques for defining goals such as increasing website traffic, boosting sales, nurturing leads, promoting content, or enhancing brand awareness.

2.2 Audience Segmentation and Targeting:

- Explore the significance of audience segmentation and targeting in email marketing.
- Discuss techniques for segmenting email lists based on demographics, behavior, interests, or lifecycle stage, and targeting specific segments with tailored messaging and offers.

2.3 Content Strategy and Planning:

- Discuss the importance of developing a content strategy for email marketing campaigns.
- Explore techniques for planning and creating compelling email content, including newsletters, promotional offers, product updates, educational content, and personalized messages.

Chapter 3: Building and Growing Email Lists

3.1 Permission-Based Email Marketing:

- Discuss the importance of permission-based email marketing and compliance with anti-spam regulations.
- Explore techniques for building email lists organically through opt-in forms, website sign-ups, lead magnets, and incentive-based offers.

3.2 List Building Strategies:

- Explore effective strategies for growing email lists and expanding subscriber bases.
- Discuss techniques such as offering gated content, hosting webinars or events, running contests or giveaways, and leveraging social media and partnerships for list building.

3.3 Managing Subscriber Relationships:

- Discuss strategies for managing subscriber relationships and minimizing subscriber churn.
- Explore techniques for maintaining email list hygiene, segmenting subscribers based on engagement levels, re-engaging inactive subscribers, and providing value-added content to retain subscribers.

Chapter 4: Email Campaign Design and Execution

4.1 Designing Effective Email Campaigns:

- Discuss best practices for designing effective email campaigns that drive engagement and conversions.
- Explore techniques for creating visually appealing email templates, optimizing for mobile responsiveness, using compelling subject lines and preview text, and incorporating clear calls-to-action (CTAs).

4.2 Email Automation and Personalization:

- Explore the benefits of email automation and personalization in improving campaign effectiveness.
- Discuss techniques for setting up automated email workflows such as welcome series, abandoned cart reminders, birthday or anniversary emails, and personalizing content based on subscriber preferences and behavior.

4.3 A/B Testing and Optimization:

- Discuss the importance of A/B testing and optimization in refining email marketing campaigns.
- Explore techniques for testing variables such as subject lines, content layout, CTAs, send times, and audience segments, and optimizing campaigns based on performance data and insights.

Chapter 5: Deliverability and Compliance

5.1 Email Deliverability Best Practices:

- Discuss best practices for improving email deliverability and inbox placement.
- Explore techniques for maintaining sender reputation, optimizing email content and formatting, avoiding spam triggers, and monitoring deliverability metrics such as open rates, click-through rates, and bounce rates.

5.2 Compliance with Email Regulations:

- Explore compliance requirements and regulations governing email marketing practices.
- Discuss laws such as CAN-SPAM (Controlling the Assault of Non-Solicited Pornography And Marketing Act) and GDPR (General Data Protection Regulation), and best practices for obtaining consent, providing opt-out options, and honoring subscriber preferences.

Chapter 6: Measuring and Analyzing Email Performance

6.1 Key Email Marketing Metrics:

- Discuss key email marketing metrics for measuring campaign performance and effectiveness.
- Explore metrics such as open rates, click-through rates, conversion rates, bounce rates, and unsubscribe rates, and their significance in evaluating campaign success.

6.2 Email Analytics Tools:

- Explore popular email analytics tools for tracking and analyzing campaign performance.
- Discuss features and functionalities of tools such as email marketing platforms, Google Analytics, and third-party analytics integrations for monitoring campaign metrics, segmenting data, and gaining actionable insights.

Chapter 7: Email Marketing Integration with Other Channels

7.1 Integration with Content Marketing:

- Discuss strategies for integrating email marketing with content marketing efforts.

- Explore techniques for promoting blog posts, articles, videos, or downloadable content through email newsletters, nurturing leads with educational content, and driving traffic to website resources.

7.2 Integration with Social Media Marketing:

- Discuss strategies for integrating email marketing with social media marketing activities.
- Explore techniques for growing email lists through social media channels, promoting email sign-ups on social profiles, and amplifying email content through social sharing and engagement.

Chapter 8: Conclusion and Next Steps

8.1 Summary of Key Insights:

- Recap key concepts and strategies discussed in the chapter.
- Emphasize the importance of strategic planning, audience segmentation, compelling content, and data-driven optimization in successful email marketing campaigns.

8.2 Implementation Strategies:

- Provide implementation strategies for readers to apply the knowledge gained from the chapter.
- Discuss steps for developing and executing effective email marketing campaigns, including list building, content creation, campaign design, automation setup, and performance measurement.

8.3 Future Directions:

- Reflect on the future of email marketing and emerging trends in the industry.
- Discuss innovations such as AI-powered personalization, interactive email experiences, and integrations with emerging technologies, and encourage readers to stay abreast of developments to remain competitive in the email marketing landscape.

Introduction to Search Engine Marketing

1.1 Understanding Search Engine Marketing (SEM):

- Define SEM and its significance in digital marketing strategies.
- Discuss the role of SEM in increasing website visibility, driving targeted traffic, and generating leads and conversions through paid search advertising.

1.2 Differentiating SEM from SEO:

- Explore the differences between SEM and SEO (Search Engine Optimization).
- Discuss how SEM involves paid advertising placements on search engine results pages (SERPs), while SEO focuses on optimizing organic search rankings through content and technical optimizations.

Chapter 2: Components of Search Engine Marketing

2.1 Paid Search Advertising:

- Discuss paid search advertising as a core component of SEM.
- Explore how paid search ads appear at the top or bottom of search engine results pages (SERPs) based on bidding and relevance, and discuss ad formats such as text ads, shopping ads, and responsive search ads.

2.2 Keywords and Ad Targeting:

- Discuss the importance of keywords and ad targeting in SEM campaigns.
- Explore techniques for conducting keyword research, selecting relevant keywords, organizing keywords into ad groups, and targeting specific audiences based on demographics, interests, and behaviors.

2.3 Ad Copy and Creative:

- Explore best practices for creating compelling ad copy and creative elements.
- Discuss techniques for crafting attention-grabbing headlines, writing persuasive ad copy, incorporating keywords, and using ad extensions such as sitelinks, callouts, and structured snippets to enhance ad visibility and engagement.

Chapter 3: Setting Up SEM Campaigns

3.1 Campaign Structure and Organization:

- Discuss strategies for structuring and organizing SEM campaigns effectively.

- Explore techniques for setting up campaigns, ad groups, and keywords in a logical hierarchy, aligning campaign structure with business objectives and targeting criteria.

3.2 Bidding Strategies and Budget Management:

- Discuss bidding strategies and budget management techniques for SEM campaigns.
- Explore options such as manual bidding, automated bidding, and bid modifiers, as well as strategies for optimizing bidding based on performance metrics and maximizing ROI within budget constraints.

3.3 Ad Extensions and Enhancements:

- Discuss the importance of ad extensions and enhancements in SEM campaigns.
- Explore various ad extensions such as sitelinks, callouts, location extensions, and promotion extensions, and discuss how they improve ad visibility, relevance, and click-through rates.

Chapter 4: Tracking and Measurement

4.1 Conversion Tracking:

- Discuss the importance of conversion tracking in SEM campaigns.
- Explore techniques for setting up conversion tracking pixels or tags, defining conversion actions such as form submissions or purchases, and measuring campaign performance based on conversion metrics.

4.2 Performance Metrics and Reporting:

- Explore key performance metrics for evaluating SEM campaign effectiveness.
- Discuss metrics such as click-through rate (CTR), conversion rate (CVR), cost per click (CPC), return on ad spend (ROAS), and quality score, and explore tools and platforms for generating performance reports and insights.

Chapter 5: Advanced SEM Strategies

5.1 Remarketing and Retargeting:

- Discuss remarketing and retargeting strategies in SEM campaigns.
- Explore techniques for targeting previous website visitors or engaged users with personalized ads based on their interactions and behaviors, and discuss the benefits of remarketing for increasing conversions and ROI.

5.2 Dynamic Search Ads (DSA):

- Discuss dynamic search ads (DSA) as an advanced SEM strategy.

- Explore how DSA automatically generate ad headlines and landing pages based on website content, dynamically matching search queries to relevant pages, and discuss best practices for implementing and optimizing DSA campaigns.

5.3 Local Search Advertising:

- Discuss local search advertising strategies for businesses targeting geographically specific audiences.
- Explore techniques for optimizing campaigns for local search intent, targeting local keywords, using location extensions, and leveraging Google My Business for enhanced local visibility and engagement.

Chapter 6: Optimization and Testing

6.1 Ad Copy and Landing Page Optimization:

- Discuss the importance of ad copy and landing page optimization in SEM campaigns.
- Explore techniques for testing ad variations, optimizing landing page experiences, and aligning ad messaging with landing page content to improve relevance and conversion rates.

6.2 A/B Testing and Experimentation:

- Explore the role of A/B testing and experimentation in optimizing SEM campaigns.
- Discuss techniques for testing different ad elements, bidding strategies, targeting parameters, and landing page designs, and leveraging experimentation to identify high-performing tactics and refine campaign performance.

Chapter 7: Compliance and Ethical Considerations

7.1 Ad Policies and Guidelines:

- Discuss compliance requirements and ethical considerations in SEM advertising.
- Explore search engine ad policies, guidelines, and best practices for ensuring ad compliance, transparency, and user trust, and discuss consequences of violating ad policies.

7.2 Ethical Advertising Practices:

- Explore ethical advertising practices and considerations in SEM campaigns.

- Discuss issues such as deceptive advertising, misleading claims, user privacy, and data protection, and emphasize the importance of ethical conduct and integrity in SEM advertising.

Chapter 8: Future Trends and Innovations

8.1 Emerging Trends in SEM:

- Reflect on future trends and innovations in SEM.
- Discuss emerging technologies, features, and trends such as voice search, visual search, machine learning, and automation, and their potential impact on the future of SEM advertising.

8.2 Adaptation and Agility:

- Discuss the importance of adaptation and agility in navigating evolving SEM landscapes.
- Encourage readers to stay informed, experiment with new strategies and technologies, and adapt their SEM campaigns to capitalize on emerging opportunities and stay competitive in dynamic digital environments.

Chapter 9: Conclusion and Next Steps

9.1 Summary of Key Insights:

- Recap key concepts and strategies discussed in the chapter.
- Emphasize the importance of strategic planning, targeting, optimization, and measurement in successful SEM campaigns.

9.2 Implementation Strategies:

- Provide implementation strategies for readers to apply the knowledge gained from the chapter.
- Discuss steps for developing and executing effective SEM campaigns, including campaign setup, optimization, tracking, and continuous improvement.

9.3 Future Directions and Continued Learning:

- Encourage readers to stay informed about SEM trends, experiment with new strategies, and pursue ongoing education and certification to enhance their SEM skills and expertise.

Introduction to Analyzing and Measuring Results

1.1 Understanding the Importance:

- Define the significance of analyzing and measuring results in digital marketing campaigns.
- Discuss how data-driven insights help marketers understand campaign performance, make informed decisions, and optimize strategies for better results.

1.2 Objectives of Analysis:

- Explore the primary objectives of analyzing and measuring campaign results.
- Discuss goals such as evaluating campaign effectiveness, identifying areas for improvement, optimizing ROI, and informing future marketing strategies.

Chapter 2: Key Performance Indicators (KPIs)

2.1 Selection of KPIs:

- Discuss the process of selecting relevant Key Performance Indicators (KPIs) for digital marketing campaigns.
- Explore common KPIs such as Click-Through Rate (CTR), Conversion Rate, Return on Investment (ROI), Cost per Acquisition (CPA), and Customer Lifetime Value (CLV), and their significance in measuring campaign success.

2.2 Setting Benchmarks and Goals:

- Explore strategies for setting benchmarks and goals for KPIs.
- Discuss techniques for establishing realistic targets based on historical data, industry benchmarks, and business objectives, and tracking progress towards goals over time.

Chapter 3: Data Collection and Analysis Tools

3.1 Analytics Platforms:

- Explore popular analytics platforms for collecting and analyzing campaign data.
- Discuss features and functionalities of platforms such as Google Analytics, Adobe Analytics, and HubSpot Analytics, and their capabilities for tracking website traffic, user behavior, and conversion metrics.

3.2 Data Visualization Tools:

- Discuss the importance of data visualization tools in presenting and interpreting campaign data.
- Explore visualization tools such as Google Data Studio, Tableau, and Microsoft Power BI, and their capabilities for creating interactive dashboards, charts, and reports to visualize campaign performance metrics.

Chapter 4: Performance Analysis Techniques

4.1 Comparative Analysis:

- Discuss the importance of comparative analysis in evaluating campaign performance.
- Explore techniques for comparing performance across different time periods, channels, campaigns, or segments to identify trends, patterns, and areas for improvement.

4.2 Cohort Analysis:

- Explore cohort analysis as a technique for understanding user behavior over time.
- Discuss how cohort analysis groups users based on shared characteristics or actions, and tracks their behavior and engagement patterns to assess campaign effectiveness and customer retention.

Chapter 5: Attribution Modeling

5.1 Understanding Attribution Models:

- Define attribution modeling and its significance in determining the impact of marketing channels on conversions.
- Explore common attribution models such as First Click, Last Click, Linear, Time Decay, and Position-Based, and discuss their strengths, limitations, and applicability in different scenarios.

5.2 Multi-Touch Attribution:

- Discuss multi-touch attribution as an advanced technique for assigning value to multiple touchpoints in the customer journey.
- Explore methodologies for weighting and assigning credit to various marketing channels and touchpoints based on their influence on conversions, and discuss challenges and best practices in implementing multi-touch attribution models.

Chapter 6: A/B Testing and Experimentation

6.1 Principles of A/B Testing:

- Discuss the principles of A/B testing and experimentation in digital marketing.
- Explore techniques for testing variables such as ad copy, landing page design, call-to-action buttons, and email subject lines, and measuring the impact on conversion rates and KPIs.

6.2 Test Design and Analysis:

- Explore best practices for designing and analyzing A/B tests.
- Discuss techniques for defining hypotheses, setting up experiments, randomizing test groups, collecting data, and interpreting results to draw meaningful insights and make data-driven decisions.

Chapter 7: Actionable Insights and Optimization Strategies

7.1 Identifying Insights:

- Discuss strategies for identifying actionable insights from campaign data.
- Explore techniques for drilling down into data, segmenting audiences, and identifying trends, patterns, and correlations that inform optimization strategies and drive performance improvements.

7.2 Optimization Strategies:

- Explore optimization strategies based on data-driven insights.
- Discuss techniques for refining targeting parameters, adjusting bidding strategies, optimizing ad creative and messaging, improving website usability and conversion pathways, and reallocating budgets to high-performing channels or campaigns.

Chapter 8: Reporting and Communication

8.1 Data Visualization and Reporting:

- Discuss best practices for data visualization and reporting.
- Explore techniques for presenting campaign performance data in clear, concise, and visually appealing formats, and tailoring reports to different stakeholders' needs and preferences.

8.2 Stakeholder Communication:

- Discuss strategies for effective communication of analysis findings and recommendations to stakeholders.

- Explore techniques for translating technical data into actionable insights, fostering collaboration and alignment across teams, and driving decision-making based on data-driven evidence.

Chapter 9: Continuous Improvement and Iteration

9.1 Iterative Approach to Optimization:

- Discuss the importance of continuous improvement and iteration in digital marketing.
- Explore the iterative approach to campaign optimization, where insights from analysis inform ongoing refinements, experiments, and iterations to maximize performance and ROI.

9.2 Learning from Failures:

- Discuss the value of learning from failures and setbacks in digital marketing campaigns.
- Explore techniques for conducting post-mortem analyses, identifying root causes of underperformance, and applying lessons learned to future campaigns to avoid repeating mistakes.

Chapter 10: Conclusion and Next Steps

10.1 Summary of Key Insights:

- Recap key concepts and strategies discussed in the chapter.
- Emphasize the importance of data analysis, measurement, and optimization in driving success in digital marketing campaigns.

10.2 Implementation Strategies:

- Provide implementation strategies for readers to apply the knowledge gained from the chapter.
- Discuss steps for developing robust measurement frameworks, leveraging analytics tools effectively, and continuously optimizing campaigns for better results and ROI.

10.3 Future Directions and Continued Learning:

- Encourage readers to stay informed about emerging trends, technologies, and best practices in data analysis and measurement.
- Recommend resources for further learning and professional development in the field of digital marketing analytics and optimization.

Introduction to Advanced Design Techniques

1.1 Understanding Design Principles:

- Recap foundational design principles such as balance, hierarchy, contrast, alignment, and repetition.
- Discuss how advanced design techniques build upon these principles to create visually engaging and effective designs.

1.2 Importance of Advanced Design:

- Explore the significance of advanced design techniques in elevating the quality and impact of visual communication.
- Discuss how mastery of advanced design techniques allows designers to push creative boundaries, differentiate their work, and captivate audiences.

Chapter 2: Typography and Text Effects

2.1 Typography Trends:

- Discuss current typography trends and their impact on modern design aesthetics.
- Explore techniques for pairing fonts, experimenting with typography styles, and integrating typography as a visual element in design compositions.

2.2 Creative Text Effects:

- Explore advanced text effects to enhance typographic elements.
- Discuss techniques for creating custom lettering, applying text shadows, gradients, textures, and other effects to add depth and visual interest to text.

2.3 Kinetic Typography:

- Introduce kinetic typography as a dynamic design technique.
- Discuss how to animate text elements to convey meaning, enhance storytelling, and create engaging visual experiences in motion graphics and multimedia projects.

Chapter 3: Advanced Color Theory and Application

3.1 Color Psychology:

- Explore the psychological impact of color in design.
- Discuss how advanced color theory can be used to evoke emotions, convey messages, and influence user behavior in design compositions.

3.2 Color Harmony and Schemes:

- Discuss advanced color harmony principles and schemes.
- Explore techniques for creating harmonious color palettes, experimenting with complementary, analogous, triadic, and split-complementary color schemes, and using color effectively in design compositions.

3.3 Color Gradients and Blends:

- Explore advanced techniques for using color gradients and blends.
- Discuss methods for creating smooth gradient transitions, incorporating duotone effects, and leveraging gradient maps to add depth and dimension to design elements.

Chapter 4: Advanced Layout and Composition

4.1 Grid Systems and Layout Structures:

- Discuss advanced grid systems and layout structures.
- Explore techniques for designing complex layouts using modular grids, asymmetrical compositions, and dynamic grid-based frameworks to create visually engaging and organized designs.

4.2 Visual Hierarchy and Information Architecture:

- Explore advanced techniques for establishing visual hierarchy and information architecture.
- Discuss strategies for prioritizing content, structuring information, and guiding user attention through strategic placement, sizing, and styling of design elements.

4.3 Depth and Dimensionality:

- Discuss techniques for creating depth and dimensionality in design compositions.
- Explore methods for incorporating shadows, lighting effects, perspective, and layering to simulate three-dimensional space and enhance the visual impact of designs.

Chapter 5: Advanced Image Manipulation and Illustration

5.1 Advanced Image Editing Techniques:

- Explore advanced image manipulation techniques.
- Discuss methods for retouching, compositing, and blending images, as well as incorporating special effects, filters, and textures to enhance visual appeal.

5.2 Vector Illustration:

- Introduce advanced vector illustration techniques.
- Discuss techniques for creating complex vector graphics, illustrations, and icons using tools such as Adobe Illustrator, and explore methods for achieving precision and scalability in vector artwork.

5.3 Digital Painting and Mixed Media:

- Explore advanced digital painting and mixed media techniques.
- Discuss methods for creating digital paintings, textures, and mixed media artworks using digital brushes, blending modes, and layer effects to achieve expressive and immersive visual experiences.

Chapter 6: Advanced Animation and Motion Graphics

6.1 Motion Principles:

- Recap fundamental principles of motion design.
- Discuss concepts such as timing, easing, anticipation, and follow-through, and explore how these principles are applied in advanced animation and motion graphics projects.

6.2 Character Animation:

- Introduce advanced techniques for character animation.
- Discuss methods for rigging characters, creating expressive animations, and adding personality and realism to character movements in animated projects.

6.3 Interactive Animation:

- Explore techniques for creating interactive animations.
- Discuss methods for integrating animation with user interactions, designing animated UI elements, and creating immersive experiences in web and mobile interfaces.

Chapter 7: Responsive and Adaptive Design

7.1 Responsive Design Principles:

- Recap principles of responsive web design.
- Discuss advanced techniques for designing responsive layouts, fluid grids, and flexible media to ensure optimal user experiences across devices and screen sizes.

7.2 Adaptive Design Strategies:

- Introduce adaptive design strategies for addressing diverse user contexts.
- Discuss techniques for adapting design layouts, content, and interactions based on factors such as device capabilities, user preferences, and environmental conditions.

Chapter 8: Advanced Design Tools and Technologies

8.1 Advanced Design Software:

- Explore advanced design software tools and technologies.
- Discuss features and capabilities of industry-standard design software such as Adobe Creative Cloud, Sketch, Figma, and Affinity Designer, and explore emerging tools for VR/AR design, prototyping, and collaboration.

8.2 Design Systems and Component Libraries:

- Discuss the importance of design systems and component libraries in advanced design workflows.
- Explore techniques for creating and maintaining design systems, building reusable components, and fostering consistency and efficiency in design processes.

Chapter 9: Accessibility and Inclusive Design

9.1 Principles of Inclusive Design:

- Introduce principles of inclusive design and accessibility.
- Discuss the importance of designing for diverse audiences, including users with disabilities, and explore techniques for creating accessible interfaces and content.

9.2 Advanced Accessibility Techniques:

- Explore advanced accessibility techniques for design.
- Discuss methods for implementing ARIA attributes, keyboard navigation, focus management, and other accessibility features to ensure equal access and usability for all users.

Chapter 10: Conclusion and Next Steps

10.1 Summary of Key Insights:

- Recap key concepts and techniques discussed in the chapter.

- Emphasize the importance of continuous learning and experimentation in mastering advanced design techniques.

10.2 Implementation Strategies:

- Provide implementation strategies for readers to apply advanced design techniques in their projects.
- Discuss steps for exploring and practicing advanced design techniques, seeking inspiration, and expanding creative horizons through experimentation and collaboration.

10.3 Future Trends and Continued Learning:

- Encourage readers to stay informed about emerging trends and technologies in design.
- Recommend resources for further learning and professional development in advanced design techniques and practice

Chapter 1: Introduction to Customizing with Code

1.1 Understanding the Role of Code:

- Define the role of code in website customization.
- Discuss how custom code can be used to extend the functionality, design, and interactivity of websites beyond the limitations of visual editors.

1.2 Importance of Customization:

- Explore the significance of customization in achieving unique and tailored website experiences.
- Discuss how custom code allows users to implement specific features, styles, and behaviors that align with their brand identity and user requirements.

Introduction to Customizing with Code

1.1 Understanding the Role of Code:

- Define the role of code in website customization.
- Discuss how custom code can be used to extend the functionality, design, and interactivity of websites beyond the limitations of visual editors.

1.2 Importance of Customization:

- Explore the significance of customization in achieving unique and tailored website experiences.
- Discuss how custom code allows users to implement specific features, styles, and behaviors that align with their brand identity and user requirements.

Chapter 2: HTML, CSS, and JavaScript Basics

2.1 HTML Fundamentals:

- Introduce the basics of HTML (Hypertext Markup Language).
- Discuss HTML tags, elements, attributes, and semantic markup for structuring content on web pages.

2.2 CSS Essentials:

- Introduce the fundamentals of CSS (Cascading Style Sheets).
- Discuss CSS selectors, properties, values, and the box model for styling and formatting HTML elements.

2.3 JavaScript Introduction:

- Introduce the basics of JavaScript programming language.
- Discuss JavaScript syntax, variables, data types, functions, and control flow for adding interactivity and dynamic behavior to web pages.

Chapter 3: Customizing Design with CSS

3.1 Advanced CSS Techniques:

- Explore advanced CSS techniques for customizing design elements.
- Discuss techniques for styling typography, colors, backgrounds, borders, and positioning using CSS properties and selectors.

3.2 CSS Animations and Transitions:

- Discuss CSS animations and transitions for adding movement and interactivity to design elements.
- Explore techniques for creating smooth transitions, keyframe animations, and interactive effects using CSS animation properties.

3.3 Responsive Design with CSS Media Queries:

- Introduce CSS media queries for implementing responsive design.
- Discuss techniques for adapting layout, typography, and styling based on device characteristics such as screen size, resolution, and orientation.

Chapter 4: Enhancing Interactivity with JavaScript

4.1 DOM Manipulation:

- Explore DOM (Document Object Model) manipulation with JavaScript.
- Discuss methods for selecting, modifying, and manipulating HTML elements and their attributes dynamically using JavaScript.

4.2 Event Handling:

- Discuss event handling in JavaScript for adding interactivity to web pages.
- Explore techniques for handling user interactions such as clicks, mouse movements, keyboard inputs, and form submissions using event listeners and event objects.

4.3 AJAX and Asynchronous JavaScript:

- Introduce AJAX (Asynchronous JavaScript and XML) for fetching data asynchronously from servers.
- Discuss techniques for making asynchronous HTTP requests, handling responses, and updating web page content dynamically without reloading the entire page.

Chapter 5: Implementing Custom Features

5.1 Custom Navigation Menus:

- Discuss techniques for creating custom navigation menus using HTML, CSS, and JavaScript.
- Explore methods for implementing responsive navigation, dropdown menus, off-canvas menus, and other custom navigation patterns.

5.2 Interactive Forms:

- Explore techniques for enhancing forms with custom features and interactivity.

- Discuss methods for validating form inputs, providing real-time feedback, and implementing custom form controls and behaviors using JavaScript.

5.3 Custom UI Components:

- Discuss techniques for creating custom user interface (UI) components.
- Explore methods for building custom sliders, tabs, accordions, modal dialogs, and other interactive elements using HTML, CSS, and JavaScript.

Chapter 6: Integrating Third-Party Libraries and APIs

6.1 Introduction to Libraries and APIs:

- Define libraries and APIs (Application Programming Interfaces) and their role in web development.
- Discuss how libraries and APIs provide pre-built functionality and data access for integrating custom features into websites.

6.2 Popular JavaScript Libraries:

- Explore popular JavaScript libraries for adding advanced functionality to websites.
- Discuss libraries such as jQuery, React, Vue.js, and AngularJS, and their capabilities for DOM manipulation, component-based development, and building interactive user interfaces.

6.3 Using Web APIs:

- Introduce web APIs for accessing external data and services.
- Discuss techniques for integrating APIs such as Google Maps API, Twitter API, and Weather API to fetch data, display dynamic content, and enhance website functionality.

Chapter 7: Debugging and Optimization

7.1 Debugging Techniques:

- Discuss techniques for debugging and troubleshooting code issues.
- Explore methods for using browser developer tools, console logging, breakpoints, and error handling to identify and fix errors in HTML, CSS, and JavaScript code.

7.2 Performance Optimization:

- Explore strategies for optimizing website performance with custom code.

- Discuss techniques for minimizing file sizes, reducing HTTP requests, optimizing code execution, and improving loading speed and responsiveness for better user experiences.

Chapter 8: Cross-Browser Compatibility and Accessibility

8.1 Cross-Browser Compatibility:

- Discuss strategies for ensuring cross-browser compatibility of custom code.
- Explore techniques for testing and debugging code across different web browsers and platforms to ensure consistent behavior and appearance.

8.2 Accessibility Best Practices:

- Introduce accessibility best practices for custom code.
- Discuss techniques for designing and coding websites with accessibility features such as keyboard navigation, screen reader compatibility, and semantic markup to ensure inclusivity for all users.

Chapter 9: Version Control and Collaboration

9.1 Version Control Basics:

- Introduce version control systems and their benefits for code management.
- Discuss concepts such as repositories, commits, branches, and merges, and explore popular version control platforms such as Git and GitHub.

9.2 Collaborative Workflows:

- Discuss collaborative workflows for managing custom code in teams.
- Explore techniques for branching, merging, code review, and collaboration using version control systems, and discuss best practices for maintaining code quality and consistency in collaborative projects.

Chapter 10: Conclusion and Next Steps

10.1 Summary of Key Insights:

- Recap key concepts and techniques discussed in the chapter.
- Emphasize the importance of customizing with code for creating unique and tailored website experiences.

10.2 Implementation Strategies:

- Provide implementation strategies for readers to apply custom code techniques in their projects.
- Discuss steps for experimenting, practicing, and integrating custom code effectively into website development workflows.

10.3 Continued Learning:

- Encourage readers to continue learning and exploring advanced coding techniques.
- Recommend resources for further learning, including online tutorials, documentation, forums, and communities for web developers.

Introduction to Advanced SEO Strategies

1.1 Understanding the Importance of SEO:

- Recap the importance of Search Engine Optimization (SEO) in driving organic traffic to websites.
- Discuss how advanced SEO strategies go beyond basic optimization techniques to improve search engine rankings, increase visibility, and attract qualified traffic.

1.2 Evolution of SEO:

- Trace the evolution of SEO from keyword stuffing and link building to more sophisticated strategies.
- Explore how search engine algorithms have evolved to prioritize user intent, relevance, and quality content, shaping modern SEO practices.

Chapter 2: Technical SEO Optimization

2.1 Website Performance Optimization:

- Discuss techniques for optimizing website performance to improve SEO.
- Explore strategies for improving page load speed, optimizing images, reducing server response time, and leveraging browser caching to enhance user experience and search engine rankings.

2.2 Mobile Optimization:

- Explore advanced techniques for optimizing websites for mobile devices.
- Discuss responsive design, mobile-friendly layouts, AMP (Accelerated Mobile Pages), and techniques for improving mobile usability and performance to comply with Google's mobile-first indexing.

2.3 Structured Data Markup:

- Introduce structured data markup and its role in enhancing search results.
- Discuss Schema.org markup, rich snippets, and featured snippets, and explore how structured data can improve search visibility and click-through rates.

Chapter 3: Content Optimization Strategies

3.1 Advanced Keyword Research:

- Discuss advanced keyword research techniques for identifying high-value search terms.

- Explore long-tail keywords, semantic search, keyword intent, and competitor analysis to discover opportunities for content optimization.

3.2 Content Quality and Relevance:

- Explore strategies for creating high-quality, relevant content that resonates with target audiences and search engines.
- Discuss content depth, comprehensiveness, originality, and user engagement metrics, and explore techniques for optimizing content for E-A-T (Expertise, Authoritativeness, Trustworthiness).

3.3 Content Optimization for Featured Snippets:

- Discuss techniques for optimizing content to appear in featured snippets.
- Explore formatting, answering questions directly, providing concise summaries, and optimizing for voice search to increase the chances of being featured in Google's rich snippets.

Chapter 4: Advanced Link Building Strategies

4.1 Link Quality and Authority:

- Discuss the importance of link quality and authority in modern link building strategies.
- Explore techniques for earning high-quality backlinks from authoritative websites through outreach, guest blogging, influencer partnerships, and content promotion.

4.2 Link Diversity and Natural Link Profiles:

- Discuss the importance of link diversity and natural link profiles in SEO.
- Explore strategies for building a diverse backlink portfolio, including links from different domains, anchor text variations, and a mix of do-follow and no-follow links to maintain a natural link profile.

4.3 Competitor Backlink Analysis:

- Introduce competitor backlink analysis as a strategy for identifying link-building opportunities.
- Discuss tools and techniques for analyzing competitor backlink profiles, identifying top-performing content, and replicating or improving upon their link-building strategies.

Chapter 5: Advanced On-Page Optimization

5.1 On-Page Technical Optimization:

- Discuss advanced on-page technical optimization techniques.
- Explore strategies for optimizing meta tags, URL structures, headings, image alt attributes, and internal linking to improve crawlability, indexation, and relevancy.

5.2 User Experience (UX) Optimization:

- Discuss the impact of user experience (UX) on SEO and rankings.
- Explore techniques for optimizing site navigation, readability, accessibility, and mobile-friendliness to enhance user experience and satisfy search engine algorithms.

5.3 Advanced Content Formatting and Structuring:

- Discuss advanced content formatting and structuring techniques for SEO.
- Explore methods for using headers, bullet points, lists, tables, and other formatting elements to improve content readability, scanability, and relevance for both users and search engines.

Chapter 6: Local SEO Strategies

6.1 Local Keyword Targeting:

- Discuss advanced strategies for targeting local search queries.
- Explore techniques for optimizing content, meta tags, and website structure to rank for location-based keywords and attract local customers.

6.2 Google My Business Optimization:

- Discuss the importance of Google My Business (GMB) optimization for local SEO.
- Explore strategies for claiming and optimizing GMB listings, managing reviews, and leveraging GMB features such as posts, Q&A, and photos to enhance local visibility.

6.3 Local Link Building and Citations:

- Introduce local link building and citation strategies for improving local search rankings.
- Discuss techniques for earning local backlinks from relevant businesses, organizations, and directories, and optimizing NAP (Name, Address, Phone Number) citations for local consistency.

Chapter 7: Advanced Analytics and Reporting

7.1 Advanced SEO Metrics:

- Discuss advanced SEO metrics for measuring performance and effectiveness.
- Explore metrics such as organic traffic, keyword rankings, backlink quality, user engagement, and conversion rates, and discuss how to interpret and analyze these metrics to inform optimization strategies.

7.2 SEO Reporting and Insights:

- Explore strategies for creating comprehensive SEO reports and insights.
- Discuss tools and techniques for tracking, monitoring, and reporting SEO performance, identifying trends, opportunities, and challenges, and communicating insights effectively to stakeholders.

7.3 A/B Testing and Experimentation:

- Introduce A/B testing and experimentation as strategies for optimizing SEO efforts.
- Discuss techniques for conducting controlled experiments, testing hypotheses, and measuring the impact of changes on SEO performance to inform data-driven decision-making.

Chapter 8: Advanced SEO Tools and Technologies

8.1 SEO Tools Landscape:

- Explore the landscape of advanced SEO tools and technologies.
- Discuss popular tools for keyword research, rank tracking, backlink analysis, site audit, and technical optimization, and explore emerging technologies such as AI-driven SEO platforms and predictive analytics.

8.2 SEO Automation and Workflow Optimization:

- Discuss the role of automation and workflow optimization in advanced SEO strategies.
- Explore techniques for streamlining repetitive tasks, automating reporting, and integrating SEO tools into workflows to improve efficiency and productivity.

Chapter 9: International and Multilingual SEO

9.1 International SEO Strategies:

- Discuss strategies for optimizing websites for international audiences and markets.
- Explore techniques for handling multilingual content, hreflang tags, country-specific domains, and other considerations for international SEO success.

9.2 Global Website Structure and Geotargeting:

- Explore best practices for structuring global websites and implementing geotargeting.
- Discuss strategies for organizing content, managing domains, and using geotargeting settings in Google Search Console to ensure the right content is served to the right audience in different regions.

Chapter 10: Future Trends in SEO

10.1 Emerging Trends and Technologies:

- Explore emerging trends and technologies shaping the future of SEO.
- Discuss topics such as voice search, mobile-first indexing, AI and machine learning, visual search, and the impact of emerging technologies on SEO strategies and practices.

10.2 Continuous Learning and Adaptation:

- Emphasize the importance of continuous learning and adaptation in the ever-evolving field of SEO.
- Encourage readers to stay informed about industry trends, experiment with new strategies and technologies, and adapt their SEO approaches to meet evolving user behaviors and search engine algorithms.

Chapter 11: Conclusion and Next Steps

11.1 Summary of Key Insights:

- Recap key insights and takeaways from the chapter.
- Emphasize the importance of implementing advanced SEO strategies to stay competitive and achieve sustainable organic growth.

11.2 Actionable Recommendations:

- Provide actionable recommendations for implementing advanced SEO strategies.
- Discuss steps for conducting SEO audits, prioritizing optimization efforts, and aligning strategies with business goals to drive long-term success.

11.3 Continued Learning Resources:

- Recommend resources for readers to further their knowledge and skills in advanced SEO.
- Provide a list of books, online courses, blogs, forums, and industry events where readers can continue their learning journey and stay updated on the latest SEO trends and best practices.

Introduction to E-commerce Optimization

1.1 Understanding E-commerce Optimization:

- Define e-commerce optimization as the process of improving various aspects of an online store to increase sales, conversions, and overall performance.
- Highlight the importance of optimization in enhancing user experience, maximizing revenue, and staying competitive in the e-commerce landscape.

1.2 The Importance of E-commerce Optimization:

- Discuss the significance of e-commerce optimization in driving business growth and profitability.
- Explore how optimized product pages, checkout processes, and marketing strategies can impact conversion rates and customer satisfaction.

Chapter 2: Optimizing Product Pages

2.1 Product Descriptions and Images:

- Discuss the importance of compelling product descriptions and high-quality images in driving conversions.
- Explore strategies for writing persuasive copy, highlighting key features and benefits, and optimizing product images for clarity and appeal.

2.2 Product Reviews and Social Proof:

- Explore the role of product reviews and social proof in building trust and credibility with customers.
- Discuss techniques for encouraging and showcasing customer reviews, testimonials, and user-generated content to influence purchasing decisions.

2.3 Product Recommendations and Cross-Selling:

- Discuss the benefits of personalized product recommendations and cross-selling techniques.
- Explore strategies for using data-driven algorithms, user behavior analysis, and strategic placement to suggest relevant products and increase average order value.

Chapter 3: Streamlining the Checkout Process

3.1 Simplifying Checkout Forms:

- Discuss the importance of a streamlined checkout process in reducing cart abandonment.
- Explore techniques for minimizing form fields, enabling guest checkout, and implementing auto-fill options to simplify the checkout experience.

3.2 Secure Payment Options:

- Explore the significance of offering secure payment options to build trust and confidence with customers.
- Discuss popular payment gateways, SSL certificates, and fraud prevention measures to ensure a secure transaction environment.

3.3 Optimizing for Mobile Checkout:

- Discuss the growing importance of optimizing the checkout process for mobile users.
- Explore responsive design principles, mobile-friendly payment gateways, and mobile-specific optimizations to enhance the mobile checkout experience.

Chapter 4: E-commerce Marketing Strategies

4.1 Search Engine Optimization (SEO):

- Discuss the role of SEO in driving organic traffic and visibility for e-commerce websites.
- Explore strategies for optimizing product pages, category pages, and content to rank higher in search engine results pages (SERPs).

4.2 Pay-Per-Click (PPC) Advertising:

- Explore the benefits of PPC advertising in generating targeted traffic and driving immediate results.
- Discuss strategies for creating compelling ad copy, targeting relevant keywords, and optimizing campaigns for maximum ROI.

4.3 Email Marketing Campaigns:

- Discuss the effectiveness of email marketing in nurturing leads and driving repeat purchases.
- Explore strategies for building an email list, segmenting subscribers, and crafting personalized email campaigns to engage customers and drive conversions.

Chapter 5: Conversion Rate Optimization (CRO)

5.1 Understanding Conversion Rate Optimization:

- Define conversion rate optimization (CRO) as the process of improving the percentage of website visitors who take a desired action.
- Discuss the importance of CRO in maximizing the effectiveness of e-commerce websites and marketing efforts.

5.2 A/B Testing and Experimentation:

- Explore the role of A/B testing and experimentation in identifying and implementing optimization strategies.
- Discuss techniques for testing various elements such as headlines, images, calls-to-action, and page layouts to determine the most effective combinations.

5.3 User Experience (UX) Design:

- Discuss the impact of user experience (UX) design on e-commerce conversion rates.
- Explore principles of usability, navigation, and visual design to create an intuitive and engaging shopping experience for customers.

Chapter 6: E-commerce Analytics and Insights

6.1 Key Performance Indicators (KPIs):

- Discuss essential e-commerce KPIs for measuring and monitoring performance.
- Explore metrics such as conversion rate, average order value, customer acquisition cost, and customer lifetime value to evaluate the effectiveness of optimization efforts.

6.2 Google Analytics and Data Analysis:

- Explore the role of Google Analytics in tracking and analyzing e-commerce website data.
- Discuss techniques for setting up e-commerce tracking, creating custom reports, and interpreting analytics data to gain insights into customer behavior and preferences.

6.3 Heatmaps and User Behavior Analysis:

- Discuss the use of heatmaps and user behavior analysis tools in understanding how visitors interact with e-commerce websites.
- Explore techniques for identifying areas of friction, optimizing user flow, and improving overall website usability based on behavioral data.

Chapter 7: E-commerce Platform Optimization

7.1 Choosing the Right E-commerce Platform:

- Discuss considerations for selecting the most suitable e-commerce platform for specific business needs and requirements.
- Explore popular platforms such as Shopify, WooCommerce, Magento, and BigCommerce, and discuss their features, scalability, and customization options.

7.2 Customizing and Extending Platform Functionality:

- Explore techniques for customizing and extending e-commerce platforms to meet unique business needs.
- Discuss the use of plugins, extensions, and custom development to add features, improve performance, and enhance the overall user experience.

7.3 Mobile Optimization and Responsive Design:

- Discuss the importance of mobile optimization and responsive design in e-commerce platform optimization.
- Explore strategies for ensuring seamless user experience across different devices and screen sizes to cater to the growing number of mobile shoppers.

Chapter 8: Customer Retention Strategies

8.1 Loyalty Programs and Rewards:

- Discuss the effectiveness of loyalty programs and rewards in fostering customer loyalty and retention.
- Explore strategies for implementing tiered rewards, points systems, and exclusive offers to incentivize repeat purchases and increase customer lifetime value.

8.2 Personalized Recommendations and Email Campaigns:

- Discuss the role of personalized recommendations and email campaigns in driving customer engagement and retention.
- Explore strategies for leveraging customer data, purchase history, and browsing behavior to deliver targeted product recommendations and relevant email content.

8.3 Customer Support and Communication:

- Discuss the importance of exceptional customer support and communication in building trust and loyalty.
- Explore strategies for providing responsive customer service, addressing inquiries and concerns promptly, and maintaining open lines of communication with customers through various channels.

Chapter 9: E-commerce Security and Compliance

9.1 Secure Payment Processing:

- Discuss the importance of secure payment processing in e-commerce transactions.
- Explore PCI DSS compliance, SSL encryption, and fraud prevention measures to protect sensitive customer data and ensure secure transactions.

9.2 GDPR and Data Privacy Compliance:

- Discuss the implications of GDPR (General Data Protection Regulation) and data privacy regulations on e-commerce businesses.
- Explore strategies for obtaining consent, protecting customer data, and ensuring compliance with relevant privacy laws and regulations.

9.3 Website Security and Vulnerability Management:

- Discuss the importance of website security and vulnerability management in safeguarding against cyber threats.
- Explore techniques for implementing security best practices, conducting regular security audits, and staying vigilant against potential security risks and vulnerabilities.

Chapter 10: Future Trends in E-commerce Optimization

10.1 Emerging Technologies and Innovations:

- Explore emerging technologies and innovations shaping the future of e-commerce optimization.
- Discuss topics such as artificial intelligence (AI), machine learning, augmented reality (AR), virtual reality (VR), and the Internet of Things (IoT) and their potential impact on e-commerce strategies and customer experiences.

10.2 Continuous Adaptation and Innovation:

- Emphasize the importance of continuous adaptation and innovation in the rapidly evolving e-commerce landscape.
- Encourage businesses to stay informed about emerging trends, experiment with new technologies and strategies, and adapt their optimization efforts to meet evolving customer expectations and market dynamics.

Chapter 11: Conclusion and Next Steps

11.1 Summary of Key Insights:

- Recap key insights and takeaways from the chapter.

- Emphasize the importance of e-commerce optimization in driving business growth, improving user experience, and staying competitive in the digital marketplace.

11.2 Actionable Recommendations:

- Provide actionable recommendations for implementing e-commerce optimization strategies.
- Discuss steps for conducting website audits, prioritizing optimization efforts, and leveraging analytics and insights to drive continuous improvement and achieve business objectives.

11.3 Continued Learning Resources:

- Recommend resources for readers to further their knowledge and skills in e-commerce optimization.
- Provide a list of books, online courses, industry blogs, and conferences where readers can continue their learning journey and stay updated on the latest e-commerce trends and best practices.

Introduction to Multilingual Websites

1.1 Understanding Multilingual Websites:

- Define multilingual websites as online platforms that offer content in multiple languages to cater to diverse audiences.
- Discuss the importance of multilingualism in reaching global markets, expanding audience reach, and fostering inclusivity.

1.2 Benefits of Multilingual Websites:

- Explore the benefits of multilingual websites for businesses, including increased visibility, enhanced user experience, and improved search engine optimization (SEO).
- Discuss how multilingualism can drive customer engagement, boost conversion rates, and foster brand loyalty.

Chapter 2: Planning and Strategy for Multilingual Websites

2.1 Market Research and Audience Analysis:

- Discuss the importance of market research and audience analysis in determining target markets and languages for multilingual websites.
- Explore techniques for identifying language preferences, cultural nuances, and market trends to inform localization strategies.

2.2 Content Localization Strategies:

- Explore content localization strategies for adapting website content to target languages and cultures.
- Discuss techniques for translating and adapting text, images, videos, and other multimedia elements to resonate with diverse audiences.

2.3 Website Structure and Navigation:

- Discuss considerations for website structure and navigation in multilingual websites.
- Explore strategies for organizing content, implementing language switchers, and ensuring intuitive navigation for users across different language versions.

Chapter 3: Implementing Multilingual Features

3.1 Language Switchers and Navigation:

- Discuss the role of language switchers and navigation elements in facilitating user access to multilingual content.
- Explore techniques for implementing language selectors, dropdown menus, flags, and other navigation tools for seamless language switching.

3.2 Multilingual Content Management Systems (CMS):

- Explore multilingual content management systems (CMS) and platforms for building and managing multilingual websites.
- Discuss features, plugins, and extensions that support multilingual content creation, translation, and management.

3.3 Multilingual SEO Optimization:

- Discuss the importance of multilingual SEO optimization in improving visibility and ranking in search engine results across different language markets.
- Explore techniques for optimizing metadata, hreflang tags, and localized content to enhance search engine visibility for multilingual websites.

Chapter 4: Content Translation and Localization

4.1 Professional Translation Services:

- Discuss the role of professional translation services in ensuring accurate and culturally appropriate translations for multilingual websites.
- Explore considerations for selecting translation partners, managing translation projects, and maintaining consistency across language versions.

4.2 User-Generated Content and Community Translation:

- Discuss the benefits of user-generated content and community translation in supplementing professional translations for multilingual websites.
- Explore techniques for encouraging user contributions, moderating user-generated content, and leveraging community-driven translation platforms.

4.3 Cultural Adaptation and Localization:

- Discuss the importance of cultural adaptation and localization in resonating with target audiences across different regions and languages.
- Explore techniques for adapting content, imagery, colors, symbols, and design elements to align with cultural preferences and sensitivities.

Chapter 5: Website Performance and Technical Considerations

5.1 Performance Optimization for Multilingual Websites:

- Discuss performance optimization strategies for multilingual websites to ensure fast loading times and smooth user experiences across different language versions.
- Explore techniques for optimizing images, caching, content delivery networks (CDNs), and server response times for improved website performance.

5.2 Responsive Design and Mobile Optimization:

- Discuss the importance of responsive design and mobile optimization for multilingual websites to ensure compatibility and usability across various devices and screen sizes.
- Explore techniques for designing flexible layouts, optimizing touch interactions, and implementing mobile-friendly navigation for improved user experience.

5.3 Website Security and Compliance:

- Discuss website security and compliance considerations for multilingual websites to protect user data and ensure regulatory compliance across different regions.
- Explore techniques for implementing SSL encryption, data protection measures, and compliance with privacy laws and regulations such as GDPR (General Data Protection Regulation).

Chapter 6: Multilingual E-commerce Strategies

6.1 Localized Product Listings and Descriptions:

- Discuss the importance of localized product listings and descriptions in e-commerce websites to cater to diverse language markets.
- Explore techniques for translating product information, specifications, pricing, and promotional content to appeal to international customers.

6.2 Multilingual Customer Support and Communication:

- Discuss the role of multilingual customer support and communication in providing personalized assistance and resolving inquiries for international customers.
- Explore techniques for offering multilingual live chat, email support, and self-service resources to address customer needs in their preferred languages.

6.3 Payment and Checkout Localization:

- Discuss the importance of payment and checkout localization in facilitating seamless transactions and improving conversion rates for international customers.

- Explore techniques for offering localized payment methods, currencies, and shipping options to accommodate diverse payment preferences and shipping requirements.

Chapter 7: Multilingual Content Marketing Strategies

7.1 Localized Content Marketing Campaigns:

- Discuss the importance of localized content marketing campaigns in engaging international audiences and driving brand awareness and engagement.
- Explore techniques for creating culturally relevant content, targeting local keywords, and distributing content through localized channels and platforms.

7.2 Multilingual Social Media Marketing:

- Discuss the role of multilingual social media marketing in reaching global audiences and building relationships with international customers.
- Explore techniques for creating multilingual social media content, engaging with followers in their preferred languages, and leveraging social media platforms for cross-cultural communication.

7.3 Influencer Marketing and Partnerships:

- Discuss the effectiveness of influencer marketing and partnerships in reaching international audiences and driving engagement and conversions.
- Explore techniques for collaborating with influencers and partners in different regions and languages to amplify brand messaging and reach new audiences.

Chapter 8: Measuring Success and Performance

8.1 Key Performance Indicators (KPIs) for Multilingual Websites:

- Discuss key performance indicators (KPIs) for measuring the success and performance of multilingual websites.
- Explore metrics such as traffic, engagement, conversion rates, and ROI (Return on Investment) to evaluate the effectiveness of localization efforts and inform optimization strategies.

8.2 Website Analytics and Insights:

- Explore the role of website analytics and insights in tracking user behavior, preferences, and interactions across different language versions.
- Discuss techniques for analyzing multilingual website data, identifying trends, and gaining actionable insights to optimize content, navigation, and user experience.

8.3 Continuous Improvement and Optimization:

- Emphasize the importance of continuous improvement and optimization in maintaining the effectiveness and relevance of multilingual websites.
- Discuss strategies for ongoing testing, experimentation, and iteration to refine content, functionality, and user experience based on data-driven insights and feedback.

Chapter 9: Challenges and Best Practices

9.1 Common Challenges in Multilingual Website Management:

- Discuss common challenges and pitfalls in managing multilingual websites and localization projects.
- Explore issues such as language consistency, cultural nuances, technical complexities, and resource constraints, and provide solutions and best practices for addressing these challenges.

9.2 Best Practices for Multilingual Website Management:

- Provide best practices and guidelines for successful multilingual website management and optimization.
- Discuss strategies for maintaining language consistency, streamlining translation workflows, fostering cross-functional collaboration, and staying agile and responsive to evolving market dynamics.

Chapter 10: Future Trends and Innovations

10.1 Emerging Technologies and Innovations:

- Explore emerging technologies and innovations shaping the future of multilingual website development and optimization.
- Discuss topics such as artificial intelligence (AI), natural language processing (NLP), machine translation, and localization automation, and their potential impact on streamlining localization processes and improving translation quality and efficiency.

10.2 Personalization and Hyper-Localization:

- Discuss the trend towards personalized and hyper-localized content experiences in multilingual websites.
- Explore techniques for leveraging data-driven insights, user segmentation, and geo-targeting to deliver tailored content and experiences to diverse audiences based on their preferences, behaviors, and location.

10.3 Voice Search and Multimodal Interfaces:

- Discuss the rise of voice search and multimodal interfaces in shaping the future of multilingual website interactions.
- Explore opportunities for optimizing multilingual content for voice search, integrating voice-enabled interfaces, and supporting diverse input modalities to enhance accessibility and user experience across languages and devices.

Chapter 11: Conclusion and Next Steps

11.1 Summary of Key Insights:

- Recap key insights and takeaways from the chapter on multilingual websites.
- Emphasize the importance of multilingualism in reaching global audiences, fostering cultural inclusivity, and driving business growth.

11.2 Actionable Recommendations:

- Provide actionable recommendations for implementing multilingual website strategies and optimization efforts.
- Discuss steps for conducting market research, developing localization plans, and leveraging technology solutions to create and maintain successful multilingual websites.

11.3 Continued Learning Resources:

- Recommend resources for further exploration of multilingual website development and optimization.
- Provide a list of books, online courses, industry blogs, and professional associations where readers can deepen their knowledge and skills in multilingual website management and localization best practices.

Introduction to Website Security and Maintenance

1.1 Understanding the Importance of Website Security:

- Define website security and its significance in protecting against cyber threats, data breaches, and malicious attacks.
- Discuss the potential consequences of compromised website security, including loss of data, damage to reputation, and financial repercussions.

1.2 The Role of Website Maintenance:

- Explain the concept of website maintenance and its importance in ensuring optimal performance, functionality, and security.
- Discuss the relationship between website maintenance and user experience, SEO rankings, and overall business success.

Chapter 2: Common Threats and Vulnerabilities

2.1 Overview of Common Cyber Threats:

- Identify common cyber threats targeting websites, including malware infections, hacking attempts, DDoS (Distributed Denial of Service) attacks, and phishing scams.
- Discuss the motivations behind cyber attacks and the potential impact on website owners and users.

2.2 Understanding Vulnerabilities:

- Explore common vulnerabilities in website infrastructure, including outdated software, weak passwords, insecure plugins, and misconfigured servers.
- Discuss how vulnerabilities can be exploited by attackers to gain unauthorized access to websites and sensitive data.

Chapter 3: Implementing Robust Security Measures

3.1 Secure Hosting and Server Configuration:

- Discuss the importance of choosing a secure hosting provider and configuring servers properly to mitigate security risks.
- Explore techniques for implementing firewalls, SSL/TLS encryption, and access control measures to protect server environments.

3.2 Website Encryption and SSL/TLS Certificates:

- Explain the role of encryption in securing website data transmission and user interactions.
- Discuss the importance of SSL/TLS certificates in establishing secure HTTPS connections and protecting against man-in-the-middle attacks.

3.3 Web Application Firewalls (WAFs):

- Introduce web application firewalls (WAFs) and their role in protecting websites from common web-based attacks.
- Discuss features and functionalities of WAF solutions and best practices for implementing and configuring WAF rules to block malicious traffic.

Chapter 4: Secure Coding Practices

4.1 Importance of Secure Coding:

- Highlight the importance of secure coding practices in building resilient and secure websites.
- Discuss how insecure coding practices can lead to vulnerabilities such as SQL injection, cross-site scripting (XSS), and insecure deserialization.

4.2 Best Practices for Secure Development:

- Discuss best practices for secure web development, including input validation, parameterized queries, secure authentication, and session management.
- Explore techniques for sanitizing user input, implementing least privilege access controls, and validating and escaping output to prevent security vulnerabilities.

Chapter 5: Website Backup and Disaster Recovery

5.1 Importance of Website Backup:

- Emphasize the importance of regular website backups as a crucial component of disaster recovery and business continuity planning.
- Discuss the potential risks of data loss due to hardware failures, cyber attacks, or accidental deletion, and the role of backups in mitigating these risks.

5.2 Backup Strategies and Best Practices:

- Discuss backup strategies and best practices for ensuring comprehensive data protection and recovery.
- Explore techniques for scheduling automated backups, storing backups securely offsite, and testing backup integrity and restoration procedures regularly.

Chapter 6: Routine Maintenance and Patch Management

6.1 Importance of Routine Maintenance:

- Highlight the importance of routine maintenance in keeping websites secure, stable, and up-to-date.
- Discuss how regular maintenance activities can help identify and address security vulnerabilities, performance issues, and software bugs.

6.2 Patch Management Strategies:

- Discuss patch management strategies for keeping software, plugins, themes, and other components of a website up-to-date.
- Explore techniques for monitoring security advisories, applying patches promptly, and testing patches in a staging environment before deployment.

Chapter 7: User Authentication and Access Control

7.1 Secure User Authentication:

- Discuss the importance of secure user authentication mechanisms in preventing unauthorized access to website resources.
- Explore best practices for implementing strong password policies, multi-factor authentication (MFA), and CAPTCHA challenges to verify user identities.

7.2 Access Control Policies:

- Discuss the role of access control policies in enforcing least privilege principles and restricting user permissions based on roles and responsibilities.
- Explore techniques for implementing role-based access control (RBAC), access control lists (ACLs), and granular permission settings to limit access to sensitive data and functionality.

Chapter 8: Continuous Monitoring and Threat Detection

8.1 Importance of Continuous Monitoring:

- Discuss the importance of continuous monitoring for detecting security incidents and anomalous behavior in real-time.
- Explore the role of monitoring tools and techniques in identifying unauthorized access attempts, suspicious activities, and potential security breaches.

8.2 Threat Detection and Incident Response:

- Discuss strategies for threat detection and incident response to mitigate the impact of security breaches and contain threats effectively.

- Explore techniques for implementing intrusion detection systems (IDS), security information and event management (SIEM) solutions, and incident response plans to respond to security incidents promptly.

Chapter 9: Compliance and Regulatory Requirements

9.1 Compliance Standards and Regulations:

- Discuss common compliance standards and regulatory requirements related to website security, data protection, and privacy.
- Explore standards such as GDPR (General Data Protection Regulation), PCI DSS (Payment Card Industry Data Security Standard), and HIPAA (Health Insurance Portability and Accountability Act), and their implications for website owners.

9.2 Compliance Implementation Strategies:

- Discuss strategies for achieving compliance with relevant standards and regulations through effective security controls and risk management practices.
- Explore techniques for conducting risk assessments, implementing security policies and procedures, and documenting compliance efforts to meet regulatory requirements.

Chapter 10: Educating Users and Building Security Awareness

10.1 Importance of Security Awareness:

- Highlight the importance of security awareness training in educating users and fostering a culture of security within organizations.
- Discuss how security awareness programs can empower users to recognize and report security threats, avoid phishing scams, and follow best practices for online security.

10.2 Training and Education Initiatives:

- Discuss initiatives for implementing security training and education programs for employees, website administrators, and end-users.
- Explore techniques for delivering engaging and interactive training sessions, creating security awareness materials, and conducting simulated phishing exercises to reinforce security awareness.

Chapter 11: Conclusion and Next Steps

11.1 Summary of Key Insights:

- Recap key insights and takeaways from the chapter on website security and maintenance.
- Emphasize the importance of adopting a proactive approach to security and implementing robust security measures to protect websites from cyber threats.

11.2 Actionable Recommendations:

- Provide actionable recommendations for implementing security best practices and maintaining website security and resilience.
- Discuss steps for conducting security assessments, implementing security controls, and staying informed about emerging threats and vulnerabilities.

11.3 Continued Learning Resources:

- Recommend resources for further exploration of website security and maintenance best practices.
- Provide a list of books, online courses, industry certifications, and security forums where readers can deepen their knowledge and skills in website security and cybersecurity.

Table of Contents

/